Awaken Children

Volume 4

AWAKEN, CHILDREN!

Dialogues With
Sri Mata Amritanandamayi

VOLUME 4

Adaptation & Translation

SWAMI AMRITASWARUPANANDA

Mata Amritanandamayi Center, San Ramon
California, United States

AWAKEN, CHILDREN!
Volume 4

Published by:
Mata Amritanandamayi Center
P.O. Box 613
San Ramon, CA 94583
United States

In India:
www.amritapuri.org
inform@amritapuri.org

In Europe:
www.amma-europe.org

In US:
www.amma.org

This Book is Humbly Offered at the
LOTUS FEET OF HER HOLINESS
SRI MATA AMRITANANDAMAYI
The Resplendent Luminary Immanent
In the Hearts of All Beings

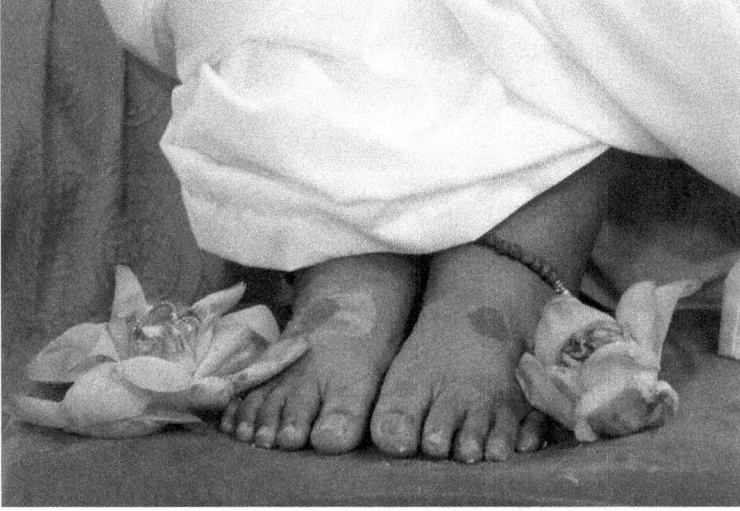

Vandeham saccidānandam bhāvātītam jagatgurum |
Nityam pūrnam nirākāram nirgunam svātmasamsthitam | |
I prostrate to the Universal Teacher, Who is Satchidananda (Pure
Being-Knowledge-Absolute Bliss), Who is beyond all differences,
Who is eternal, all-full, attributeless, formless and ever-centered
in the Self.
Saptasāgaraparyantam tīrthasnānaphalam tu yat |
Gurupādapayōvindōh sahasrāmsena tatphalam | |
Whatever merit is acquired by one, through pilgrimmages and
from bathing in the Sacred Waters extending to the seven seas,
cannot be equal to even one thousandth part of the merit derived
from partaking the water with which the Guru's Feet are washed.
Guru Gita, verses 157, 87

Contents

Preface   9

Introduction   11

Chapter 1   17
   Beyond duality   17
   Spiritual qualities of women   26

Chapter 2   33
   Trip to Kanyakumari   33
   Receiving the Guru's prasad   40
   Subtle food of the Guru   45
   Nayanar Swami   54
   Humility   58
   Suffering of the poor   63
   Sadhana, self-surrender and love   66

Chapter 3   75
   Work in praise of God   75
   A family in distress   80

Chapter 4   89
   Do not laugh at others   91

Chapter 5   101
   Believers and non-believers   103
   Difference between a devotee and a disciple   111
   Innocent faith and how to study the scriptures   119

Chapter 6   129
   Concentration and meditation   129
   Infinite masks of the Mother   132

Chapter 7   138
   Questions asked by Westerners: which path to follow   138
   Formation of qualities in children   142

Family life as an ashram 144
Fear of surrendering 147
The incomprehensible Mother 150

Chapter 8 156
A profound teaching illustrated in everyday cooking 156
Householders and spiritual life 163
Oneness with God through Love 174

Chapter 9 180
Young man from Rishikesh 180
The nature of the Guru 186

Chapter 10 200
Work as worship 200
Two Mothers 205

Chapter 11 212
Spiritual Love and worldly love 212

Chapter 12 236
A devotee's experience of Kali 236
Do not judge others 239

Chapter 13 244
Inevitability of death 244

Chapter 14 252
Remembering God while eating food 252

Chapter 15 260
A miracle in court evidence 260
A question about tantra 265
Mind and no-mind 274

Glossary 277

Preface

Rebirth! Death of the old and birth of the new – a new life, a new vision. This is the real boon of a Mahatma. But this death is coming back to life, to really live not in death but in life, a life pulsating with full vitality, peace and joy. This return from death is not to cry, not to worry, not to become tense about anything, but to heartfully smile, blissfully laugh while looking at everything, even death. Mahatmas want everyone to experience this everlasting peace and joy. They sincerely wish that everyone should become like them, and they strive hard to accomplish this goal.

Our beloved Mother Amritanandamayi's whole life is dedicated to awakening Her children from their inner sleep. For that alone She speaks, for that alone She acts, and that alone is the reason She is here in this world of plurality, in this name and form. But remember, don't be calculative; don't be too analytical; don't be too logical, for you will miss Her real Being.

Amma teaches us to be in the heart, not in the head. A heart full of love can know Her, see Her and experience Her. Therefore, while going through this book, let your heart be in the forefront. Somebody asked Mother, "Amma, what is the place of reasoning in spirituality?" "To finish off reason is the place of reasoning in spirituality," was the answer.

Mother is love – love of God, that love which is our real nature. Amma says, "Intellect cannot experience love, for love is silence. Intellect is always noisy. Only faith can know love. Faith is in the heart. Therefore, only faith springing forth from the heart can imbibe the silence of love." Let us be in the heart so that we can at least have a peep into that ocean of love.

The pure love and compassion which manifests in a never-ending stream through this Great Master and Mother can equally be experienced through each and every word She utters in the form of teachings. Amma will continue conversing until we stop talking, until our minds stop babbling. When we stop talking, we will realize that the Mother was not speaking at all, that She was always still, steady and silent. Until then, let us keenly listen with our heart and soul to this Great Master's voice with *sraddha* (faith) and *bhakti* (devotion).

Introduction

Herein is contained a direct translation of the Holy Mother's *divya upadesha* (divine advice) into the English language. A tremendous blessing is bestowed by presenting Mother's teaching to the English-speaking world. It is left to the reader to sanctify his or her life by a careful reading of the material and a whole-hearted practice of it in daily life.

Several points should be remembered in order that this translation be approached with the right understanding. First of all, most of these conversations have occurred between Mother and Indian householders and renunciates in the cultural context of India. Also, Mother's advice is given according to the level of understanding of each person to whom She is speaking. Often a word-for-word English translation falls short of conveying the totality of what Mother has expressed in Her mother tongue, Malayalam. One must consider these factors when contemplating Her words in order to achieve deeper insight.

It is next to impossible to do full justice to the greatness of what Mother is. When we say that Mother is the *Satguru* (Supreme Guru), we should understand that this being is not an ordinary teacher. A teacher communicates the wisdom that passes through his intellectual understanding, ideally supported by his own experience. The *Satguru*, however, speaks directly from the state of Oneness. He uses logical thinking as a tool, but his thought may be paradoxical. From his God-intoxicated state of fullness, of mystical union with the Divine, words of wisdom spill out from the Guru. Sometimes these words and pronouncements may seem shocking to the unprepared seeker. The reason for this is that the Guru does not always take into account the whole framework of values and projections associated with certain concepts, but instead, he reveals the truth of what he sees, often with the intention of shocking the seeker into right vision.

By definition, the mystic shocks. The example of Mother giving *darshan* bears witness to this. That the 'young lady,' however mystic or guru She may be, embraces so tenderly all people who come to Her – including men – is, to say the least, unusual and exceptional in a traditional society. In this motherly way, the mystic in Mother takes the total liberty to bypass socio-cultural norms, and expresses Her intimate nature in action, in oneness and in Her endless compassion for all creatures. When the same mystic makes a seemingly denigrating remark about 'worldly pleasures,' there is no value judgment behind such a thought. Seen from the state of Supreme Bliss in which She abides, worldly pleasures may seem to be deprecatory. If some of the statements of the Guru are shocking, it is because we helplessly see them through the numerous veils of social values, moral principles, projections, misunderstood prejudices, psychological reactions or even misapplied principles. Can this really, in all honesty, be called 'seeing'? Our natural reaction is then to project all these veils onto the Guru. When we cannot digest one of the insights spilled out to us, we say, "This Guru is wonderful, but how can he speak so outrageously?" It is our duty as seekers to patiently open up and catch the drops of wisdom and receive the teachings, working with them until the maturity comes to us to understand them in the right light.

The mystic may also sometimes spill out words that seem incoherent, expressing ideas half-developed. It is particularly delicate to translate such words because we may, more often than not, in our ignorance, be tempted to give a coherence to such words. The apparent incoherence of such sayings do reveal their deeper sense when meditated upon.

Secondly, Mother's use of language is direct and earthy. We often forget that the truth coming from the Guru's unqualified state of Reality remains still clothed in the language spoken by him. The *Satguru* is the Reality, but this Reality is manifested in a body and, as such, is born in one particular place at one particular point in time with all the cultural conditions that this may imply. The reader himself is bound by his own language, his own socio-cultural context, and the struggle of his own people trying to liberate themselves from the weight of projections and value judgements. For example, when Mother uses the term 'worldly people,' the term She uses does not have the connotations of moralistic value judgements that it has in the English language. Her words convey an immediacy and intensity of purpose to transmit the Essential, particularly when speaking to *sadhaks* (spiritual aspirants). When it comes time to bring a point across to a renunciate, Mother does not mince words. Thus we can understand Her advice to renounce the enjoyment of worldly pleasures to be sound advice to one whose sole aim is God-Realization.

In a separate conversation with a householder, the Mother's advice takes on an entirely different tone. "Mother doesn't say that you must give up all desires. You can enjoy them, but do not think that this life is for that only." Keep in mind that in the Mother's language, the word 'world' literally means 'that which is seen,' as opposed to the invisible Reality or God. Knowing this will be of great help in interpreting Her use of the word 'worldly.' When the Mother contrasts that which is spiritual to that which is worldly, She refers to the attitude with which actions are done. Spiritual actions are those which lead one to God through selflessness and purity. Worldly actions are those actions which lead one away from God, performed as they are in a spirit of selfishness.

Thirdly, for one who has traveled and mingled with cultures vastly different from his own, it is obvious that not only verbal language changes, but changes must also occur in the way one relates to the world and the way one reaches out to things with the weave of one's feelings and thoughts. What is presented of the Mother's teaching is from dialogues with Her. Sometimes She will repeat what She says to emphasize a particular point or to make a certain impression on the listeners. Thus we may find some ideas repeated in this collection of gems.

In regards to Her concern for women, the Mother – Herself appearing in the body of a woman – gives a timely message. In truth, no one but this woman mystic, who is the intimate confident of tens of thousands of female devotees, knows the plight of women in general, and of Indian women in particular, in the often misused and misapplied traditional context that stifles their lives. She not only encourages but urges women to utilize their innate nature to develop spiritually.

Finally, the Mother speaks to us from the exalted state of *sahaja samadhi*, a Self- Realized Master's natural state of abidance in the Absolute Reality. Much of Her manner of teaching and expressing glorification of the Divine is through singing devotional songs. While we have included the translation of some of the songs in the text, no words can transmit the quality of Her ecstatic singing. We are herein trying to retransmit the gems that have been spilled out to us, appealing in all humility for the grace and right understanding to do full justice to the wisdom of that being who has so compassionately stretched out Her hand to us to take us back into Her. The challenge in translating is to render the Mother's transcendent vision into English for the layman. The vital ingredient in this process is the contemplative mind of the reader. Abandoning all superficiality, may our mind and intellect become subtle to assimilate the Eternal Wisdom of the Mother's words. Firmly established in our practice, may we revel in the direct experience of the Supreme Absolute without delay.

Swami Amritaswarupananda

Chapter 1

Beyond duality

In the tropics on the southwestern coast of India, the summer sun often blazes throughout the day. Yet even during the peak of this season in Kerala, the Ashram and its surroundings are not much affected by the intensity of the heat. A canopy of coconut palms provides abundant shade, and the breeze that blows constantly off the nearby Arabian Sea cools the air.

Although the Mother's first spiritual children had come to stay with Her many years before, the Ashram officially began in 1981. In those early years, before anyone dreamed of an Ashram or disciples and devotees from all over the world, days and nights spent with the Mother were a continuous series of wondrous adventures and intimate teachings, of discovering the many facets of this enigmatic Mother, and through these, discovering one's own Self.

Since 1982, the Ashram residents followed a regular schedule as more and more spiritual aspirants came to live there. Rising at 4:00 a.m. to chant the *Lalita Sahasranama*, the Thousand Names of the Divine Mother Sri Lalita, residents gathered for morning and late afternoon meditations and for classes on the ancient scriptures. The daily schedule ended with evening *bhajans* as dusk released the sun to rest in the western ocean.

Each day visiting devotees came to see the Mother. While She kept no specific hours for these daily *darshans*, the Mother was sure to see every person who came. Although there were still times when She met with devotees out in the open under the palm trees, *darshan* was usually held in a special hut built for the purpose.

16 April 1984

At nine o'clock in the morning the Ashram was calm and peaceful. The residents were still meditating in the hall, and the melodious singing of a nightingale added a delicate charm to the tranquility of the morning. The Holy Mother came out of the meditation hall where She had been sitting with the brahmacharis, observing their meditation. With Her hands held behind Her back, the Mother began walking back and forth in front of the temple. There was a majestic appearance about Her. One of the residents approached the Mother and stood beside Her, as if he had something to say. Realizing his wish, the Mother stopped walking and stood in front of him.

He said, "Amma, people are scandalizing Amma and the Ashram, gossiping and speaking a lot of nonsense. They are saying that it is not proper for Amma to embrace people. How can we make them understand that Amma is One with the Supreme Being?"

The Mother replied, "Those people who are supposed to know will know and understand. The others are not familiar with a Mother who considers all as Her children. Therefore, though they criticize, Mother does not blame them. Son, they are like that. They cannot be otherwise. It is their nature.

"Petrol (gasoline) can be used for running a car as well as for burning a house. People who use petrol for burning want only to destroy. They do not consider the creative aspect of petrol. Most people love only for selfish motives and do not know Mother's unconditional love. They do not know that love can be expanded to embrace the whole universe. They are familiar only with a limited capacity for love. Mother's life is for giving happiness and peace to people, but people do not understand this. A needle can be used to stitch and sew things together as well as to injure someone. People live in too much strife and division. Mother's aim is to unite people's hearts with God and to make them one with Him. But these people who criticize the Ashram want to hurt and injure people.

"People judge things according to their mental dispositions and tendencies which are limited. Due to this limitation their judgements are wrong most of the time and they miss the essence of things.

"A plant in which an ayurvedic physician sees great medicinal value is nothing but grass for a person who harvests food for cows. Likewise, people differ according to their individual *samskaras* (illusions). It is through the glasses of their *vasanas* (accumulated tendencies) that each one views and judges the world. The color of the glasses differs according to a person's tendencies, but in all people identification with these *vasanas* is so strong that they feel that their judgements, and their judgements alone, are correct.

"People in ignorance, people who have no spiritual grounding or even any spiritual tendencies, will not see or understand what Mother is doing. They live in total ignorance, unaware of such things. Let us pray to the Lord and seek forgiveness for them. But those who are supposed to know will know. They will come here, overcoming all obstacles."

"Amma, what makes these people live in ignorance? Why are they blind? What covers their vision?" asked the resident.

"It is nothing outside which envelopes their vision, but it is their own mind," answered the Mother. "The mind full of thoughts is ignorance; the same mind devoid of thoughts is *Atman*, the Self. People are so identified with the body that they miss the Reality, the Essential Principle. They see the waves and forget about the ocean. They see only the clouds and miss the vast expansive sky. They see the flower and fall in love with it, but they overlook the plant. The waves come and go, appear and disappear, but the ocean remains the same. The same can be said about the clouds in the sky and the flower on the plant. People miss the Reality, the Substratum, which is the Enlivening Principle, and this is a big loss. To forget It is the biggest loss.

"Duality exists only when you are identified with the body. Once this identification is transcended, all dualities disappear. In the state of Supreme Oneness, the pot (the body), breaks, and the space inside the pot becomes one with the total space. There is no more conditioning; only the One exists. All differences such as man and woman, healthy and unhealthy, rich and poor, beautiful and ugly, pure and impure, vanish. You will then see and experience the electricity, rather than the bulb or the fan or the refrigerator, which are objects powered by electricity. Once this happens, how can one say, 'I will only do this, not that' or, 'I will receive only women, not men.' In this state of total non-identification with the body, all differences disappear."

At this point the Mother sat down on the front verandah of the temple. She continued, "Even the feeling that there are men and there are women is one of degree because in every man there is woman and in every woman there is man. People are half man and half woman. Some men are more womanly than manly, and of course, the opposite is also true. One's actions and thoughts will reveal masculine or feminine traits. What is a real human being? A real human being is one who is endowed with self-control and mental strength. But who is without any weakness? Even a dictator, who may seem like a strong-minded person, is a weakling because he rules, tortures and kills people out of fear for his own security. Fear is the greatest weakness.

"The elements which constitute the bodies of both men and women are the same. God used a little more flesh to make women, that's all. What is there to be ashamed of in considering both men and women equally if one is fully established in that Non-Dual state of Reality?

"Son, Mother never has the feeling, 'woman' or 'man.' Mother's only feeling is that all are Her children. There should be at least one person who hugs one and all, seeing them as Her children, shouldn't there? Who else is there to do that? Mother cannot change Her innate nature, out of fear of what people might say."

One of the brahmacharis asked, "Amma, may I go to Mookambika Temple and come back in a few days?"

Amma cautioned him, "Son, why do you wander here and there? This is another tendency of the mind. You think that by going to Mookambika or some other holy place you are fulfilling a divine desire and that it is therefore not harmful. Of course it is not harmful if you have the right attitude and faith. But when such a desire arises, you should observe the mind closely in order to make sure the desire is genuine. The desire is usually just a product of your craving to travel and go sightseeing. But you cannot confess that to me; therefore, you express it in the guise of a pilgrimage with a divine purpose.

"This is a strong *vasana* in many people, to think that they are doing the 'right thing' when really all they want to do is satisfy their usual desires. Merry-making, sight-seeing, traveling around and seeking entertainment are common *vasanas* in people. These *vasanas* will still follow a person even if he abandons one way of living and chooses another. The only difference is that the mind will express it in another way. But the basic *vasana* will remain the same. It is just like renouncing chocolate and switching to ice cream. The object changes, but the desire remains the same. You do not know how skillfully the mind tricks and fools you. Beware, and use your discriminative power on such occasions.

"Once you accept a Perfect Soul as your Guru, stop wandering, both mentally and physically. Stay with the Guru; surrender to Him or Her. That is it. Cast off all worries and unnecessary brooding over incidents and experiences of the past, and mentally and physically travel towards Him, toward His real Being. This is the real journey.

"When you are in the presence of a Self-Realized Master, try to be firm and unshakable, whatever may happen. Everything should be left to the Guru's will. You will be in trouble if you move around, straying away from the Master in order to fulfill your desires and wishes. Self-surrender is very much needed."

Next a devotee asked a question, "Amma, what is the explanation for Realized Souls expressing desires in childhood, like wanting to play on a swing or wanting toys, when they take on a new birth after having given up the body of the previous life?"

To this the Mother explained, "A Self-Realized Soul might express desires, but there is a big difference between the attitude of a Self-Realized Soul and that of an ordinary human being. When an ordinary human being develops a desire for an object, he creates a chain by becoming attached to the object. This chain of attachments gets longer and longer and goes on binding him. He has no control. He will be haunted all the time by all kinds of desires, whether they are necessary or unnecessary, helpful or unhelpful, permitted or prohibited. His mind becomes a real marketplace.

"A Realized Soul, too, will sometimes express desires, but He is of an entirely different calibre. He has complete control over the desires. You might see Him eating, sleeping or dressing like an ordinary person, but He is not attached to whatever He does. He can give it up easily. He is just like a child. A child is not attached to anything. He will move easily from one activity to another, let go of one object when another interests him more. If a Realized Soul takes another birth after casting off the previous life's body, He might express desires in His childhood, asking for this or that. But even though a child, He will remain a witness, and He will be fully aware of His Real Self. He might act like other children, but what harm is there in this? A child should be like a child, shouldn't he? A child should be mischievous, sport about, play with toys, and cry for his mother's milk; otherwise, he is not a child. That innocence is the attractive thing about children.

"It is said that Sri Krishna, the All-Knowing One, wanted His father to capture the moon for Him when He was a child. He was full of playfulness. He expressed desires like all children do, but He was fully aware of His nature. So this is the difference. An ordinary human being has no control over the mind, but a Realized Soul, whatever his age, has one hundred percent control. His mind and desires function without compromise as he instructs them. In a mortal man's case, the mind and the desires function as they like, uncontrolled. The Realized Soul, whether he is a child or a grown-up person, creates a desire by his will, and he has the power to destroy it whenever he wants. Other people create desires but are incapable of destroying them."

A householder devotee arrived who had only recently started coming to the Ashram. He bowed down in front of the Mother and offered Her the fruit which he had brought. This devotee was very keen to know more about the Ashram. Seeing how young the brahmacharis were, he asked the Mother, "Should they be required to lead a spiritual life at such a young age?"

"Son," the Mother said laughingly, "it is not due to Mother's insistence that these children have chosen a spiritual life. When they first came, Mother told them, 'I don't have any faith in you who come here, deluded by an ordinary girl.' And do you know how they replied? 'Until we met Mother, we never even considered living a spiritual life or becoming monks. But we believe in that power that is in You which has created an effortless transformation in us.' Therefore, son, it was purely their choice, not Mother's.

"Do you think that somebody can be dragged into spiritual life unless they chose it wholeheartedly? No one can ever make you eat something that you do not like. Just to please someone, you might taste a little, but you will not eat the whole plate. If you eat only due to someone else's insistence, the food will not stay in your stomach. You will vomit. If this is the case with ordinary things, then what can be said about choosing a spiritual life and renouncing all other choices? This is something which must happen spontaneously. Nobody can force spirituality onto someone else. It happens out of urgency. In this state of urgency, a person cannot do anything but choose spirituality. There is no explanation for this; it just happens."

Another householder devotee requested clarification concerning Self-Realization: "Amma, it is said that the 'I' will disappear when one attains Self-Realization. How does that happen?"

"The 'I' ceases to exist when the mind attains perfect concentration," the Mother answered. "The feelings of 'I' and 'mine' are due to the ego. The ego is nothing but identification with the body and mind. The mind is thoughts. When thoughts are present, we remain a little ego. There is no spontaneous expression. Everything is filtered through the ego. Through the narrow vision of the little ego, we see only the waves of the sea. When thoughts are eradicated through constant practice and concentration, the ego, 'I', disappears. When through our concentration, the little ego is reduced to ashes, we become the Limitless and Impersonal and can thus comprehend the Ocean of Bliss. The remains of what looks like the ego will be there, but it is not real. It is not productive.

"Ask a scholar, 'Sir, what is your opinion about this planet and the people on it?' He will probably answer, 'This is a world full of useless fools!' Furthermore, he will most probably feel that he is the only wise person on the planet. Such a scholar has the most inflated 'little ego' you can find. He is a man who sees only the waves. He cannot even take a peep at the Ocean of Bliss. He can see only separate entities, only individuals, only differences and divisions. He cannot see the whole; he sees only the parts and pieces.

"Ask the same question of a *Mahatma* (great soul) and He will reply, 'There is only the Self, nothing else. God alone exists. Everything is beautiful; all are good and wise.' He beholds the Whole, the Oneness. The *Mahatma* experiences unity in diversity, in everything, in all circumstances, irrespective of time and place. For him everything is an extension of his own Self. He cannot blame, criticize or hate anyone. His small 'I' has disappeared and he has become the 'big, impersonal I'. This state comes only when the ego disappears. In order to attain this, one needs a one-pointed mind.

"God Himself will be the servant of the person who has gained one-pointedness of mind. Mother guarantees this, children. You try and see what happens."

The Mother's bold assurance struck the householder devotee with wonder. His eyes were fixed on the Mother's face. After a short while, he said, "Amma, how do we even begin..."

"Even while in the midst of numerous worldly problems, you children still think of God and show great interest in doing spiritual practice. This in itself makes Mother feel very happy." The Mother's reassurance was encouraging.

Another question was raised: "Amma, it seems that God didn't think before creating the world. Had He thought about it, there would not be so many complications and troubles."

"From His point of view," said the Mother, "the 'Old Man' has not created the world at all. He is flawless. We are the ones who create shadows and reflections. Again and again we create them, giving them reality. Running after these shadows and reflections, we fantasize and thus create our own world of chaos and confusion.

"Son, who is responsible for all this complication and trouble? Is it God? No. It is you. You alone are the cause. God created day and night to make us happy. Both are beautiful unless we act improperly. Day is the time to act and discharge one's duties, and night is the time to rest and relax. Who is responsible if somebody covets another's possessions and steals things at night, or if someone is a terrorist and uses the time to make bombs in secret? Is it God or is it the person doing those things? Animals, which are considered to be less evolved than humans, do not have problems like us, the so-called intelligent beings. Animals live much more in tune with nature. But it is arrogant and selfish human beings who are always disturbing nature's harmony."

Spiritual qualities of women

At around ten o'clock, some householder devotees arrived with their families. Some of the children were students in grade school and some were in college. The Holy Mother led all of them to the room above the meditation hall where She spoke to them for some time, showing great interest in their household affairs and inquiring about how their children were doing in their studies. Just like a loving mother, very much concerned about her family, the Mother conversed with them about various topics, filling them with warm feelings of motherly love and concern. It was obvious that the Mother's soothing and affectionate words made them very happy and relaxed. She took a piece of rock-candy, broke it up into several pieces and distributed it to the devotees as *prasad* (a blessing in the form of a gift).

The conversation slowly evolved to spiritual matters. There were more women present than men, and perhaps taking this into account, the Mother began talking about women. "Woman is *Shakti* (power). She is much more powerful than man. Though it may be difficult for a woman to have a determined mind, once she does, no power can stop her. She cannot be defeated then. Spiritual realization is easier for a woman to attain than for a man, provided she has the proper discrimination and determination. But by nature, women are yielding and giving and this often results in being unsteady. This unsteadiness should be overcome through constant repetition of one's mantra and remembrance of God. A woman's self-confidence is often weak, but she can make it unshakably firm. A woman can do it, for she has the patience to achieve. A man cannot raise children because he lacks patience. Men are impatient for results. Women have both patience and love, but in general, they lack determination and self-confidence. While men generally have the latter two qualities, they should develop patience and love. Because determination and self-confidence do exist within them, women should try to awaken these qualities and make them strong.

"Many people live with the misconception that women are only supposed to give birth and raise children. These same people might also think that men are the only ones who can rule and command. Both ideas are wrong. A woman can rule as well as a man if she brings out the dormant masculine qualities within her. And a man can be as loving and affectionate as a mother if he works on that unmanifested feminine aspect within him. But there is an important point to remember: while developing and even practicing patience and love, a man should retain his determination and self-confidence and a woman should maintain her patience and love even after she has cultivated determination and self-confidence.

"Women are the repositories of infinite power. In spiritual matters they can surpass what many men attempt to do; therefore, do not think that women are lower than men.

"Women should wake up from their sleep, wake up to spiritual awareness. There is infinite spiritual power within them. They are not weaklings and they must realize this. They have at their disposal two very powerful tools, love and patience, which are the sharpest and the strongest weapons of all. These two qualities are capable of conquering anything with ease."

"Amma, what do you say about people in India imitating the West?" asked one of the devotees.

"Children," the Mother replied, "it is a pity that India is trying to imitate the West. That is not our culture. It does not belong to us. It is a very dangerous tendency to imitate Western culture. But look at the Westerners; they are trying to follow us. They want spirituality, whereas we crave material wealth. If you must imitate the Westerners, imitate their good qualities like the sincerity that they show to the work they undertake and the external discipline that they have. Instead, we imitate them blindly. Each nation has a culture of its own. The very existence of a country is dependent on that. If that root culture is not preserved, the country will face its downfall. India's cultural heritage is spirituality. Spirituality is the vital energy of India. If that is gone, the nation will perish. Therefore, that should be protected. In order to save the coming generation, parents should wake up. Their children's future is in their hands, and they can help them to a certain extent. Parents should try to inculcate in their children's minds the value of leading a spiritual life. This is the most valuable wealth that parents can give to their children. Material wealth will perish, but spiritual wealth is imperishable.

"Problems will arise in married life. When a time of crisis comes, spiritual truths will save a man or a woman from mental turmoil and emotional distress, which are quite common in modern society today. While feeding children food and providing them with other necessities, remember to feed them with some spiritual values as well. If you don't do this, you will spoil your children in the name of motherly love or fatherly love.

"In the olden days when people felt sorrow, they did *tapas* (intense spiritual practice, literally 'heat'). They engaged in austerities in order to remember God. In this way they gained strength to face their problems. Nowadays, unable to confront unhappy moments in life, people resort to liquor and drugs. Unable to face problems, they seek to escape them. Such a pity! They do not know what they are doing. In relying on intoxicants to avoid their problems, they are paving the way for their own destruction.

"Once a person becomes addicted to intoxicants like liquor, marijuana, cocaine, heroine, or other drugs, the addiction swallows him completely. He becomes so dependent on intoxicants that he is not able to function normally without them. In the beginning he may feel that the drugs or alcohol are enjoyable. But as he becomes dependent on them, needing more and more to get the desired effect in order to forget his problems, he realizes that the drugs are no longer pleasurable. Addiction to habit-forming drugs forces an addict to rely on them totally; they become a biological need and he becomes obsessed with always needing the drug. So obsessed is an addict that he neglects his loved ones, his family and friends, and he neglects his duties and responsibilities in order to obtain his drugs. Ultimately, he neglects himself; his health becomes ruined. His physical body weakens, and he becomes susceptible to disease. What is worse, he does not care about himself. Habit-forming drugs cause the brain to deteriorate and cause damage to the nervous system as well as to other organs of the body. If an addict produces children, they may be born mentally retarded or physically deformed. Therefore, parents, take good care of your children. Do not let them fall victim to alcohol or drugs. Give them the necessary spiritual education while they are still young."

Speaking humbly, a woman devotee said to the Mother, "Amma, I have brought you some *parippuvada* (a delicacy made of dal, deep-fried in oil). It is not very good. Will you have some?

With a radiant smile on Her face, the Mother said, "Certainly. Mother likes whatever is brought by people with devotion. Even if it is poison, it will be made good and pure by the innocence of their hearts."

Taking a small steel container out of her handbag, the woman joyfully handed it over to the Mother, who, removing the lid, took one piece out and had a bite. Beaming a smile at the devotee, She exclaimed, "Good! Very delicious!"

The Mother then fed the other half to the woman, who was overflowing with joy. Then She fed each person present a small piece from the container. When there was still one *parippuvada* left in Her hand, the Mother broke it into two pieces. Again She fed the woman devotee with one piece, and upon handing her the remaining half, the Mother, with a mischievous smile on Her face, said, "Daughter, you feed Mother now." Sitting in front of the devotee, She opened Her mouth. The woman looked as if she were in a dream or in another world. Such astonishment and such tremendous joy lit up her face. As she put the treat into the Mother's mouth, the devotee struggled to control her tears. Immediately after feeding the Mother, she broke down and sobbed like a child.

Through her tears, she said, "I cherished the desire to feed you while I was making this food. And when you fed me and the others, that wish again became strong. O Amma, you have fulfilled my heart's desire."

The woman could not control her tears. Still sobbing, she sang

Ellam Ariyunna Ammayodu

No need to tell anything to the all-knowing Mother,
Walking beside us,
She sees and understands everything,
The Primordial Being
Sees all thoughts of the inner self.

It is never possible for anyone to do anything,
Without Her knowledge.
The Primordial Lord abides in all.
Let us all worship with joy the
Embodiment of Truth and Awareness.

The other devotees sang the response[1] to the song as they silently wept, visibly moved by what had taken place. Absorbed in Her own world, the Mother sat with eyes closed.

❧ ☙

---

[1] Bhajans or devotional songs are usually sung with one singer leading and a chorus responding.

Chapter 2

Trip to Kanyakumari

19 April 1984

After the evening *bhajan*, everyone made preparations to go to Kanyakumari, a holy place and pilgrimage center which is situated on the southernmost tip of India where three seas meet – the Arabian Sea, the Indian Ocean and the Bay of Bengal. The famous Devi temple there is dedicated to the Goddess as the Eternal Virgin, and it is the center of attraction for thousands of devotees from all over India. Mother's devotees had expressed a strong desire for Her to visit this place. They were not so much interested in seeing the Cape, and if it were not for Mother's presence, most of them would not go on their own. The real secret behind their desire was that such trips provided an opportunity for the devotees to spend more time with the Mother. Furthermore, traveling with Mother is always a unique experience, something the devotees can cherish in their hearts forever.

The preparations were completed and more than fifty people gathered together, among them both Ashram residents and householder devotees. The devotees had hired a tourist bus for this trip and had procured cooking vessels, sacks of rice, and other ingredients and items necessary for making food. This was to avoid, as far as possible, having to eat at restaurants and other public places.

After crossing the backwaters, the brahmacharis, with the help of the householder devotees, tied all the luggage on top of the bus and finally everyone was seated inside. At this point, Mother suddenly said, "Look, children, this is not a picnic or a sight-seeing trip. Consider this as part of your *sadhana* (spiritual practice). Tempting circumstances may arise, but always be aware of your goal. As far as Mother is concerned, She has no special interest in making this trip. She has no reason in agreeing to go other than the happiness of Her children. Try to consider this journey as an effort to journey into your own Self. Talk less. Try to chant your mantra as much as you can. Remember God or your beloved deity whenever you have time. Do not pay any attention to the objects or events which you might see on either side of the road. The mind is already full of images, do not burden it with more. We are trying to remove the existing ones. Let us finish with those and not add any more. If you must speak, do so, but softly and moderately. Do not talk about unnecessary matters. Time is very precious for us. Mother is not at all worried if you lose one *lakh* (100,000) rupees, but if She sees Her children wasting even a second, Mother feels very worried and sad. Lost time will not be retrieved.

"While traveling, many of our *vasanas* will manifest. Be aware of that and try to control your thoughts and sense organs. Children, when you are all alone, staying away from crowds and not mingling with people, you may not be aware of the latent tendencies dormant in you. Rather, you may feel peaceful, happy and content when you are alone or in favorable company. But if you cannot maintain that peace and contentment while you are in the midst of people whom you do not like or while you are in a tempting situation, that peace or contentment is not genuine. To maintain that peace and contentment in all circumstances is our goal. Therefore, children, try to have maximum mental control. Practice love, patience and forbearance during this trip. This is a good opportunity for you to put those qualities into practice. Someone may disagree with you and another may argue with you. Don't react; try to be calm. Your calmness will disarm the other person. If you have any complaints, come tell Mother about it, but do not get angry; do not speak roughly or use harsh words.

"If anger arises in you, do not express it immediately. Leave the place. Go and sit somewhere by yourself. Contemplate and meditate. You will find that the cause of your anger is not in the other person but within you. It is not the other person that causes it, but your past. The past is your reference book. Anger is within you. Someone accidentally touches the anger in you, and you erupt.

"Anger is like an infected wound. When somebody touches it, you feel the pain. And if the touch is hard, pus and blood will come out, creating more pain. Yes, anger is a deep, infected wound. It is a disease and needs to be treated. It needs your compassion and loving attention. Therefore, when someone gets angry, remember that he is a sick person. Do not make him more sick; do not let more pus and blood flow out of his wound. Do not make him experience more pain by pressing and squeezing harder and harder. This means that we should not return anger. By getting angry with a person who is angry with us, we are not treating the wound but making it only bigger and deeper. What an angry person needs is condolence. Take pity on him and soothe his wound of anger. Children, once again, Mother wants to remind you that this is an opportunity. Mother knows very well that it is quite natural to have conflicts and arguments when we are in a group. None of you are Self-Realized; therefore, disagreements among you can happen. But try to practice love and patience."

Mother paused for a while and then She said, "Let us now begin our journey." As the driver started the engine, the devotees called out together, *"Jai Bolo Satguru Mata Amritanandamayi Devi!"* (Victory to the Perfect Master Mata Amritanandamayi Devi). Again Mother's voice was heard, "Sing a *bhajan* in praise of Ganesha," and they sang

Gajanana

O Elephant-faced One
O Son of Parvati,
Abode of Compassion, Supreme Cause
Destroyer of Obstacles who is served by the virtuous,
Pure Consciousness, of dark blue hue,
Eternal One, bereft of sorrow,
One who gives good results
O Protector of the afflicted,
Illuminator of the Self, full of Bliss
And worshipped even by Indra

The time was 11:00 p.m. as the bus began to slowly move. The devotees continued singing. Everybody was very enthusiastic and happy. It seemed that all were full of blissful anticipation. Mother's instructions had instilled the spirit and strength of a genuine pilgrimage in the minds of the devotees. Everybody looked forward to a wondrous spiritual journey.

For most people, a picnic provides the opportunity to temporarily forget their daily routine and to enjoy pleasure objects as much as they want. On such occasions people in the world go on eating, drinking and indulging as they try to be happy. They want to forget everything, all their worries, tensions and strains. And to achieve this they depend on objects which they think will give them pleasure. Of course they do get a certain degree of happiness and will succeed in forgetting their worries for a short time. But afterwards, when they return to their daily lives, they will be thrown back into the midst of worries and problems. Not only that, through over-indulgence they will have dissipated all their energies and will not be able to function effectively. Caught-up in a vicious cycle, they end up worse than ever, heading towards disaster.

This journey also looked like a picnic. But it was a spiritual picnic under the guidance and leadership of a Perfect Master, a Knower of the Self. With such a leader it was not really necessary to select an idyllic place for the picnic, for a *Mahatma* could create waves of spiritual vibration all around, immersing the participants in the bliss that issues from within. At this picnic the food was the Divine Name. On an ordinary picnic people seek pleasure in external objects, letting all their energies drain away as they depend on things outside themselves for satisfaction and happiness. But the spiritual seeker conserves energy by relying on his own Self, the source of happiness. While people in the world descend until they break down and succumb to the morass of a meaningless life, spiritual people have the opportunity to rise up and ultimately ascend to the state of Bliss and Immortality.

Life is a picnic. We have a choice of two places to have this picnic. One site is beautiful and alluring to the senses which perceive the external world, but this place offers only a mass of confusion within one's mind. The other is not so attractive or appealing on the outside but filled with immense bliss and peace for one's inner being. We are free to choose. Ordinary people in the world and spiritual people are both looking for happiness. Whether it will be a temporary happiness which will culminate in never-ending sorrow or in a temporary endurance of trials which will lead to everlasting bliss, is for us to decide. One site is found within and the other is the external world. One is the path of eternal bliss and the other is the path of temporary happiness.

The devotees clapped their hands and kept on singing. The night was under the cover of rain clouds. The darkness reminded one of the dark blue hue of Mother Kali. The moon peeped through the rain clouds as they were scattered by the wind. The devotees stopped singing as Mother said in a loud voice, "Count the heads." One resident approached Her and said, "Amma, we have a list of the names of everybody traveling in the bus." "Okay, then call each name and let the person respond by chanting 'Om Namah Shivaya'," Mother said. This brahmachari began calling out the names one by one, and the devotees responded as instructed by the Mother. She laughed and apparently enjoyed this very much and remarked, "Just like being in school."

When the roll call was completed, Mother started singing

Maname Nara Jivita Makum

O mind, this human birth is like a field,
If not cultivated properly
It becomes dry and barren.

You know neither how to sow the seeds properly
Nor how to grow them well,
Neither have you the wish to know.

By removing the weeds and applying fertilizer,
By taking proper care,
You may have a good harvest.

As the singing continued, the rain clouds slowly disappeared. Both heaven and earth were lit up by the shimmering moonlight. Immersed in a completely indrawn state, Mother kept on singing while Her eyes were fixed on the silvery sky above.

Radha Ramana.

O Beloved of Radha, Lord of my heart,
Destroyer of misery and Support of all,
Is it not Thee, O Embodiment of Consciousness,
Who occupies my mind solely?

20 April 1984

The next morning at around five o'clock, the bus carrying Mother and Her children reached Kanyakumari. They at once proceeded to a small ashram which belonged to a swami who had great respect for the Mother, and he was very delighted to see Her. Everyone had a chance to rest from their all-night journey.

At 6:00 a.m. they went to another spiritual center and rented rooms. Half an hour later everyone went with Mother to see the sunrise. She stood on a rock facing east as the sun slowly emerged from the sea. Yellow rays of sunlight blended with the reddish glow of the sky, and this light slowly pervaded the eastern horizon and was reflected in the sea. The Mother stood like a statue on the rock, gazing at the sun, beholding its glory and splendor. Her countenance shone with a radiant smile. Raising both Her arms, She sang

Vandikyunnen

In order that You dance within me,
O Mother, O Adorable One
I bow and surrender to Thee.

Existing as the Power of Life
Within the individual soul,
If You should leave, all would become still.

O Universal Energy, the Self of Perfect Bliss,
Come, come, O Supreme Light
Remain, never abandon me.

O Thou Atom of atoms,
Who pervades the Universe,
Dweller in the Thousand-petalled Lotus,
Come, come.

Thou Whose brilliance equals millions of suns,
Dweller within myself,
That Mother alone is the only hope
For getting merged in Her.

The devotees sang the response. Afterwards, with everyone feeling as if they had been bathed in the eternal glory of the Supreme Light, they slowly walked back to their rooms. Each cherished the vision of the rising sun glowing on the horizon, the soothing sounds of the ocean waves lapping on the shore, and the divine feeling which the Mother had created through Her physical presence and Her singing. The charm and beauty of this occasion was utterly inexplicable.

Receiving the Guru's prasad

Later Mother and the group went into the city of Kanyakumari to visit the Devi Temple. By the seashore on the southern side of this temple lived Mayi Amma, an *avadhuta* (one in a state of bliss, beyond the observance of social mores).

A few years earlier, during the first visit that Mother had made to the Cape, a devotee who accompanied Her had a wonderful experience with this *avadhuta* who lived with her pack of dogs. No one knew much about her. She was said to be more than 150 years old. She very seldom spoke, and if she did utter something, it was hardly understandable. She was indeed a totally incomprehensible character.

Just the day before that first visit to Kanyakumari, that particular devotee had come to the Ashram and was with the Mother when She was eating Her lunch. A few of the brahmacharis were also present, and as it was Her custom in those days, Mother would feed all those who sat near Her before She Herself would eat. Mother offered a ball of rice to everyone, including that devotee, who was a strict vegetarian. Because the Ashram was right in the middle of a fishing village and fish was generally eaten by the villagers, the man was worried that there was fish in the rice and therefore was hesitant to accept the Mother's *prasad.* Since only vegetarian food was made at the ashram, there was no fish in the rice at all. Mother did not insist, so he did not take the *prasad.*

The next day the same devotee was among the people in Mother's party who happened to be with Mayi Amma while she was having her lunch. Mayi Amma, too, gave *prasad* to everyone. When it was the devotee's turn to receive *prasad,* Mayi Amma put aside the rice and vegetables she had been distributing and uncovered a separate dish, took out a big piece of fried fish and pushed it into his mouth. This was quite unexpected! Nobody even suspected that there was fish in the *biksha* (alms) she had received. No fish had been given to anyone else, except that devotee who had refused the prasad from the Holy Mother the day before. Everyone else had received plain rice mixed with vegetables. The devotee turned pale and sat with the fish between his teeth while everyone burst into laughter. He could neither swallow it nor could he spit it out. He was in a dilemma. For although he was a strict vegetarian, this fish was *prasad,* therefore sacred. Finally he had to swallow it, closing both his eyes tightly.

Later he confessed, "That was God's punishment for my having doubts about Amma in not accepting the *prasad* which She had offered me. That was a good lesson for me."

Another incident of someone refusing the Holy Mother's *prasad* is worth relating at this time. It happened in 1979, back in the days when devotees from the neighboring houses used to bring food to the Mother. The Mother never cared what they brought as an offering, and sometimes they brought fish as a side dish for the rice. She knew that for the local villagers fish was a staple food and one of their favorite dishes. About this the Mother has said, "While cooking the food, the devotees constantly chant their mantras. These children bring it with great *sankalpa*[2] and devotion. How can Mother refuse it when their devotion and *sankalpa* are so pure and innocent?" And so even though all the Ashramites were pure vegetarians, the Mother would lovingly accept this favorite food of the villagers.

A second particular incident involved a woman devotee who had come for the Mother's *darshan*. As she was sitting next to Mother, another devotee from a neighboring house arrived with *biksha* for Mother. A side dish of fish came with the rice she brought, and, as was Her custom, Mother offered one ball of rice with curry to this woman devotee beside Her. The woman took it in her hands, but she did not eat it. After the woman had left, Mother commented to some of the remaining devotees, "What a pity! That daughter did not eat the rice," When the woman had returned to her home, she became sick, vomiting constantly whenever she ate or drank anything. Day by day her condition grew worse. She could eat nothing at all, and, as a result, she became very weak. Although she tried different medications, nothing relieved her condition. A whole week passed in this manner when suddenly she was struck with the revelation that her vomiting condition was caused by the fact that she had refused to eat the Holy Mother's *prasad*.

Immediately she returned to the Ashram, and as she stepped into the *darshan* hut, the woman heard the Mother saying to another devotee the very words she needed to hear, "The Guru is God. Whatever the Guru gives should be accepted with utmost reverence and devotion. Even if it is a seemingly insignificant object like a stone or a blade of grass, one should accept it as one would the most precious thing. One should not refuse the Guru's *prasad*, whatever it might be. Ordinary human beings

---

[2] The creative power of thought and will manifesting as feelings, prayers, attitudes and resolves.

cannot understand with what *sankalpa* the Guru gives the *prasad*. *Satgurus* know what to give and when to give it. Therefore, accept whatever they give. Never deny the Guru's *prasad*."

Hearing these words, the woman was overcome with emotion. Now she was fully convinced about the cause of her sickness. She fell at the Mother's feet and sought forgiveness for her ignorant behavior. Mother consoled her and fed her with a small piece of banana which she ate. Thereafter, the vomiting completely stopped. It had taken her a whole week to realize the cause of her troubles, but it was a lesson duly learned. Such incidents with the Mother are worth remembering because they illustrate how to respond in the presence of a Perfect Master.

After spending the day visiting the temple and different parts of the shore around Kanyakumari, Mother returned in the evening to the ashram, accepting the invitation the swami had extended to Her that morning. At five o'clock the swami spoke a few words about the Mother before the evening *bhajan* began. He said, "Even today there are *jivanmuktas* (Self-Realized souls) and *avatars* (Divine Incarnations) in this country. Amma is this kind of Divine Incarnation. But people do not have the eyes to see it. Those who have not inherited from their previous birth the ability to recognize them will scandalize *jivanmuktas* and *avatars*, thus making it impossible for others to come to know and worship these great souls. This is a very sad situation."

The *bhajan* lasted for an hour or so. One of the songs led by Mother was

Amme Yennu Loru

Why is it that my hairs stand on end
When I remember the word 'Amma'?
Why do I forget everything else
When I think of Mother, my Mother?

Thirst and hunger have left me,
I have also forgotten my daily bath,
I know not what day or date this is,
I forget everything in the thought of Mother.

What is my mind pining for?
Why does my body tremble when I look
At the blue sea, the blue sky
And the white clouds?

Mother's sweet form
Is a solace to suffering minds,
Now my only thought is
When will I see Her again?
When will Mother come to me?

After the *bhajan*, the group returned to the center where they had booked rooms. Mother also returned but remained outside, still in a blissful state after Her ecstatic singing. She did not want others around Her at this particular time. All alone She walked a short distance away from the building and sat under a neem tree. At ten o'clock, the center and its environs were quiet even though there were many people staying there. Half an hour passed. Everyone was still waiting outside the building, with the hope that they could once again see Mother before they went to bed. As if in response to their wishes and prayers, Mother's voice emerged from the dark, "Gayatri-*mol*."[3] Everyone's attention turned in the direction of Her voice as the glow of expectation shone on their faces. "Call all the children." That was enough. Gayatri did

---

[3] Brahmacharini Gayatri ("mol" means "daughter" in Mother's language, Malayalam) is Mother's personal attendant. In 1984 there were only two brahmacharinis who lived with Mother, Gayatri and Kunjumol, both of whom looked after Her personal needs. There were other women who came for extended visits and some householder residents.

not have to inform them, for the whole group immediately ran toward Mother. Each one wanted to sit as close to Her as possible. Jostling, they tried to get closer and closer. When at last everyone had settled down, a silence prevailed which was broken only by Mother's voice, "Children, if any of you are too tired or feel sleepy, don't strain yourself. Don't feel that because Mother has called, you must sit here. Mother just wanted to see all Her children together; that's why She called you." But none of them wanted to go to bed, for their hearts craved to spend as much time as they could with Mother.

Subtle food of the Guru

One of the devotees remarked, "We are hungry children, Amma. Give us something to eat. How can you ask us to go to bed when we are badly in need of food? We cannot sleep when you are going to serve food here."

Amma said, "This is subtle food. To taste this subtle food one needs a subtle tongue. Children, the Guru is, in fact, your food. A true disciple should try to eat him up. The Guru is waiting to be swallowed by the disciple. But most disciples are unable to do that, for they lack the subtlety to do so. They know only about the gross body of the Guru."

"Amma," asked one of the devotees, "what do you mean by subtle food? And what do you mean by 'eating up the Guru'?"

Her reply came, "It doesn't mean that you should bite him and eat him up." All laughed, the Mother included.

When the laughter subsided, Amma continued, "The Guru's real form is something far beyond the physical plane of existence. It transcends even the Trimurti (the Trinity – Brahma, the Creator; Vishnu, the Preserver; and Maheshwara, the Destroyer). It is the Supreme Principle itself. One should try to see through the physical form of the Guru to his inner form, the subtle form. One

45

needs subtlety of mind to know and realize this subtle nature of the Guru. Through *sadhana* one should try to attain that state of mind. This food is not something which can be taken through the mouth. It is to be imbibed through the heart. Imbibing the higher principles in which the Guru lives is eating up the Guru. If you see only the Guru's physical form, without trying to understand his inner nature, you will always end up in danger. Let Mother tell you a story to illustrate this point.

"There was once a Master who had two disciples who always competed with each other. One day while he was resting the Guru called both of them to massage his legs. The Guru was lying down and the two disciples sat on either side of him. The first disciple said, 'Look here, the right leg is mine, and the left is yours, okay?' The second disciple replied, 'Agreed. And don't encroach on my territory. If I am going to take care of the left leg, don't butt in.' The first one answered back, 'I and my right leg will not interfere with you and your left leg.' So they started massaging. The poor Guru was not aware of this division. He fell asleep, and as he shifted positions, he unknowingly lifted his right leg onto his left. This was enough to enrage the second disciple. The furious disciple stood up and accosted the first disciple, 'You broke the ageement. Remove your right leg from my left leg this very moment. If you don't, you will see who I am and what I can do!' Upon hearing this, the first disciple also got up, yelling, 'Shut up, you braggart! Go ahead, let me see what you can do to my right leg! Do it, if you dare!'

"Both of the disciples grabbed two long sticks. The second disciple got ready to break the right leg while the first was bent on taking revenge by breaking the left leg. Hearing the argument between the two disciples, the Guru woke up and and was surprised to see them standing one on either side of him, furiously glaring at each other while brandishing sticks. He exclaimed,

'What is this? What are you two doing?' The disciples cooly retorted, 'Go back to sleep. This is none of your business. We can settle this matter.'

"This is what happens if one does not try to see beyond the physical Guru. One should strive hard to see the real nature of the Guru. That real nature is something beyond His physical form. To perceive that essential nature of the Guru one needs subtlety, subtlety to penetrate the Guru. Otherwise, it could culminate in something like this incident of the two disciples trying to break the Guru's leg.

"Subtlety of mind can only be attained through concentration. It comes when the mind is completely focused on the Supreme Principle, when all thought waves have ceased. In that state your mind becomes as expansive and vast as the unclouded sky.

"The Guru is the Creator, the Sustainer and the Destroyer, and at the same time He is beyond these. The Guru is the Supreme Principle made manifest in the form of one who sheds light upon the disciple. By sowing the seed of spirituality in the disciple, the Guru wakes him up from the sleep of ignorance. Externally we are wide awake, that is, we are in an ordinary state of being awake to the world of objects. We are wide awake to the plural world of objects and fast asleep to the real world of Consciousness. From this standpoint, one may wonder, "How can I wake up again?" It is the inner awakening that is the real waking up. Even though every morning we wake up to the external world of objects, we are fast asleep internally. We are asleep, not awake to the Reality of the Self within. The Guru makes the disciple understand and realize that he is sleeping, that he is in ignorance. In order to remove something, one should, first of all, know that it is there. The Guru makes the disciple aware of his own ignorance. Having done this, a Satguru makes the disciple work in his spiritual practice in order to remove this ignorance.

"More precisely, the Guru wakes the disciple up from sleep, makes him aware that he is sleeping deep within, and by putting him through rigorous spiritual training, he awakens the spiritual energy within him. Working side by side with the disciple, the Guru breaks the shell of his ego. Thus the Guru becomes the destroyer, the destroyer of the ego.

"A Great Master is the embodiment of the 'subtler than the subtlest' principle.[4] Only when the disciple becomes as subtle as the Guru can he realize his unity with such a Perfect Master."

The Mother paused. All could clearly see Her face as they sat around Her under the neem tree. The moon was shining in the sky and its glow caressed the earth. The moon which enhanced that night was like the Mother who beautified human hearts. In that peaceful atmosphere everyone seemed very much absorbed both in the Mother's form and in Her words. Someone in the group commented, "Amma, you are that Guru. You are that subtle principle."

Amma did not pay any attention to him. She just sat gazing at the moon. Another devotee reminded Her that She had not said anything about 'eating up the Guru.' But She did not reply. She remained looking at the moon. She was in a rapture, for Her eyes were still and fixed. Realizing that the Mother was in an absorbed mood, the devotees kept quiet. It took a few minutes for Her to come down.

She then continued, " 'Eating the Guru up' means to merge in him completely. You should dissolve. The 'I' or the ego should dissolve and disappear. Disappearance of your little self and total identification with the Guru's inner Self is what is meant by 'eating up.' This is total Oneness. Forgetting all about yourself, your entire being should enter into and disappear in his Pure Being.

---

[4] *Anoraniyan Mahatomahiyan* in Sanskrit, meaning "subtler than the subtlest, bigger than the biggest."

This is 'eating up the Guru.' It is possible only through love, only through the heart, not with the head. Love can easily consume the Guru. Love can easily consume your ego. Once the ego is fully consumed by Love, the Guru will simply enter into you or you can simply enter into Him. Both are one and the same because then there is nothing to obstruct, nothing to stop the flow. This flow of love goes both ways and becomes one. The Guru is already flowing constantly, flowing and overflowing the brim with love. And through love you flow into Him.

"In the state of pure innocent love, the lover is always hungry. He wants to eat up his beloved. There is an insatiable hunger in pure love. One can see and experience this intense hunger even in worldly love. But in spiritual love the intensity reaches its peak. That apex is the extreme point, the ultimate limit which is limitless, for this love is all-expansive. In a true seeker this love becomes like a forest fire, yet it is even more intense, more consuming. His whole being will burn with the intensity of that fire of love. In that blazing fire he himself gets consumed and then comes the complete merging.

"What happens when you eat food? The digestive process makes it one with your body. The food will become one with you. It will become your body, mind and intellect. Similarly, the Guru is your spiritual food. Eat him up if you can. Imbibe him. Let his light and love fill your body, mind and intellect. If you do this then there will be no more body, mind or intellect. You will become love. The Guru is waiting to be consumed. If you are hungry, swallow him up. If you are not hungry, starve in order to feel hunger."

Astonished by the imagery, a devotee exclaimed, "Starve! It's not about giving up food that you are talking, is it? Could you please make this clearer?"

"Son, you are right," Amma said. "Mother does not mean physical starvation. Make the mind starve. Stop feeding the mind with thoughts. We continue feeding the mind with the food of desires and thoughts. This has become a habit, and the mind now thinks that this is the best food. This is a habit which should be removed. The mind should know that this food will give us a 'stomach ache,' if not now, then later. The mind should know that this food of thoughts and desires is harmful and that there is food far tastier and healthier than this. The various spiritual practices make up the most delicious and healthful food. Once you experience this, start to feed the mind regularly with the Divine Name, *japa* (chanting one's mantra), *dhyana* (meditation) and other spiritual practices. Slowly the hunger to have more and more of this spiritual food will grow until at last it becomes a terrible hunger. You will want to swallow God. But to attain this, starve the mind. Stop feeding the mind with worldly thoughts and desires."

Mother stopped. After a few moments of silence, She asked Balu to sing a *kirtan* (devotional song)

Katutta Sokamam

O Mother, let me not fall into this
Deep dark pit of sorrow.
I am neither a scholar
Nor one born under a lucky star.

Nevertheless, intense are my thoughts
Fixed on Thee,
O Mother, walk not away,
Simply casting a smile at me.

Renouncing all other forms of happiness
And constantly remembering Thy purity,
I chant Thy transcendent Names.

O Eternal Auspiciousness,
To remember Thy words
That this birth is to exhaust
All errors from my past births, I console myself.

O Embodiment of Compassion,
Remove my ignorance.
Bestow pure intelligence on me.

In the midst of worldly pleasures,
I always gaze upon Thee
Yet unhappy am I. O Ruler of all worlds,
Giver of greatness, light the lamp
Of equal vision in my innermost self.

It was nearly eleven o'clock. Mother said, "Children, all of you go to bed now." After having prostrated to the Mother, all got up and went to their rooms. Mother, accompanied by Gayatri, sat under the neem tree for a while longer. She put Her head on Gayatri's lap and lay there in silence. It was not quite midnight when She finally went to Her room.

A few brahmacharis and householder devotees did not go to bed on returning to their shared rooms. Instead, they sat on their beds and began discussing the day's conversations with the Mother. The late-night discussion quickly evolved into a dispute, for each one of them had his own interpretation of Her wisdom-filled words. As the lively discussion continued, someone knocked on the door. All wondered who it could be at such a late hour, for it was already 1:30 a.m. They thought that it was perhaps the caretaker or a guard. Assuming it must be the night watchman, they opened the door. How surprised they were to see the Mother standing there, with Gayatri just behind! The Mother had a serious look on Her face.

A few moments passed before She spoke, "Have you forgotten so quickly about all the things which Mother told you before we started this trip? It is one-thirty in the morning; you know that it is wrong to be talking so loudly at this hour. You are not the only ones staying here, you know. There are many, many others. Why do you disturb their sleep by making so much noise? To share your ideas about the *satsang* (spiritual talk) is all right. But to enter into a dispute about it, and adamantly say that what you felt is the only correct interpretation is wrong, totally wrong. By doing this you are narrowing your mind. Sharing ideas is different from disputing. In sharing both parties listen and tell, give and accept. This gives you a broader attitude. It helps you grow. There is no harm in that. But when disputing, you talk – you don't listen. You give your ideas but don't accept the ideas of others even if they express a genuine idea. Thus you are closing yourself, narrowing and limiting yourself. This is dangerous. Moreover, whatever Mother said was meant for contemplation, not for dispute. It was meant to be exercised, not analyzed. It was not to be cut and chopped into pieces with your head."

Having said this much, the Mother left. The devotees and brahmacharis were full of remorse for what they had done. They did not speak another word. They switched off the light and went to bed, feeling a bit sad about the whole incident.

In a few minutes there was another knock at the door. Almost in unison they jumped out of bed and in a split second, the light was turned on. Opening the door, they found Mother standing there, smiling this time. She said, "Mother could not remain in the room after having scolded Her children. She felt restless. Children, did you feel sad?" She was full of compassion.

Together they replied, "No, Amma, not at all." One devotee added, "We realized our mistake. We should not have done that. Amma, we are all ignorant children, so ignorant!" and he began to cry.

With great affection, Amma consoled him and the others. Dividing the plantain She held into small pieces, She fed a bit to each person and once again spoke a few consoling words, "Children, don't be sad. Mother can only do things which are good for you, things which will make you grow spiritually. She cannot act otherwise. Mother feels that freedom with Her children; therefore, She cannot help correcting you when you make mistakes, for She thinks that you will take it in the right way. Mother feels that you are Her own. Children, you should also try to feel the same way, that Mother is your own. Then there will not be any sadness or mental agitation."

Her words were so full of concern and love that the devotees and brahmacharis could not control their tears. Each one of them cried privately while lying in bed that night, cherishing in his heart the Mother's innocent love for Her children. They all felt themselves cradled to sleep in the Mother's arms.

21 April 1984

The next morning at seven o'clock, the entire group left for Marutvamala, a sacred hill. Also called Medicine Hill, this little mountain is famous for the ayurvedic herbs which grow on it. The ancient *Puranas* (epics) say that Hanuman, the great servant devotee of Lord Sri Rama, was sent to obtain some divine herbs to heal Lakshmana, Rama's devoted brother who was wounded in the battle against Ravana in Sri Lanka (Ceylon). Ravana had abducted Sita, the wife of Rama, and the battle was fought to rescue Sita. Lakshmana was wounded by a spear thrown by Ravana and was lying in a coma. Only herbs obtained from Mt.

Kailash could restore him to consciousness. Rather than waste time looking for the individual herbs, Hanuman uprooted an entire portion of the mountain and flew back to Sri Lanka. As he rounded the tip of India, a piece of the mountain fell off near Kanyakumari, forming this sacred medicine hill, Marutvamala. Today many seekers come here on their pilgrimage, climbing this hill to make offerings at its Hanuman shrine, and *sadhaks* (spiritual aspirants) can be found performing *tapas* in small caves dispersed on this hill.

Nayanar Swami

A short distance away from the main road, where the path leading to Marutvamala Hill began, there was a small house where another *avadhuta* (this one an old man) used to live. His name was Nayanar Swami. Mother had met him on Her first visit to Kanyakumari three years before.

During his lifetime, Nayanar Swami had stayed in one very small room in the house which belonged to a lower class Tamil family. The dark room from which he is said never to have emerged was filled with sacks and pieces of wood, and all sorts of other seemingly useless things which he had used to make images of goddesses and gods. He was a very strange character whose actions were incomprehensible to most people. Yet many divine powers were attributed to him. Nayanar Swami had left his body one year before this present visit. In fact, just after returning from Her visit with Nayanar Swami three years earlier, Mother had predicted that he would leave his body after two years' time.

Some very interesting things took place at that first meeting of Mother and this *avadhuta*. The Holy Mother and a group of about twenty devotees were on their return trip to Vallickavu after having spent three days in Kanyakumari. During those three days, most of their time was spent in *satsang*, *bhajan* and meditation on the rocks by the seashore and in the Devi temple by the side of the ocean. Traveling in a hired van, the group began to proceed north. Hardly had they gone ten kilometers when all of a sudden a strange looking old man jumped in front of the van, waving his hands as if to signal the vehicle to stop. "Stop the van! There is Nayanar Swami!" Mother shouted.

The van was stopped and everyone got up from his seat. Seeing the swami enter a small house, Mother and all Her devotees followed him inside. Mother sat down in front of Nayanar Swami and everyone gathered around. The *avadhuta* swami was very excited. He muttered a few words in Hindi and then, pointing his finger towards the Holy Mother, he called out, "Kali! Kali! Deathless One!" As he shouted these words over and over again, the Mother's *bhava* (mood) suddenly changed.

Her tongue stuck out, Her eyes bulged, and She produced a peculiar sound which was similar to that of the seed letter 'Hrim' being chanted constantly in an unbroken stream. As She manifested all these gestures, the Mother levitated. She was not touching the floor at all! The fingers of both Her hands held divine *mudras* (yogic gestures). The Mother was portraying the fierce aspect of Mother Kali, and the swami appeared to be very excited and delighted indeed.

The brahmacharis and devotees began singing a *kirtan* (devotional song). They were all a bit frightened and worried to see the unexpected changes in the Mother's mood. Some of the women even began to cry. Eventually the Holy Mother returned to the physical plane of consciousness, and Her normal self. The swami also grew calm. At this point, one of the Mother's devotees reached out with his palm towards him and asked, "Swami, will you give me *brahmatvam* (the state of Brahman)?" Nayanar Swami forcibly turned the devotee's hand towards the Mother and said in Hindi, "Here, you ask Her. She is the right person to ask."

Later when the brahmacharis asked Mother why She manifested the divine mood in the swami's presence, She answered,
"He desired to see it." They did not know what She meant.

Now, three year later, as Mother and the group left the bus
to climb the sacred hill, they were greeted by the local people.
Upon seeing the Mother and Her devotees, the family with
whom Nayanar Swami had lived came running towards them
and offered their prostrations to Her. They expressed their wish
to have a picture of Amma and the address of the Ashram saying,
"Three years ago, when all of you left after visiting the swami,
he exclaimed to us, "Do you know who that was? She is Kali,
Bhadrakali!" They also told us that as the van had moved away,
the swami had come out of the house again and stood there star-
ing at it until it disappeared from his sight. They added that the
swami had never come out of his room, not before nor since,
except for those two times, that is, when he had jumped in front
of the van to make it stop, and when he had come out to watch
the Mother drive away.

One of the devotees gave the lady of the house a picture of
the Mother and the Ashram address, which the family was very
happy to receive. Mother and the group of devotees took leave
of them and started to climb the hill.

Marutvamala was very beautiful. There were shady trees,
rocks and caves on the hill, making it an ideal setting for a life
of asceticism and contemplation. Everyone climbed the hill with
great enthusiasm, even the elderly people who had come with the
group in a separate car which followed the bus. All were so happy
to make this pilgrimage with Mother that they did not feel any
weariness or fatigue. Occasionally Mother turned around and
asked the elderly devotees, "Do you feel tired? If you do, sit down
and rest for a while." They always replied, "No, we are not tired.
When Amma is with us, how can we feel tired?" It was actually

amazing to see how these elderly people climbed the hill which was quite steep in some parts along the way.

As She walked, the Holy Mother started singing devotional songs. Everyone responded blissfully. With arms outstretched in ecstasy, the Mother sang as She ascended the hill. One devotee was carrying a tin container full of banana chips on his head and set it down in front of Mother who distributed the food to everyone. Again, She sang

Hariyude Kalil

Without falling at the Feet of God,
None can extinguish the fire
Of the sorrow of transmigration.

Without bowing forever to the Guru,
None will gain the bliss of Liberation.
None can reach the Lord
Without getting absorbed in chanting the Name.

None can attain the state of Liberation
Without merging in the sweetness of devotion.
He who does not meditate, do japa
Or other spiritual practices,
Will not partake of the nectar of Bliss.

Without righteousness and compassion,
Good actions cannot be performed.
In this world, only God is the Friend
Of the devotee and the Supporter of the helpless.
When He is with us,
How can we be without support?

Humility

The group reached a place on the hill where there was a beautiful temple, and everyone stopped there for a short while to rest. Two monks of the place came up to the Mother and bowed down before Her. They had heard about the Mother and wanted to meet Her, they explained. She talked to them for a few minutes, and when they left, She said, "One of them is a good *sadhak*. Mother knew this immediately upon looking in his eyes. He is very humble too."

Reminding the devotees about the importance of humility in spiritual life, Amma again spoke: "Humility will come as one progresses in *sadhana*. Humility means seeing God in everything or perceiving one's own Self everywhere. Humility means accepting the Will of the Supreme. Humility means self- surrender, surrendering our will to the Will of God. Once that is done, one can only be humble because one sees that whatever happens in his life, whether positive or negative, is His will. In this state, all reactions disappear. There are no more reactions, only acceptance. Therefore, humility can also be interpreted as total acceptance."

Mother got up from where She sat, saying, "Let us continue climbing." As the group moved up the hill, Mother led the chant, "Shyam Radhe," to which the devotees joyfully responded with "Radhe, Radhe." Sometimes Mother switched and chanted "Radhe, Radhe," and the group replied, "Shyam, Radhe."

Although it was a hot day, the breeze lessened the intensity of the heat. Mother kept on chanting, "Shyam, Radhe." All of a sudden, She stopped chanting and stood still. She was in *samadhi* (absorption in the Self or God). With both hands raised forming a divine *mudra,* the Mother remained perfectly still. Her eyes were half- closed, and a beautiful smile glowed on Her face. Minutes passed. Slowly She regained consciousness but remained unmoving for a little while longer before proceeding. Silence prevailed for some time. No one spoke.

It was Mother who broke the silence, "Children, don't forget to chant your mantra. The period of *sadhana* is like climbing a high mountain. You need a lot of strength and energy. Mountain climbers use rope for pulling themselves up. For you, the only rope is *japa*. Therefore, children, try to repeat your mantra constantly. Once you reach the peak, you can relax and rest forever."

The sun became more and more intense. Someone tried to hold an umbrella for Mother, but She refused it, "No, no. Mother doesn't need an umbrella. How can She stay under an umbrella when all Her children are walking in the sun? Besides, She is used to it. Come rain or shine Mother used to spend all Her days and nights outside in the open air. Sugunanandan-*acchan* (father) and Damayanti Amma used to get so worried about Mother's staying outside that they built a raised shelter in order to protect Her from the rain and the sun. But She never remained there. Mother was very determined to transcend both heat and cold by enduring them. The heat of obstacles will not affect a person who constantly remembers God."

As the group continued climbing, Mother noticed some people relaxing under some shady trees. Another wise saying followed, "When the time comes, the leaves will fall off of even shade-giving trees, and you who sit under them will again have to sweat and toil in the sun's heat."

This was a hint which meant that God alone gives eternal shade, and that none of the worldly places of refuge is permanent. These temporal shelters will perish one day or another, pushing one again into deep sorrow.

Mother continued, "Only a few, very few among the millions who have tried for it, have ever reached the goal. It will certainly not be possible to reach the goal if you forget the goal while sitting in the shade along the way.

"Some *sadhaks* come and ask Mother the day, date and even the time of their realization. Poor people, they don't understand that thinking and brooding about such things are distractions from the goal. Children, there are express buses and local ones. Once the express bus starts from its point of origin, it never stops until it reaches its destination. One can easily predict that the express bus will reach its destination on time. However, the local bus will stop and take people from every junction, and one cannot state the exact time that it will arrive at the destination. Similarly, the determination and *lakshya bodha* (intent to reach the goal) of some *sadhaks* are so strong that they won't stop until they reach the goal. Such *sadhaks* are like the express bus, and a Satguru can tell when they will reach the goal. On the other hand, most *sadhaks* are like the local bus. They lack determination and *lakshya bodha*; therefore, it is difficult to say when they will reach the goal. They are like people who sit in the 'shade' forgetting the goal."

A devotee remarked, "Amma, you are always sitting, aren't you? It is we who walk, isn't that so?"

"If Mother sits, everyone will sit, and then no climbing will take place," came the Mother's immediate answer.

Everyone felt that She was indicating that the wheel of creation will come to a standstill if God becomes inactive.

Some *sannyasins* (renunciates) were sitting on either side of the path. Mother asked the householder devotees to give them alms, explaining, "In order to sustain the body, these *sannyasins* need food. By giving alms to them, householders gain merit. In order to lead a happy life in the world, a householder needs such merit. Giving alms to the deserving is a way of acquiring merit. But a true spiritual seeker tries to go beyond both merit and demerit; therefore, he does not care about its gain or loss."

Eventually Mother and the whole party reached the peak which was named Pillattadam. It was an especially lovely place from which one could see all the surrounding areas. There was a shelter here with a natural rock covering for a roof, and several large, flat rocks where one could sit comfortably. Just below there was a natural cave which was occupied by a *sannyasin*.

As Mother and all Her children sat on the rocks, She gazed at the eastern horizon for a long time. The atmosphere was peaceful and serene, as this place was totally isolated from the outside world. A strong wind blew from the west, but that slowly subsided after a short while. Mother seemed to be revelling in Her own world, and the whole group remained silent. Some time passed and then She sang

Kodanukodi

O Truth Eternal,
Mankind has searched for Thee
For millions and millions of years.

Renouncing everything, the ancient sages
Performed endless years of austerities
In order to make the Self flow
Into Thy Divine Stream through meditation.

Thy infinitesimal Flame, inaccessible to all,
Glowing like the effulgence of the sun,
Stands still without dancing
Even in the fiercely blowing cyclone.

Then Mother asked Balu to sing a song. He sang one which he had composed once when he had to be away from Mother for a few weeks

Sokamitentinu Sandhye

O Twilight, why are you sad?
Are you also wandering on the shores
Of past memories?
O Dusk, bathed in reddish hue,
Is the fire of sorrow burning within you too?

O Twilight, have you a Mother like mine?
Or have you seen my Mother
Who radiates the beauty
And coolness of purity like the full moon?

O Dusk, should you see Her, please convey
The message of this helpless son who cannot speak
Due to deep sorrow caused by the pain of separation.

O Twilight, please offer
These flower petals at Her Feet
And kindly convey my humble prostrations to Her.
When you return I will confide in you
The heart-rending stories of my former days.

After singing more songs, Mother asked everyone to close his eyes and meditate. She also closed Her eyes and became deeply absorbed. Many of the devotees preferred to sit gazing at the Mother, as most of them had chosen Her as their beloved deity. Yet, bound by Mother's words, everyone turned his gaze inward.

Having spent an hour or so at the top of the hill, at 1:30 p.m. the party began climbing down. There was not much talking during the descent, but *bhajans* filled the air. Mother sang mostly *namavalis* (simple songs chanting the Divine Names). Clapping their hands joyfully and enjoying the nectar of devotional singing, everyone followed Mother down the hill.

Suffering of the poor

Upon reaching the foot of the hill, Mother approached some huts where extremely poor Tamil families lived. She spent some time with each of them. Conversing lovingly, She inquired how they earned their livelihood, whether or not they received any support from the government, and asked specifically about other problems they had. Mother seemed very concerned, and expressed much compassion and love for these people, hugging and kissing every one of them, and, with Her own hands, She distributed some sweets and other food.

Upon leaving, Mother said, "Poor children. Mother is deeply wounded in Her mind, seeing these people's suffering. Who will take care of them? People talk about helping the poor, but no one seems to be doing anything for them. Children, compared to the suffering of these people, our suffering is nothing. God has provided us with food, clothing and shelter. But these children have nothing. Let us use our God-given faculties with utmost discrimination. We must not cheat Him by misusing them. These children might have misused such gifts in their previous births, and that is why they are suffering now. Still it is our duty to have compassion for them. In fact God created the rich to help the poor, the healthy to assist the unhealthy, and normal human beings to help and serve the mentally retarded and physically deformed."

A devotee asked, "Amma, why does God keep quiet when people are suffering like this? Can't He do something to remove it?"

"Yes, He did something, son," came the Mother's answer. "He created us, hoping that we would do something to help them. We should think of them. We should try to feel their suffering. In order to do this, we should try to put ourselves in their place. We have never suffered in our lives, so we don't even know what suffering is. We consider our personal problems as big and important. But children, there are more important things in this world. There are far bigger problems to solve. Yet we think of our own problems only. We do not consider others' problems nor feel any compassion for them. That is our biggest problem. Only a person who has really suffered can understand the suffering of others. We have never dived deep to the bottom of the sea to collect pearls. We do not know how difficult a task it is, for we are used to buying pearls from a shop. Therefore, we do not know the immense task behind the matter."

By now the group had reached the bus. Mother was the first to get in and the others followed. When all were settled in their seats, She continued, "There are two occasions when most human beings are happy or unhappy. They are happy when their enemy or one whom they dislike is unhappy or suffering. But they are unhappy when they hear that he is having a good time or a contented life. Mother will tell you an anecdote.

"There were two neighbors who were enemies. One day one of them went to buy some wood to do some maintenance work on his house. Unfortunately, upon returning home, he realized that both pieces of wood that he had purchased were decayed inside, and thus he felt very unhappy about the waste of his money. He then left the house in that state, but when he returned, he was laughing and rejoicing. His wife was curious and asked, 'Why are you laughing like this? What is the matter?' He replied, 'How can I not laugh? You know, in buying the two pieces of rotten wood we did not lose so much money, but our neighbor suffered a huge loss. He bought twenty pieces of the wood from the same shop, and all of it turned out to be just as useless!'" Everybody in the bus burst into laughter.

"Children, this is our attitude," Amma said after the laughter ended. "We do not have a heart that feels the sorrow of others. We feel happy when our neighbors are unhappy, and we feel unhappy when they are glad. But *Mahatmas* reflect both the happiness and unhappiness of others and express them sincerely. That is the difference between a mortal being and a *Mahatma*. He has the heart to feel others' sorrow and suffering. The sorrow of others is his sorrow, and the happiness of others is his own happiness. But ordinary human beings are totally self-centered. Children, try to hear the cries and know the pains of suffering people."

The bus stopped in front of the center where the group was staying. It was now almost three o'clock. Mother went immediately to Her room, while the others had lunch before going to their rooms to rest. Two hours later the group gathered again and went walking to the seashore with Mother in the lead.

Among the devotees there was an eighty-five year old scholar who was an authority on Sanskrit grammar and logic. He was constantly talking, introducing a topic and asking the others to pose questions about the subject. He was very restless and clearly wanted to show off his vast knowledge. He debated, argued and disputed. As the group neared the seashore, Mother called to him, "*Pundit mon* (scholar-son)." Although he boasted in front of others, this learned old man was like a three year-old boy in front of the Mother. His devotion to Her was very steady and firm. His age did not affect his health at all. He had been practising *hatha yoga* for many, many years, and therefore, he was very strong, cheerful and vigorous.

Upon hearing Mother calling him, the pundit ran towards Her. She looked at him and smiled mischievously, for She had been listening to everything he had said. He bowed low in front of Her. With one hand She caught hold of his hands, and with the fingers of Her other hand, She playfully tapped the top of his bald head as if it were a drum. "Son," Mother remarked, "you have wasted eighty long years with your Sanskrit and logic. After so many years of study, you should try to move from the head to the heart. It is too late for you to do it alone, so Mother is trying to tune you, intellectually at least, by strumming on your head."

Everyone laughed, except for the pundit, who turned pale and said, "Amma, forgive me for my ignorance." He looked a bit distressed. The Mother's words had obviously made him reflect on his life.

After a fifteen-minute walk they reached the seashore. Mother stood still for quite some time, looking out at the vast expanse of the sea. Then She asked everyone to sit down and meditate. Before they began, Mother gave instructions: "Visualize a fully-bloomed lotus flower in the ocean and imagine that your beloved deity is sitting on it. Try to imagine that the deity is looking at you, smiling at you, calling you near and blessing you. Try to see clearly each and every part of your beloved's form—the eyes, eyebrows, nose, lips, cheeks, forehead, hair, crown, everything. If you don't like to do this, you can simply concentrate on the sound of the ocean waves."

Having given these suggestions, the Mother Herself became immersed in meditation. Everyone meditated with Her as they sat before the ocean, its waves unceasingly washing up on the shore, creating a rhythmic drone. The evening light became diffuse as the glow of twilight softened into dusk, and the seagulls emitted a final cry to mark the close of day.

Sadhana, self-surrender and love

After returning from the seashore, Mother and Her children sang *bhajans* in a hall at the place where they were staying. A good-sized crowd came to listen to the Mother and to receive Her blessing. By nine o'clock the *bhajan* and *darshan* were over and Mother returned to Her room. Some very sincere *sadhaks* and a few other devotees who wanted a private audience with the Mother came to see Her. She sat on the front verandah of Her room and invited them to sit in front of Her. They prostrated and sat down.

After a few minutes of light conversation, one of the *sadhaks* asked a question: "Amma, how should one do *sadhana*?"

Mother answered, "Children, you can adopt any path you like. Son, one path cannot be advised for all. *Sadhana* should be prescribed according to each one's personal inclinations and mental constitution. It is like prescribing different kinds of medicine for people with different diseases. The same medicine cannot be prescribed for all. The medicine and its dosage must differ according to each patient's disease. The same applies to our *sadhana*. Each person is different in nature and, therefore, should be instructed in such a way as to help him personally to progress spiritually. Spiritual practice is a medicine which can eliminate all diseases caused by the nature of existence.[5] But if the prescription is not correct, like the wrong medicine for a patient, it can cause harm.

"*Lakshya bodha* and effort coupled with patience are needed. In the beginning, one can meditate on the personal aspect of God. But later one should go beyond the form. To attain this, mere reading and studying the scriptures will not suffice. One should also contemplate, 'For what purpose do I read, what is my real goal in life, and what should I do to attain that goal?' Try to keep the mind on God no matter what you are doing. Only if we attain mental maturity can we remain calm, even if somebody scolds us.

"Which path to follow depends on the spiritual disposition one has inherited from the previous birth. This birth is a continuation of the previous one. Whatever path you follow, the mind should flow spontaneously towards it. Love is necessary. To approach a Perfect Master is another way to find your path.

"Regarding *sadhana*, the most important thing one should remember is to maintain the spirit and practice it until you reach

---

[5] *Bhava roga* or the disease of worldly existence.

the goal. It is always a deliberate attempt in the beginning. You have to remember it constantly and try to do it without fail. Now, *maya* (illusion, illusory power) is much more powerful than God in us. This means that negative qualities are more powerful than positive qualities. As a result, the chances of losing enthusiasm and giving up the practice completely or decreasing its intensity are stronger than the chances of continuing it. Therefore, you must deliberately continue doing your practices, putting forth as much effort as possible until they become spontaneous."

Another asked, "How can one attain complete surrender?"

"*Saranagati* (complete self-surrender) is not something which can be taught verbally," explained the Mother. "It will come if you develop love and faith. Pure and innocent love for God is what is really needed. The mind should long to become one with God.

"Like love, surrender cannot be studied or learned from any books or from any particular person or from a university. Self-surrender comes as love grows. In fact, the two grow simultaneously. The more you love a person, the more you surrender to him. This is what happens even in a normal love affair between a man and a woman. The lover and the beloved surrender to each other's wishes and wills, as the love between them grows into fullness. His likes become hers and vice versa. Surrender is nothing but giving up one's individuality, giving up one's likes and dislikes for a higher goal. Even in ordinary love both the lover and the beloved give up their likes and dislikes, which constitute their individuality, for the sake of their love. In spirituality, the seeker renounces all that he has to the Supreme Principle, God. All that one can claim as one's own, all the attachments and aversions one has are the product of one's ego. They can also be referred to as *vasanas* or accumulated tendencies. All these things which we claim as our own do not, in fact, belong to us since we have no control over them. Reputation, fame, position, our homes, wives, husbands, children – none of these can stay with us permanently. We may have such things now, but who knows what is going to happen the next moment? But this is not the case with the accumulated tendencies, with the ego. The ego is our own. It belongs to us. Nobody else can claim it. Therefore, real self-surrender is surrendering or renouncing one's ego at the feet of the Supreme Self."

From that answer arose another question: "Amma, you said that love could not be learned from a university or by reading books. But we feel inspired when we read or hear about Divine Love, don't we?"

"That's true," came the Mother's reply. "But if you observe closely, you will see that people who feel so inspired after reading or hearing about Divine Love, will quickly forget it and can easily feel the opposite if they become provoked. Are you able to dive deep into this feeling of Divine Love? Are you able to sustain that spirit of inspiration within your heart? If so, what you said is correct. But in most cases, this does not happen. People read and feel inspired, and then they forget. Mother is not trying to say that reading and hearing about Divine Love is insignificant. No. But this is what is meant: reading gives us an intellectual understanding of Love, but love is not of the intellect. Love is in the heart. Love is not associated with logic, but with faith. Love is religion; logic is science. Love joins and unites; logic cuts and divides. Love is oneness; logic is multiplicity. Love is deep; logic is superficial. Logic can be taught because it is concerned with the head, but love cannot be taught because it is the language of the heart. This language cannot be expressed through words. It is a spontaneous feeling. Something in the intellect can be expressed verbally, but feelings in the heart cannot be put into words. Ask a lover, 'How much do you love your beloved?' He will say, 'Oh, I love her so much!' or maybe he will say, 'I love her with all my heart and soul.' What feeling do you get from this statement? None."

Another question was asked: "Amma, then what is the way to develop love?"

Mother answered, "Son, in order to develop love one should be in a place where the circumstances are suitable for this goal. To live in the presence of a Perfect Master is the best way to develop love. The Guru helps you by creating the circumstances necessary to fill your heart with love. These circumstances are not only external, but internal as well. The Guru creates both. He works directly with the disciple's *vasanas*, which stand as the main obstacle in the path of love. Through created circumstances, he first attracts and binds the disciple with his person. Once the Guru is fully aware that the disciple is totally attached to him, the next step is elimination of the ego. For that to happen, the Guru again creates situations, working with both the gross and the subtle ego. Once the ego is removed, your inside becomes empty. All the old stuff has been removed, and you can now fill yourself with love. The removal of the old and the filling with the new happens simultaneously.

"The circumstances created by the Guru are so powerful, so precious and alluring, that the disciple will start cherishing and memorizing each moment that he spends with the Guru, and he will start loving the Guru with his body, mind and intellect. The disciple's love will flow both to the physical and the spiritual forms of the Guru. When he comes to know that his Guru is the very Consciousness that shines within and through all objects, the disciple starts to love everything.

"The Guru's words and deeds are beautiful. Through His beautiful words and deeds, He creates unforgettable moments and events in the disciple's life. The Guru's love intoxicates the disciple. His desire to love and to be loved by the Guru becomes like a blazing flame. Slowly, in due course, the Guru removes the disciple's craving to be loved *by* Him, and he develops in its place the craving to be in loving service *to* Him. Again, in order to make the disciple understand and realize that the Guru is not the body but the all-pervading Self, He creates circumstances for the disciple to see Him in everything and to serve Him through every action. For this love to take place, the disciple must empty the mind of all its desires. That is why Perfect Masters always insist on the importance of *sadhana.*"

In his excitement, one of the brahmacharis present called out, "This is exactly what Amma does to us!" Everyone enjoyed the spontaneity and innocence of the young man's remark. They all turned to him smiling. Amma's response to this was, "You know, these children here were really afflicted with *Amma bhrant* (craving for Mother) when they met Her. But Mother always wonders why these children are so mad about this 'crazy Kali.'" A devotee responded, "Amma, it is that 'craziness' which attracts and binds us."

As it was nearly 10:30 p.m., Mother got up from Her seat. All who were present offered their prostrations to the Mother. After having expressed Her love and affection to the sadhaks and the other visitors, She proceeded alone towards the neem tree.

From the direction of the tree, one could hear Mother singing a song

Ennude Jivita

O Mother, my boat is sinking
Here in the ocean of this world.
The hurricane of delusion
Fiercely rages on every side.

Clumsy is my helmsman, the mind
Stubborn my six oarsmen, the passions.

71

Into a merciless wind
I sailed my boat,
And now it is sinking;
Split is the rudder of devotion.
Tattered is the sail of faith,
Into my boat the waters are pouring.

Tell me, what shall I do?
Alas! With failing eyes,
Nothing but darkness do I see.
Here in the waves I will swim,
O Mother, clinging to the raft of Thy Name.

It sounded as if Mother were walking around as She sang. The night was cool and Her melodious haunting voice filled the air. Various people staying at the center came out of their rooms to see who was singing. They remained on the verandahs of their rooms listening to the Mother's inspiring song. When the song was over, there came a pause, but the spiritual vibration created by the song was so powerful that no one really noticed that the singing had stopped, so enraptured they were with a feeling of enchantment.

Then the Mother really soared to the heights of spiritual bliss. From where they stood on the verandah, the devotees and the brahmacharis could hear Mother laughing. It was as if She were so far beyond human feelings that the only sounds which She could make were these gentle laughs. Due to Her overflowing and uncontrollable bliss, the song automatically stopped when it was only half over.

Mother was alone under the neem tree, except for Gayatri and Kunjumol,[6] two of Her oldest and closest girl disciples who looked after all of Mother's personal needs, especially at times like

---

[6] Pronounced 'Kunyumol'—meaning "little daughter."

this when She forgot Her body completely. Like one intoxicated, Mother roamed about with faltering steps. Gayatri and Kunju-mol followed Her closely to protect Her from falling down or stumbling over something.

Half an hour had passed this way. Now, with Gayatri and Kunjumol holding Her hands and guiding Her, Mother was taken to Her room. Soon the brahmacharis and all the devotees retired to their rooms as well. Thus the last day of the visit to Kanyakumari came to an end. The next day the group journeyed back to the Ashram, singing *bhajans* as they rode in the van and reached there by two in the afternoon.

Chapter 3

Work in praise of God

25 April 1984

On this day, beginning at nine o'clock in the morning, all the Ashram residents and some visiting devotees were engrossed in cleaning the Ashram premises. It goes without saying that Mother was also present. Like everyone else, She carried sand and bricks, swept, collected trash and cleaned clogged drains. Whatever work Her children did, Mother did as well. Her presence gave vigor and enthusiasm to all those who participated.

When some people started gossiping at one point, Mother cautioned them in this manner, "No talking. This is not mere physical labor; this is spiritual work, work entrusted to you by God. Although you do not earn any monetary wages for it, payment is made by Him in the form of His Grace. In order to avail oneself of this, one should remember Him while doing the work. That 'Old Man' is a miser. He won't give anything to those who are lazy. He is very selfish, and will not think of those who do not think of Him. You must please Him, praise Him and adore Him. He likes being praised very much; He will not wake up unless you praise Him. But the praise that He likes is not ordinary praise. It is not the same as when you compliment someone or someone compliments you. When you praise someone, you do so because you want to be liked by him, thus your ego is involved. And when someone praises you, your ego gets puffed up.

"When your ego is there, you go away from God; the distance between you and Him becomes greater and greater. But through singing His glories, you become closer to Him, closer to your own Self. By praising God, you become innocent and pure, because when you glorify Him, you are not glorifying another person; you are actually glorifying your own Real Self. There is no 'person' to be glorified. He neither accepts nor rejects your praises because there is nobody there to accept or reject them. The Absolute Self alone is in that Nameless and Formless state. The form and the praises are meant for your own benefit, thus when you chant or sing the glories of God, you are glorifying the Self or the Atman which is not different from your own Real Nature.

"To forget 'doer-ship' and to go beyond the attitude of 'I do the work and I want the fruit of it' one should lift one's mind to that Supreme Principle. Do not talk while working. Talking will neither help us think of God, nor will we be able to do our work properly. Talking is an unnecessary waste of time and energy. Replace talking with the singing of the Divine Name. In this way you will be able to stop the inner babbling. Glorifying or praising the Lord is, in fact, the process of awakening your own inner Self.

"Once again, when you praise someone or when another person praises you, your ego or his ego gets inflated. But when you praise Him, your ego gets deflated until finally there is no ego at all. As God is beyond everything, nothing happens to Him. He remains as He is."

As if lost in a dream, everyone stopped working and moved towards Amma as She spoke these words. She, however, continued to sweep the ground. While the devotees had all forgotten their work, Mother remained so intent on Her sweeping that She did not even notice the assembled crowd. Suddenly She looked up and, seeing everyone standing around, Mother exclaimed, "Hey, what are you doing here? Go and do your work, you lazy bums!" One devotee said, "Amma, your nectarous words made us inactive."

Without paying much attention to this comment, Mother said, "Come on, children, let us sing together while we work," and She began to lead a chant

Thirukathukal Padam Nan

Let me sing the glories of Thy holy acts.
Please grant me a boon:
When I sing of Thy glories,
Please come into my heart.

Remove ill fate, Goddess Durga. O Kali,
Every day I beg to have a vision of Thy form.
I know not the method of meditation,
Neither is there melody in my music.

Have mercy on me
Let me immerse myself in bliss,
O Essence of the Vedas.

And then another

Chitta Vrindavanam

The melodious sound of the flute
Is rising from the Brindavan of my mind,
O Lord in the temple of my mind
Who abides in the form of awareness,
O Sweet Lover of flute music,
Lord of the world, Son of Yadu
Peacocks of the pure mind
Are eternally dancing in the service
Of that Being.

Upon hearing that beautiful music of the flute,
I enter into an ecstatic mood in deep meditation
On that One who is fond of the flute.

Each one's cup was filled to the brim with joy. Forgetting all about the world outside, and even forgetting themselves, the devotees worked and sang the glories of God. It was obvious that their minds were fully concentrated on the Mother, as She led them in song. This was an example of real *Karma Yoga.* Everyone worked without expecting anything, all the while fixing their minds on the Divine.

When the singing had finished, Mother called out "*Hari Bol!!*" (roughly equivalent to 'Praise the Lord!'). The next moment, dropping Her broom, She began to run off calling out, "Children, you continue to work! Mother will be back soon." But as soon as She had left, the devotees felt depleted of all their vitality and stood perfectly still. As if She knew that they had abandoned their work, the Mother turned around after She had gone just a few yards, saying, "Don't worry. Mother will come back in a few minutes. But we should try to finish this work before lunch. Yes, yes, now go ahead."

With this assurance from Mother that She would soon return, all felt happy and resumed their work with the same enthusiasm as before. Sure enough, in half an hour Mother came back carrying in one hand a bucket full of sweetened coffee and in the other, a packet of banana chips.

She set these down near the people working, and having asked someone to bring glasses, She called all Her children to come and began serving all the residents and devotees. In order to make sure that everybody had his share, Mother called out each person's name, asking, "Son," or "Daughter, did you get any?" One devotee asked, "Amma, are you not having any?" She answered, " Mother is full when She sees Her children eating and drinking."

There was a little more work left to do. One small heap of sand still had to be carried to fill in a spot where the land was low. Mother got up. Without calling anyone, She walked towards the sand pile, taking with Her a shovel and a basin. Upon seeing this, the devotees and the brahmacharis immediately jumped up and hurried to the sand pile, saying, "Amma, no, no. We will do it." But Mother paid no attention. Ignoring them, She began shoveling the sand into the basin. Then, carrying this on Her head, She walked towards the landfill. The devotees followed suit, and within a few minutes the work was completed. Mother then went to Her room, and the devotees were free to bathe and get cleaned up.

The Mother came down from Her room again at three o'clock in the afternoon, and sat in front of the meditation hall. Devotees and resident brahmacharis gathered around, but since there was not enough room for everyone to sit, She moved over to the *darshan* hut. Seeing that some of the brahmacharis had taken the seats closest to Her, She advised, "Let the householder children sit here. You move to the rear. You live here and always have the opportunity to see Mother. But these children get a chance only once in a while." The brahmacharis immediately obeyed, making room for the householder devotees to sit closer to the Mother.

The Holy Mother began by receiving the devotees who had come to see Her that day. She asked the brahmacharis to sing while one by one She gave *darshan* to the devotees. They sang with the accompaniment of harmonium and tabla.

Upon hearing the song, the Mother went into *samadhi*, and the devotee who was about to approach Her for *darshan* was asked by a brahmacwhari to move aside. The Mother was clearly transported to another realm. Her right hand, forming a divine mudra, was in a half-raised position, while the other hand was placed on Her chest. Her face glowed as She sat completely still, statue-like, remote yet mysteriously near.

Brahmachari Pai chanted some *slokas* (verses) from the Devi Mahatmyam, a Sanskrit work in praise of the Divine Mother

To that Ambika
Who is worthy of worship by all devas and sages,
Who pervades this world by Her power,
Who is the embodiment of all the powers
Of all the hosts of devas, we bow in devotion.

May She grant us auspicious things.
O Devi, we bow before You,
You Who are good fortune
In the dwellings of the virtuous,
And ill-fortune in those of the vicious.

You are intelligence in the hearts of the learned,
Faith in the hearts of the good
And modesty in the hearts of the high-born.
May You protect the universe.

Immersed in devotion and flooded with the Mother's spiritual power, the devotees tingled with anticipation, and all eyes were fixed on the Mother's radiant face. After about fifteen minutes the Mother regained consciousness and opened Her eyes, as She chanted "Shiva...Shiva...," and waved Her right hand in circles, a gesture familiar to the devotees yet inexplicable.

A family in distress

Darshan resumed, and the Mother continued to receive and bless each person individually. Soon a group of people entered the hut. As they came in, it was quite obvious that they were a family. Without acknowledging the next person in the *darshan*

80

line, the Mother called for this family to come forward right away. They all looked very sad. One of the two girls in this family wept uncontrollably as she moved towards Mother. "My child' daughter, do not cry," Mother said to the girl. "Do not grieve about what happened. Be consoled. After all, the flames did not consume the whole house. A great danger that could have occurred has been overcome by a smaller one. Moreover, you did not do it intentionally."

Hearing the Mother's words, the family members looked at each other in wonderment. It was quite clear that the Mother was referring to the tragic event which had happened to them even before they disclosed it to Her. With the crying girl on Her lap, Mother tried to console the family, saying, "Children, what has happened, has happened. It is past. The past is past and gone. Never is it going to come back. Even if you worry, all that has been lost is not going to return. Have confidence, courage and mental balance. If those are lost, then everything is lost. But if you maintain control of yourselves, Mother would say that nothing has been lost at all." As She spoke, the Mother rubbed the back of the man who appeared to be the father as he kneeled before Her with his head on Her lap.

Watching the Mother with these devotees, one felt that She was even more despondent over their troubles than the family members themselves. By expressing Her sympathy and motherly concern for their sorrow, She clearly helped them overcome their mental distress, and slowly they all calmed down. The father pleaded, "You are all-powerful and all-knowing. Amma, please save us from this deep sorrow." The whole family then sat around the Mother and had a long discussion with Her. Then, the Mother once again comforted and caressed each of them. While giving *prasad* to them, She assured them that everything would be all right. "Don't worry. The marriage will definitely take place." By the time they left, they were not only relieved and relaxed, but they actually seemed happy.

After they had gone, Amma turned to the next person who was waiting for Her *darshan*. She smiled at him and said this to him: "Son, don't think ill of God or of anyone. You musn't get angry without discerning and understanding the reason and real purpose behind an action. Anger will close your heart and this is where God is supposed to dwell. By getting angry, you are slamming the door of your heart right in His face. Son, don't do that. Those children are confronting a very difficult time. That is why Mother called them before calling you."

The Mother then related the cause of the family's deep sorrow. A few days before, the parents of the two girls were out during the day dealing with matters concerning their elder daughter's marriage. Both of the daughters were home, and the younger one wanted to take something out of the wooden chest that was kept in the parents' room. The room was rather dark and since there was no electricity, she carried a kerosene lamp. The girl opened the chest with the lamp still in her hands. While she was searching for what she wanted, the lamp tipped over and fell into the chest, the kerosene spilling all over the contents. Unfortunately, the chest was also where the parents kept their clothing and all their valuables. The kerosene-soaked clothing easily caught fire. The girl was shocked. She screamed and ran out of the room. She and her elder sister, the bride-to-be, screamed loudly. Hearing their shouting and screaming, the neighbors came running. They extinguished the fire, but not before the chest was completely burnt. The fire consumed part of the room, but luckily it had not spread to any other part of the house.

The parents were heart-broken because all of the money which they had saved for their daughter's marriage was put in that wooden chest. Since the marriage was scheduled for that month, they had withdrawn from the bank, just the day before, the amount required for her dowry and other expenses. Now they lost all of that money. To make matters worse, the bridegroom's parents, upon hearing about the fire, now opposed the marriage because they considered the fire to be an inauspicious omen. Thus, the whole family was in deep mourning.

The whole time the Mother narrated the story about the family, the young man whom the Mother had reprimanded sat with his head hanging down. He did not utter a single word. At last, he raised his head and spoke in an apologetic tone, "I am sorry, Amma. Please forgive me. I am not only ignorant, but a fool as well, to think that Mother would give special attention to someone without a particular reason. I also thought that I could hide my thoughts from you. But you caught me. Forgive me, Mother, forgive me." Praying thus, he lamented, for when the Mother had called the family instead of calling him, even though he was the next person in the *darshan* line, he had felt very angry towards the Mother. He had felt that the Mother was being unfair, being partial towards the family. He thought, "It is my turn to have *darshan*. How can Amma call on them, ignoring me. I have been waiting in the line for a long time and they just came. She is not impartial."

It was later revealed that the Mother's words had come true regarding this family. Even though the bridegroom's parents were against the marriage due to the fire, which they considered a bad omen, the young man loved his betrothed so much that he insisted on marrying her, in spite of the fire. He did not believe it to be an inauspicious sign. So much did he believe in this marriage that he even threatened to remain a bachelor forever if the parents did not give their consent. So adamant was he about this that the parents finally relented.

Nevertheless, though this one problem was solved, the bride's family still had the problem of the money. The whole family kept praying to the Mother. Almost seventy-five percent of the amount lost was meant for the dowry, which the bridegroom's parents had demanded, for such was the custom. Days passed. Nothing turned up. The girl's parents were very worried. They only had enough money to make the preliminary arrangements.

Three days before the marriage, a friend of the bridegroom's family brought a letter signed by the bridegroom and his parents. The letter stated that their son was absolutely against the custom of dowry. In fact, he had known nothing about it because it had been a secret arrangement made by his parents. Upon discovering it, he felt outraged that he had not been consulted in the matter. His parents, realizing how strong-willed their son was concerning this marriage, not only gave up the idea of the dowry but even offered to give whatever was necessary, in cash or kind, to make the marriage take place happily and smoothly on the scheduled date. All these miraculous changes occurred after the girl's family had gone to see the Mother. Meanwhile, after Mother had warned how anger can close one's heart to God, the *darshan* continued as the brahmacharis sang.

The Mother's *darshan* concluded around five o'clock. She emerged from the hut and sat on the front verandah of the meditation hall. Since the meditation time for the brahmacharis was from 4:30 - 6:00 in the evening, Mother looked inside the hall and upon finding only a few brahmacharis there, She asked, "Where are the others?"

One latecomer was standing just outside the door, hoping to get in without Mother noticing him. As he tried to sneak inside, Mother suddenly got up from where She was sitting and walked towards the door. Giving him a serious look, She said, "Don't you know that 4:30 is the time for meditation?" He tried to answer,

"Yes, Mother, but..." The Mother interrupted, " No buts. If 4:30 is the time for meditation, you must be here for it, unless you are engaged in some other important work. Where were you? What were you doing?" Hesitatingly, the brahmachari answered, "I was reading but fell asleep." The Mother's response to this came quickly, "Hey, what are you saying? Being a brahmachari, aren't you ashamed to say that you fell asleep while reading a book? That shows lack of awareness. You are not alert. If you can't read without sleeping, how can you hope to meditate? Meditation requires a lot of alertness! If you are alert, you can be wide awake, even if you have not slept for days on end."

Overwhelmed by the seriousness of Mother's expression and tone, the brahmachari was a bit frightened. But seeing this, Amma burst into laughter and called him to Her. She gently patted his back, but remained firm in what She said to him, "Are you afraid of your Mother? It was only a joke. Don't think that Mother is angry with you, son. Nonetheless, you should try to follow the schedule of meditation, *japa,* and yoga practices. This is very important. Discipline is needed for a *sadhak.* If we do not consider discipline as being important, then we won't take spiritual life seriously."

Mother sat with the brahmacharis and meditated for some time. She often does that to inspire them and to observe them as well. On such occasions Mother always keeps a few pebbles on hand. Whenever She sees a brahmachari dozing or losing his concentration, She throws one of these pebbles at him and says something to help him regain his one-pointedness.

The Holy Mother returned to Her room at around 5:30 p.m. and came down again for the regular evening *bhajan* at 6:30. Her ecstatic singing filled the atmosphere.

Ambike Devi Jagan Nayike Namaskaram.

O Mother, Goddess of the Universe,
I bow before Thee.
O Giver of happiness, I bow before Thee.
O Thou whose form is Peace, Who is omnipresent
Thou art the Great Deluder,
Without beginning or end.

O Thou whose form is of the Self, I bow before Thee.
Intelligence, knowledge and speech,
All are Thee only.
O Devi, it is Thou who leadest the mind.

She sang song after song, gradually building up to a crescendo of intense devotion. All hearts opened effortlessly and experienced a great wave of Divine Grace. Nobody could resist being affected, such was the power created by the Mother's singing. She Herself allowed it to carry Her to its peak. Like a boat that has lost all control and is being tossed wildly by the waves, the Mother allowed the ecstasy of singing the Divine Name to carry Her wherever it would. The outpouring of devotion surpassed all limits when She sang.

Devi Saranam Saranam Amme.

Give me refuge, O Goddess,
Give me refuge, O Mother.
O Thou Whose Divine Form
Is praised by the celestials,
Salutations to Thee, the Primal Supreme Energy!

Salutations to Mother Who is the Cause
Of all auspiciousness, Fulfiller of all desires,
Perfection Itself and the Source of Nature Herself.

Thou art the Cause of Creation, Sustenance
And Destruction.
Thou art the Destroyer of the wicked.
I bow to Thy Feet Which art of the form
Of Pure Existence and Awareness.

At a certain point, the Mother stopped singing and got up from Her seat and started dancing blissfully, with both Her hands raised halfway, and Her fingers held in a divine *mudra*. A beautiful smile lit up Her face, and every now and then She uttered a mysterious laugh.

Everybody continued to sing, drinking in the nectar of pure devotion. They were fascinated by the Mother's graceful movements as She glided around the floor in Her dance of divine rapture. Slowly the dancing ceased, but She remained swaying back and forth to the music until She finally sat and then lay on the cement floor. The singing also stopped and absolute silence prevailed. It was a beautiful, profound silence, and those present slipped easily into meditation and experienced very powerful concentration.

Over an hour passed before Mother regained ordinary consciousness. Keeping Her hands on Gayatri's shoulders, She walked to Her room leaving everyone in an elevated mood. No one wanted to disturb the feeling of Divine Love and concentration they were experiencing, not even after Mother had left. Most of the residents and visiting devotees remained meditating in the temple and on the temple verandah. Some of the brahmacharis went to the meditation hall. Not until 11:45 p.m. did anyone bother to eat dinner.

Each moment with the Holy Mother is a moment to learn love, to imbibe it, and to live in it. Singing with the Mother provides a rare opportunity to feel and experience the Divine within ourselves, the pure and innocent love in us.

Chapter 4

26 April 1984

The Mother began receiving devotees in the *darshan* hut this morning around eleven o'clock. Since it was a *Devi Bhava* day, there was a large number of people in the hut. One woman devotee was singing a lovely *bhajan* about Krishna's beauty. The first half of the traditional song described His childhood antics, the way He stole butter and milk from the homes of the *Gopis* or milk-maids and shared it with His friends. The song continued, telling about how Yashoda, His Mother, once tied Him to a huge mortar stone, hoping to keep Him out of mischief, and how He dragged it around, continuing to make trouble. The Mother, while She continued to give *darshan* to each person, was laughing and enjoying the song, making comments here and there. At one point She said, "Little Thief! How skillfully He won every person's heart. Mischievous fellow! He was a good thief, a thief who stole everything from everyone but for a higher purpose."

The woman sang with utmost devotion. Having described Krishna's childhood games, she went on about His physical beauty. The last half of the song was about Radha's love, about Her aching heart and finally, the excruciating pain She experienced when Krishna left Brindavan.

Even though a devotee was lying on Her lap, the Mother became perfectly still as She appeared to become engrossed in the song. All of a sudden She started crying out, "Krishna! Krishna!" This went on and on. Her head was tilted back and Her half-closed eyes turned upwards. As instructed by a brahmachari, the devotee slowly moved from Her lap to one side. At last the call ceased, but the Mother entered into a deep state of *samadhi*. Her right hand showed the divine *mudra* which She used to show during

Krishna Bhava, and the crying had culminated in a blissful smile that made Her look very much as She had during the Krishna Bhava. Her eyes were half-closed, and there was an indescribable glow on Her face. The devotees present felt thrilled and almost all of them either glided into deep meditation or shed tears of love and bliss. They all could feel that She was totally identified with Krishna. Everyone present felt that this was truly a feast for the eyes to behold. The woman whose singing was instrumental in prompting this to happen sang another song in praise of Krishna. After that, the brahmacharis took over, chanting some slokas from a work in praise of Krishna, the *Narayaneeyam*

I adore the Form of the Lord
Whose head is crowned with a diadem
That rivals the sun in its brilliance;
The beauty of the forehead enhanced
By the vertical mark of sandalwood paste,
With eyes brimming with mercy
And face lit up by a benevolent smile,
With nose attractive, well-proportioned,
With ears adorned with fish-marked pendants
Adding lustre to the cheeks by their reflection;
Wearing on the neck the luminous jewel, Kastubha,
The chest resplendent with a variety of decorations—
Floral wreaths, strands of pearls
And the auspicious mark called 'Srivatsa.'

This Form of Thine
Consisting of Pure Bliss Consciousness,
The sweet nectar of fascinating beauty
Is showered everywhere, captivating the minds of all
Who devotedly hear the recitation of Thy deeds
And excellences, inebriating them with bliss,

Exciting a thrill all through their limbs,
And bathing their bodies with cool streams of tears
Welling up from the ecstasy of joy.

The Holy Mother's divine mood lasted for about twenty minutes. It seemed that She had not yet come down fully to this plane, so it was with great difficulty that She continued to receive people. She asked for a glass of water. Perhaps this was a means of coming down to the world of forms, thoughts and actions. By concerning Herself with objects, She can keep Her mind down on the empirical plane. Water was offered to Her by Gayatri. She took a few sips and again closed Her eyes for a few more moments. Then She whirled Her right index finger in the air a few times, a gesture She often makes but has never explained since it does not belong to the realm of explanations. Again *darshan* resumed. After a short while, She again began to look like Her normal self.

Do not laugh at others

27 April 1984

The brahmacharis were having lunch. Two of them talked and laughed together as they ate. Suddenly the Mother's voice was heard: "Hey, fellows! Are you talking and laughing while you eat? What a shame! How can you do such a thing? You are living in an Ashram, striving to realize God. Aren't you seekers? Yet you are talking about someone, laughing at his weaknesses and making fun of his drawbacks, aren't you?"

The laughing brahmacharis were taken aback. As the Mother approached them, they stood up from their seats, with their heads hanging down. She continued to reprimand them, "Don't hang your heads down. That shows that you have committed a mistake. Innocent people never look down. They always look straight ahead. They are not afraid. Those who have not committed any errors are not afraid of anyone. But you hang your heads down. That shows you have done something wrong, and that now you are afraid of punishment. Mother does not want to punish you; She simply wants to correct you. So, look over here and tell the truth. Whom were you mocking?"

The two brahmacharis looked at the Mother's face and mentioned the name of another brahmachari. One of them said in a soft voice, "We were making fun of the way he chanted the *Lalita Sahasranama* off-key."

Now Mother burst into laughter. She turned to the other brahmacharis, saying, "Did you hear that? They were making fun of (She says that brahmachari's name) and the way he chants the *Sahasranama*." Then She said in admonishment, "What children you are! Don't you feel ashamed? This is the biggest sin—to mock others. Are you yourselves perfect? When you tease someone, remember this truth that somebody else is teasing you, laughing at your faults and flaws also. If you remember this, you will not mock anyone again.

"Children, you all know that the first mantra of the *Lalita Sahasranama* is "Sri Matre Namah," Salutations to the Great Mother. She is Mother, Mother of all. What are the greatest qualities of a Mother? Love, forgiveness and patience. Our Mother (the Divine Mother) is endowed with all the three qualities in their purest form. Therefore, even if you commit any errors, She will forgive you. No mother will instruct her children to call her 'mother' only after they have studied the *Saptaswaras*.[7] A musical voice is not needed to call one's mother." Mother stopped for a minute and then said, "Children, now sit down and eat." Before She left the dining area, She instructed all the brahmacharis to come to Her room after lunch.

---

[7] Ascending and descending notes in Indian classical music.

Upon finishing their meal, the brahmacharis climbed the steps to the Mother's room. The door was open as Mother was waiting for Her children. As a sign of devotion and reverence, each of the brahmacharis touched and saluted the floor of Mother's room as he stepped across the threshold.[8] Each one also prostrated to the Mother before he sat down. Mother waited until everyone had arrived. When all were present, including the brahmacharinis, Gayatri and Kunjumol, She had everybody chant 'OM' three times. Then, Mother asked them to meditate on the form of their beloved deity for a while. Mother also sat in meditation. Then She joined Her hands in prayer and remained in that posture for a few moments. There was pin-drop silence. Mother looked at Her children and smiled, Her face full of compassion and love for them. The serious face and stern tone of voice She adopts sometimes is only external. It is one of the masks She uses to discipline Her children. Within, the Mother is always loving and compassionate.

Amma proceeded to speak, "My children, you are Mother's wealth and health. Mother does not want anything from you except your spiritual growth. When She finds that you are not growing internally as She expects you to, Mother feels very sad. Life is a play for those who have attained the state of perfection, for them it is not so serious any more. But for you that is not true. You should take things seriously; this is a discipline for you now. Seeing and taking things too lightly is not good for a *sadhak*.

"Children, a *sadhak* is one who is striving hard to reach the goal. How can one take things lightly while striving hard to attain eternal freedom? Only after liberation will there be spontaneity in one's responses. At present, nothing comes spontaneously to

---

[8] In India it is a common practice for the spiritually inclined to salute the threshold when entering a temple or room where a *Mahatma* is present. This salutation is a gesture of touching first the floor with one's right hand and then bringing it to one's forehead or heart.

you except your old *vasanas*. You are trying to eliminate them and replace them with the higher values of life. Therefore, everything is a test, a hard test for you. Take these tests seriously. When Mother says 'seriously,' don't misunderstand and think that She is asking you to put a serious look on your face. No. The attitude you have should be serious; this seriousness should be something internal. Sharp discrimination is what is needed.

"Take the example of someone getting angry at you for no reason. For a normal person it is difficult to remain calm and undisturbed in such a situation. But you should use your discrimination in order to keep your mind well under control. For this to happen, introspection is needed. To accept the anger as a blessing sent by the Lord in order to test your patience, or to ignore it and remain unaffected, one needs sharp discrimination. In both cases a *sadhak* must make a conscious and continuous effort in order to proceed towards the ultimate goal. This is not a light matter. Do not consider it as child's play. This is the way of life that you have chosen. Your life is dedicated entirely to this purpose. When you have attained the goal, you will be able to perceive the whole world and all the happenings around you as child's play. Then you can be spontaneous. At that time all fears automatically drop away. Then you can play and laugh and be happy like a child. But until then you must take life as a serious affair.

"Obstacles and difficulties are challenges to confront and to conquer. A challenge cannot be taken as a light matter unless you are an adept. You are not an adept; therefore, take it seriously.

"To fight in the battlefield is a game for a master in the art. But for the ordinary soldier who is not experienced in the art of war, it is a struggle between life and death. The Mahabharata battle was child's play for Krishna and Arjuna because both of them were masters in using all kinds of weapons. They had all the divine weapons under their control. But for the ordinary soldiers it was a real challenge. For them the battle was something which had to be taken seriously. If they took it lightly, their lives would have ended with their heads rolling on the ground.

"In the same way, children, for a person who is established in God, all that happens around him is a play. The whole world is a play. All abuses, criticisms, insults, hatred and anger showered on him return unaccepted to those from whom they came. Whatever is not accepted is returned to the giver. Or another way of putting it is that a Realized Soul accepts everything. He accepts things, but they cannot remain with him. He is like a doorway; things just pass through him. Nothing can remain with him. Or you can say that he is like fire. What is thrown in the fire gets consumed by the flames and disappears. One who is established in the Supreme is always spontaneous. For him acceptance comes readily, but for you, it is not spontaneous. It is a real struggle, and a struggle cannot be taken lightly. What you are really dealing with is fighting your own negative nature. Fighting is a challenge which should be considered seriously.

"Children, eventually this struggle will become totally 'struggle-less.' This fighting will be completely 'non- fighting.' When this happens, then your actions and your acceptance of things will be spontaneous."

Mother stopped for a while and looked at Her children. They were all listening to Her words very attentively, marveling at Her wisdom and knowledge. Before coming to the Mother and adopting the life of renunciates, most of these young men had excelled in their various fields of study and work. And now, they were sitting in front of this ordinary-looking village girl who was almost the same age as they, listening to Her words like obedient little children. To an outside onlooker, the Mother looked like any other girl in this provincial fishing village, but in the hearts of these spiritual aspirants, they knew they were sitting before Wisdom Incarnate.

Amma resumed talking: "This afternoon Mother saw two of Her children making fun of and laughing at someone else's weakness. Children, before judging another person, try to observe your own mind, your own thoughts and your own actions. Try to see your own faults and weaknesses. Become aware of them. If you can do this sincerely, you will not find fault with others because you will realize that your own mind is more of a mess than theirs. Then you will not laugh at others.

"To laugh at somebody else's shortcomings is one of the lowest things you can do. If you must laugh, laugh at your own weaknesses; laugh at your own stupidities. This is far better than laughing at someone else. By being able to laugh at your own faults, at least you become aware of your own lower or false nature. If you can laugh at your own lower nature, this means you are evolving, and this is consoling. You will be fit for immortality, or at least, you are getting closer to it. When you laugh at yourself, this means that you are slowly becoming aware of your own ignorance. This is a good sign. Once you realize that you are ignorant, then it is easy for the Guru to work on you. Many disciples or devotees simply say they are ignorant, but they really do not mean it. Deep down in their minds they think that they know many things. Actually they do not recognize their own ignorance. A person who laughs at his own weaknesses and faults realizes and recognizes his own ignorance. He can easily evolve and rise to the Supreme State of Blissful Laughter. He can soon laugh, watching the whole universe as a play of God. Therefore, children, do not tease or make fun of others. It is very painful for Mother to see Her children behaving so cheaply."

Again there was a long pause. Amma asked the brahmacharis, "Children, is Mother's long speech boring you? If so, Mother will stop." No one replied. There was absolute silence. She resumed, "Silence means 'yes,' doesn't it?"

Immediately one of the brahmacharis who had created the problem at lunch said, "No, Mother, no. Your beautiful *satsang* has made us dumb of speech. Now we realize our stupidity and feel like laughing at our foolishness. Amma, please enlighten us by giving us more and more satsangs like this. Let our talking, both inner and outer, be stopped by contemplation of your words." As he sought forgiveness for his mistake, tears welled up in this brahmachari's eyes.

Amma consoled him, saying, "Son, don't worry. God forgave you as soon as you realized your mistake and repented."

Then She continued, "Children, you might have read this story from the life of Krishna. It happened in Brindavan. The mischievous Son of Nanda, together with His playmates, the Gopas, one day sneaked into the house of the two teachers who had taught them the alphabet. Both teachers were rather odd characters. They were fast asleep when Krishna and His friends started their mischief. As they had planned and using the paints they brought with them, Krishna and His friends painted the faces of the teachers to look like clowns. Finishing their work, Krishna and His friends left and went outside where they waited, hoping to have some fun when the teachers woke up. Soon the fun began. As one awoke, he looked at the face of the other, who was still asleep, and started laughing at him, wanting his companion to see how funny he looked with his face covered in dots and lines of various colors, so he vigorously shook his sleeping friend. The friend woke up, rubbed his eyes and started laughing, pointing at the first one's face. Both of them continued to laugh at each other until, at last, they looked in a mirror. Then they stopped laughing. At that point, they were in a hurry to wash their faces.

"Children, this is how we are. Though this story seems to be just a funny and insignificant incident among Krishna's many pranks, there is deep meaning in it. It depicts the human tendency to laugh at other people's weaknesses. When you laugh at someone, remember that someone else is laughing at your weaknesses. No one is perfect. Look in your inner mirror, and you will see the black marks in you. Once you see them and become aware of them, you will stop laughing. Then you will be in a hurry to remove them. Until then, making fun of others will continue to close your heart. Children, do not laugh at others and remain closed in your own heart. It is self-destructive. You are here to throw away the old habits which are so deep and dense within you. Don't fall victim to them. To make fun of others, to laugh at others' weaknesses is the nature of students in regular schools and colleges, but not that of a spiritual seeker. But because it is so strong a tendency, it is easy for you to fall prey to such behavior. It will defeat the very purpose for which you are here. You are here to remove the old *vasanas* and to keep from creating any more."

Suddenly the Mother's facial expression changed. With a pitying look on Her face, She said in an urgent, pleading tone, "Stop adding to them, children; stop adding to them."

Mother again stopped for a while. She closed Her eyes and a few tears rolled down Her face. Seeing the Mother crying, everyone's heart was filled with sadness, and their eyes also swelled with tears.

Then She revealed more: "Children, Mother was not sad when all the villagers were against Her. Nor did She feel dejected when Her parents and other family members turned totally antagonistic towards Her. Mother did not feel sad at all when the skeptics and nonbelievers scandalized Her. But now Her own children make Mother sad. Deep down in Mother's heart She is completely detached; there is no attachment to anything. But on the surface She has created an attachment for your own good."

For a few more minutes, the Mother sat in a meditative mood. Everyone followed Her example. When She opened Her eyes, Mother spoke again, "Let us sing a *bhajan* together before we conclude. Children, pray to the Supreme to bless you with love in your hearts. Love alone will purify. Pray for that. Pray to remove all those things which stand as obstacles to the flow of Love."

The Mother sang and the brahmacharis sang the response

Ente Kannunir.

Although You see my tears, O Mother,
How is it that You feel no compassion,
You feel no compassion?

Although many days have passed since I came
To seek refuge at Thy Feet, why aren't You pleased,
Why aren't You pleased?

O Mother, why are You remiss in granting
Peace of mind to Your devoted servant,
Why are You remiss?

Your Feet are the sole Refuge of this poor soul,
Thus grant me refuge, bless me, O Mother
Grant me refuge and bless me.

Mother's heart overflowed with Divine Love, and this was reflected in Her children. Everyone sat absorbed in meditation when the singing was over. After spending a little more time with the brahmacharis, Mother got up and went out on the terrace. As usual, Gayatri was about to follow Her, but She said, "No, Mother wants to be alone for a while." She remained there on the terrace as the brahmacharis, one by one, prostrated in front of Her bed and left the room. The time was three o'clock, and all proceeded to their afternoon chores, still contemplating the Mother's words.

Chapter 5

28 April 1984

Eight o'clock in the morning was meditation time for the brahmacharis all seated in the meditation hall. Some of them had already begun and some were just getting settled to begin, when suddenly, from Mother's room upstairs came the melodious sound of the tamboura, a stringed instrument. Knowing it was Mother who played the instrument, no one could think of meditating anymore. Opening their eyes, they all sat very much alert, as they keenly listened to the sound of the tamboura.

Some of the brahmacharis who were not satisfied just to listen went outside, hoping to catch a glimpse of Mother through the openings in Her balcony wall. Unable to see Her, they were disappointed and sat facing Her room. In a few minutes, to the accompanying sound of the tamboura, Mother's voice was heard as She sang to Krishna

Ini Oru Janmam.

O Krishna, give me not another birth
Lest I fall into the deep quagmire of delusion.
If You give, then bestow on me the boon
Of taking birth as the servant
Of Your servants forever.

O Krishna, You fill my mind
With Your Holy Name,
Reveal Your Lotus Feet, bright and clear therein.
Keep my mind ever balanced
And all will be felt to be Your manifestation.

O Krishna, Treasure of Compassion,
I salute Thee with joined palms,
I humbly salute Thee.

Hearing the Mother singing, some of the householder devotees also gathered on the side of the building under the balcony. They stood or sat there, motionless, like statues carved out of stone. The blissful singing of the Mother created an atmosphere in which one could glide easily into an introspective state. The Mother continued with another song full of pathos

Karunya Varidhe Krishna.

O Krishna, Ocean of Compassion,
The thirst for life is ever increasing,
There is no peace for the mind.

Alas! Confusion is too much.
Forgiving all wrongs,
Wipe the sweat from my brow.

O Kanna, now I have no support
Other than Thy worshipful Lotus Feet.
O Krishna, my throat is drying up,
My eyes are failing, my feet are tired,
I am falling to the ground,
O Krishna.

The song stopped abruptly as did the sound of the tamboura. It seemed that the Mother had entered a rapturous mood. At this point more than ever, everybody wanted to run upstairs and be with the Mother, but they could see that the door to Her room was closed. Even so, some of the brahmacharis made an attempt to get in, but failed and returned downstairs, where all continued to look up toward the Mother's room, mentally visualizing Her

God-intoxicated mood. Thus the morning's meditation period was spent in actually hearing the singing of the Beloved Deity and in making attempts to actually see Her physical form with eyes open rather than closed.

Each time one watches the Mother, there is something new. Each moment one spends with Her opens the door to a new experience, to a never-known aspect of the Divine. Living and moving with a *Mahatma* always gives one a feeling of ever- freshness.

The unquenchable thirst of Her devotees and disciples to always be in the Mother's presence, to gaze at Her face for hours on end, is certainly the product of this ever-fresh quality of the Supreme Consciousness. As much time as they spent with Her, the Mother's children were never satisfied; it was never enough. Thus they could not remain in meditation with their eyes closed, when there was the hope of peeking at Her form. While what is new becomes old, and what is old is quickly worn-out, the Ultimate Reality, without beginning or end, remains forever new, forever fresh. And one cannot help but experience this ever-freshness in the presence of those who are established in the Supreme Self. They are not only ever-fresh but ancient too.

Believers and non-believers

Many devotees were waiting to have Her *darshan* when the Mother came downstairs at 10 o'clock. They followed Her to the hut where She sat on the cot for a few moments with eyes closed. Upon opening Her eyes, She looked toward the back of the hut and called to a person who was sitting in the very rear. "Son..." No one responded, so She again called, "Son..." This time a man raised his head and looked behind him, thinking or perhaps pretending that She was referring to someone behind him. "No, no. Pundit-mon. You. Son, Mother is calling you," and She gestured with Her right hand for him to come. With a surprised look on his face, the pundit got up and went near the Mother. Again She gestured for him to sit down. He seemed astonished. As soon as he sat in front of Her, She playfully tapped his head a few times, smiling as She rhythmically chanted "Hanuman" with each tap. At this point, the scholar fell at the Mother's feet and burst into tears. He cried aloud saying, "O Mother, forgive me for testing you. Forgive me, forgive me for testing you." The Mother lifted him up, wiped his tears and comforted him. She asked him to sit by Her side and continued to give *darshan* to the other devotees.

This man was apparently a scholar of Sanskrit literature and scriptural texts, and this was his first meeting with the Mother. He related his experience to the residents later: "I had heard many stories about the Mother from many different sources. I wanted to see Her, but I had doubts about Her omniscience. Therefore, when I finally decided to come, I set up these conditions: 'If She is a genuine saint, She must call me first, irrespective of where I sit in Her presence or of how many people there are at the time. I also wanted Her to state the Name of my *upasana murti* (the deity that he worshipped) when I met Her. Amma did both and has filled my heart with faith and love for Her. Even before I disclosed who I was, She knew that I was a scholar. That is why She called me 'Pundit-mon.'"

As the *darshan* continued with the scholar sitting next to the Mother, the brahmacharis began to sing at Her request. When they finished, the scholar expressed a wish to chant a Sanskrit *sloka* to the Mother. It was from the *Ramayana*, of Hanuman's praise of Lord Sri Rama.

> *Please give me this blessing,*
> *That my love for You should never diminish.*
> *Do not allow me to think of anything else*
> *Or divide my love between*
> *You and any other person.*

I want to live as long as Your great Name
Is preserved among the sons of men.
Let me be Your devotee forever and ever.

Having chanted the verse, he humbly confided to the Mother, "Amma, this prayer by Hanuman to Rama is also my prayer to you."

She laughed and replied, "To this crazy one? Shiva! Mother is mad, a nut!"

The scholar responded, "Yes, you are right, Mother. For ignorant people like us, *Mahatmas* are crazy. We lack your craziness, craziness for God. We lack the craziness to love everyone equally. That is our problem. Mother, we need a little bit of your craziness to straighten out our problems."

No further remarks came from the Mother; instead, She sang a song, a *namavali, Krishna Vasudeva Hari*. The brahmacharis continued to sing, and when that song was over, a young man put forth a question: "Amma, there are believers and nonbelievers in this world, aren't there? What does the believer get from his faith in the existence of God? Does he get something that the nonbeliever does not?"

"Son," the Mother replied, "faith in God gives one the mental strength needed to confront the problems of life. Faith in the existence of God is a protective force. It makes one feel safe and protected from all the evil influences of the world. To have faith in the existence of a Supreme Power and to live accordingly is religion. When we become religious, morality arises, which, in turn, will help to keep us away from malevolent influences. We won't drink, we won't smoke, and we will stop wasting our energy through unnecessary gossip and talk. Morality or purity of character is a stepping stone to spirituality. We will also develop qualities like love, compassion, patience, mental equipoise, and other positive traits. These will help us to love and serve everyone equally. Religion is faith. Where there is faith, there is harmony, unity and love. A nonbeliever always doubts. He does not believe in unity or in love. He likes to cut and divide. Everything is food for his intellect. He cannot be at peace; he's restless. He always questions; therefore, the foundation of his entire life is unstable and scattered due to his lack of faith in a higher principle.

"But a person who is endowed with real faith will be steadfast. A person who has religion can find peace. The source of this peace is the heart, not the head. A person with faith believes in unity, love and peace, not in division and disharmony. Mother is not talking about religion in the narrow sense, but in the broader sense."

"But, Amma," the young man further inquired, "these qualities can be seen in some nonbelievers as well, can't they?"

The Mother responded, "Maybe. But due to the lack of faith in a Supreme Power, they will not have anything to hold on to and surrender to fully to when adverse circumstances arise. As far as a believer is concened, God is the Supreme. God is an experience. God lives in us through desireless love, compassion, forbearance, renunciation, and qualities like these. If a nonbeliever has any of these qualities in him, in their purest form, he will get all the benefits of a believer. What Mother means by 'believer' is not someone who has faith in a god or goddess but someone who gives value to higher principles for which he is willing to sacrifice everything. If these qualities serve as the principles by which the non-believer lives his life, he will be equal to a believer. On the other hand, if those qualities are only on the outside, if they are shallow and not deep, a person will not have the benefits of a true believer. Often nonbelievers like to talk, but they do not put their words into practice. They are shallow and talk only to put on an impressive show. They do not have anything to hold on to. They lack the faith in a Supreme Governor of the Universe to save them from the problems of life.

"If one keeps only an ideal or a principle as the goal of life, he can lose his mental stability during certain weak moments, which will result in the giving up of all the values which he has cherished in his entire life. This will not happen in the case of a true devotee. A true devotee is always optimistic. His first and foremost quality is acceptance, whatever may happen in his life. He holds on to his Lord and considers everything as His *prasad*.

"A person endowed with faith in the Supreme holds on to that Principle when a crisis occurs. It is this faith which gives him a strong and balanced mind to enable him to confront any trying situation. Qualities like desireless love, compassion, forbearance and renunciation should become integrated in our lives. A truly religious person lives with faith in the existence of a Supreme Principle. For him these qualities are greater than his life. He will give up his life but not the principles by which he lives. He is willing to die for his spiritual principles."

The Mother then proceeded to tell a story to illustrate this point. It was about the Pandavas and the horse that was chosen to roam the length and breadth of India. After they had completed the *ashwamedha yagña*,[9] the Pandavas released the chosen horse. The custom was that whoever dared to stop and seize the horse was considered to be challenging the supremacy of King Yudhisthira, who had performed the special ceremony which had culminated in the release of the sacred horse.

King Mayuradhwaja was a great devotee of Lord Krishna. He was a repository of all virtues, whose wisdom and knowledge of the *Vedas* (scriptures) were known throughout the land. Above all, he was a man of deep compassion and self-sacrifice. This king Mayuradhwaja seized the ceremonial horse of the Pandavas, and

---

[9] An ancient sacred horse ritual

thus Arjuna, the great Pandava hero, considered it his duty to fight him. But Krishna dissuaded Arjuna from doing so, for He wanted to demonstrate to the Pandava hero the power of King Mayuradhwaja, his self-sacrifice, truthfulness and devotion. The Lord also wanted to humble Arjuna's pride.

According to Krishna's plan, both He and Arjuna proceeded to King Mayuradhwaja's palace in the guise of two brahmins. They received a warm welcome, and the king offered them generous hospitality. On the eve of their arrival, at the feast that was arranged for these two guests, the Lord, still in brahmin disguise, stood up before all those who were present and began to narrate this tale of woe:

"O wise and virtuous King, as we were coming through a forest on the border of your empire, a tiger snatched away the young son of my companion. Half the body of the poor child had already been swallowed by the beast before we were able to reach him. But taking pity on us in our grief, the tiger promised to return the child alive if we fulfilled a certain condition." Feigning reluctance to disclose this condition, Krishna paused. The king, however, was eager to hear the rest of the story and urged Him to continue.

"O great King, the tiger asked for the gift of the right half of the sanctifying body of Mayuradhwaja, the pure and holy emperor of the land. Now tell us, how can we eat peacefully with this great agony gripping our hearts? Only if you promise to give the tiger half your body will my companion's boy be saved. But how, great King, can we ask such a thing of you?"

Without showing the least bit of hesitancy, the king readily and gladly agreed to give half of his body to the tiger. Thus, upon finishing his meal, the king sat on the floor and instructed his queen and his son to saw his body into two halves. Each holding one end of the saw, the queen and her son began to cut the king's body in two. As the two brahmins (Krishna and Arjuna) were witnessing this event, they noticed tears filling the left eye of the king. Immediately, Krishna interrupted and said, "Oh, you are giving the promised gift with tears. That means that you are sad to leave the body, and you are giving it up unwillingly. I cannot accept anything given with tears. A real gift is something given whole-heartedly." To this King Mayuradhwaja replied, "Sir, if I were unwilling or hesitant, both eyes would shed tears, wouldn't they? But only the left eye is crying because it will not serve a good purpose. The right half of the body is going to be used for a most sacred purpose in saving the life of a helpless boy. But since the left half will be thrown away to be eaten by dogs and vultures, it is lamenting that it, too, cannot serve a higher purpose. The right half, on the other hand, is jubilant about being sacrificed for such a meritorious purpose."

As the king finished speaking, Krishna revealed His real form to King Mayuradhwaja and blessed him with everlasting bliss and contentment. Arjuna's pride was humbled, and the king's humility and self-sacrifice were duly rewarded by the Lord Himself.

In response to the story, a devotee commented, "Amma, this is far beyond an ordinary person's conception, isn't it?"

"This is what Mother was going to say," Amma said. She further explained, "This story is, of course, not to be taken literally but figuratively. Certainly there were great souls who could act in this way, but now everything is only in words, not in actions. Here the king was willing to sacrifice his own life in order to uphold the principles by which he lived. This is something far beyond an ordinary person's thinking and understanding. But you should try to see the spirit and the principle behind the story. That is why Mother says that faith and spirituality are not to be taken lightly. Spiritual principles should become an integral part of your lives. Only when they are practiced in your daily life will you be able to experience the benefits of faith and of spiritual principles in their fullness.

"Life is full of misery and the fear of death. Nobody can escape these inevitabilities. But a courageous man can live a happy life. A man who is afraid of death, afraid of losses and afraid of sorrow can never be happy. To be fearless comes only through religious practice. A truly religious person is neither afraid of death nor is he afraid of losses. He is really courageous. He lives for the Truth, and he breathes for Love. His whole being is dedicated to that. Unlike the religious man, a nonbeliever is afraid. First of all, he is afraid of believers and the principle of God. He lives in fear that God will win. He is afraid that believers will predominate and he will lose. This fear in itself makes him a weakling. But a person who is endowed with faith in God is not afraid of nonbelievers nor of people who might scandalize him for his beliefs. His faith is so firm and intense that he strongly believes that God will take care of everything and that Truth will ultimately win. And this is what is happening everywhere. One should be daring enough to open one's eyes and see this. A real believer is full of strength, immense strength. Nothing can harm him. All of life's obstacles, whether created by human beings or by nature, will crumble when they hit against the firm and stable faith of the believer.

"While a nonbeliever will waste his life and energy in speaking against or spreading falsehoods about something which he insists does not exist, a believer really lives by his belief and acquires more strength and more energy through his faith in God. He is not wasting his time and energy in trying to prove or disprove anything. Besides, if God is something which does not exist, why do these nonbelievers walk around trying to prove it, the non-existence of a 'Not'? That's foolishness, isn't it? How many lifetimes are they going to waste like this? One day they are bound to raise both their hands and accept God as the Supreme Power.

Nature will make them acknowledge God, if not in this birth, definitely in the next life. This is because the more strongly they deny Him, the closer they become to Him. Negative thoughts about God are still thoughts about Him."

Difference between a devotee and a disciple

A scholar asked the Mother, "Amma, what is the difference between a devotee and a disciple?"

"Son, strictly speaking, a true devotee and a true disciple are one and the same," answered the Mother. "A true devotee is a true disciple and vice versa. Both a disciple and a devotee have devotion; they both begin with devotion, so to speak.

"A disciple is one who is endowed with devotion to the Guru and is willing to undergo being disciplined by him. But in the beginning stages, even the disciple's devotion will be incomplete. Complete faith will still be lacking. Questions may arise; doubts may occur. In the beginning, a disciple will have a thirst to be loved by the Guru, and he will be jealous about the attention given to other disciples. At this stage, the disciple will have an attachment to the Guru or love for the Guru, but this love will be tainted with selfishness. It is always a struggle in the beginning stages. Yet because of this attachment and love, incomplete though it may be, the disciple will not be able to quit the Guru. The Guru will bind the disciple with his love and then will gradually help him evolve. In due course, as a result of the constant practice and effort under the guidance of the Guru, the disciple will rise up in love. His devotion will become genuine. His sole aim will be to serve selflessly and love the Guru without any expectation of reward. Thus he rises up from the state of an unsteady and indiscriminative disciple to that of a steadfast and immensely discriminative disciple. He rises from the state of a selfish devotee to that of a selfless and pure devotee. When there is nothing left for him but the Guru, then he is a true disciple.

"A true disciple is one who is willing to surrender everything to God or the Guru and desires nothing but the attainment of Supreme Knowledge. He wants to be disciplined by the Master. Whatever may come, a real disciple will not leave the Master until he attains the Supreme State. He may have to go through a lot of difficulties, a lot of mental and physical taming and training, but a real disciple will happily surrender to these trials in order to win the Guru's grace. His only wish will be to serve the Guru selflessly and to do things which will please him. The Guru may try to confuse the disciple by acting and speaking in strange and contradictory ways. The Guru may accuse the disciple of mistakes that he has not committed. But a true disciple will be endowed with the mental strength, determination and discrimination to overcome all these impediments.

"A true disciple gives up his ego, his individuality. The river of the Guru carries him wherever the Guru wills. He has totally surrendered to the current of the Guru. He loses all rights on his body; he becomes like a corpse. He simply lets the Guru or God take him wherever God or the Guru wants. He doesn't judge the Guru. Such a disciple sees the inner Guru, not just the outer form. For him everything is the Guru. He himself has become a bankrupt; he has nothing of his own. He has nobody else to depend on and nothing more to claim as his own. Strongly bound to the Guru in his total surrender, he has no other choice but to seek the Guru's grace. Fully aware that Perfection cannot be attained without the Guru's grace, he knows that he needs to empty his mind completely in order to receive it. At every moment he strives to attain this. He tries to imbibe silence, which is the Guru's real nature. He knows that he should keep quiet first to experience that inner silence. The Guru or God is his Beloved.

Once he comes near the Guru, he tries to be quiet to imbibe or hear that silence.

"A real devotee also considers everything as the will of his Lord. His whole being is constantly in a prayerful mood. For him, every word and deed is a prayer, a worship of his Beloved. Having surrendered everything to his Beloved Lord, a true devotee is always in a blissful mood. There is no place for hatred or anger in him. When everything is his Lord, how can he hate or be angry? He will always be in a pleasant and peaceful mood. All conflicts and divisions cease to exist in him. Those who hate him and those who love him are equal to him. Not only love, but anger and hatred are also *prasad* for him. Not only good, but bad also is *prasad* for a true devotee. Not only believers, but nonbelievers also are nothing but his Lord for him.

"As far as a true disciple is concerned, even though he may choose a god as his beloved deity, no god or goddess is higher for him than his Guru. For him the Guru is both the means and the end; the Guru alone is the goal to be realized. But in the case of a devotee, he considers his beloved deity as everything. Still, the fact remains that in order to get the full benefit of his *sadhana*, he needs the help and guidance of a *Satguru* (Perfect Master)."

The scholar further questioned, "Many people come to see you. There are also a lot of people who are devoted to temple worship. They are also known as 'devotees,' aren't they? But the qualities that you mentioned are not seen in the majority of them. What is the difference?"

Mother answered, "Although all worshippers are generally known as 'devotees,' unlike a true devotee, they have not surrendered everything to God. They may still be involved with affairs in the world, and they may continue performing desire-prompted actions. They will still have desires, ambitions and anxieties, and are prone to crave excitement. Yet they do love God. They pray to Him, sing His glories and speak very highly of Him, but still they retain the ego – the individuality, the *vasanas*. In response to circumstances that arise in their lives their actions will be the result of the ego rather than relying on the God."

"Is this applicable to disciples too?" asked the scholar.

"Yes," said Mother, "but not to those disciples who are completely surrendered to the Guru. There are some who are still desiring to lead a material life even after meeting the Guru. Not seeing clearly who the Guru really is, that is, seeing only the outer form and not the inner nature of the Guru, they might have doubts about him. Perceiving only the outer, they judge the Guru. Unable to understand the seemingly confusing or contradictory nature of the Guru, they will not able to withstand the disciplining of the Master. Their attachment to the Guru has no 'glue.' Their determination to reach the goal is not as strong as that of the true disciple or the true devotee. Self-realization is not their primary goal and maybe not even their secondary goal. Their first choice is to fulfill their own desires through ways they think best to achieve them. They even consider the Guru or God as a person through whom they can fulfill their desires.

"Such a devotee or such a disciple is only partly devoted; whereas, a true disciple or a true devotee is fully devoted to the Guru or God. Truly devoted means to surrender everything to the Guru or God. The Guru's will becomes his wish. The Guru's words become his way of living. The Guru's deeds become his path to follow. 'I' and 'mine' disappear completely. 'He' and 'His' alone exist for one in that state, a state of total egolessness, like the cloudless sky. Thus in being totally devoted, the true devotee or the true disciple has no other choice but to be disciplined or taught by the Guru, for discipline makes one a fit instrument of the Guru or God.

"A true devotee or a true disciple is a perfect instrument in the hands of the Guru or God. The progression can be put in the following manner: First, we have devotion to the Guru. This devotion can be interpreted as love which makes us attached to the form of the Guru. When that attachment is full and complete, then the discipline starts. Discipline is nothing but demolishing and rebuilding, making a new person out of the old one. It requires operating, cutting, removing unnecessary things and obstacles, then stitching and joining to make us function again without any 'sour notes.' This part of the process is a bit painful, but once that is completed, we can feel comfort and relaxation when the smooth, unhindered playing of the Guru's music moves through us. We are then his instrument, and He can play on us in whatever way he wants, because we are totally devoted to him. Because the heaviness of the ego is gone, we become lighter in weight. Lighter in weight, we can be easily carried by the Guru to the final state of Oneness.

"Sometimes people call themselves a devotee or a disciple, but the factor which determines whether one is a devotee or disciple depends on the amount of surrender that they have towards the Guru or God. In fact, devotion to the Guru or devotion to God are one and the same because God and Guru are one and the same. The formless Supreme Principle, out of sheer compassion and love, assumes a form, and that is the Guru. Devotion to the form of the Guru takes us to the formless aspect of Him, which we call God or *Paramatman*."

Some Western devotees were present and the Mother's words were being translated for them. One of them asked a question: "Amma, how can one develop that kind of devotion to the Guru in order to be disciplined by him or her?"

"In some people it is spontaneous and in others it is a slow process," Mother said. "In order to accelerate this process, we should come under the direct guidance of a Perfect Master. Love is not something which can be taught by someone or learned from somewhere. But in the presence of a Perfect Master we can feel it and, in due course, develop it because a *Satguru* creates the necessary circumstances for love to grow within us. These circumstances created by the Guru will be so beautiful and unforgettable that we will truly cherish these moments as something precious and invaluable. They will remain as a sweet memory forever and ever. One incident of this kind will create a big wave of love in us. More incidents like this created by the Guru will make a chain of exhilarating memories which will produce waves and waves of love within us, until at last there will be only love. Through these circumstances the Guru will steal our heart and soul, filling us with pure and innocent love.

"However, all this depends on the urgency that one feels. One has to feel the need for it. An urgent need cannot be ignored. We will do anything to try to fulfill it. We will not rest if an urgent need is not fulfilled. But most of us do not feel this urgency to be devoted to God. We think that life is possible without devotion to God and live our lives depending on the world, not on Him.

"At present, God is the last item on our list. But He should be the first. If we put God first, all other things will fall into proper place in our lives. Once we have God in our lives, the world will follow. But if we place the world first, God will not follow. If we embrace the world, God will not embrace us. To have God in us is a struggle in the beginning, but if we persist, it will lead us to everlasting bliss and happiness. All struggles will end. To embrace the world is easy and things go smoothly in the beginning, but this will culminate in never-ending sorrow and suffering. We are free to choose one or the other.

"Mother knows that it is really a difficult task for you children who are from the West. But if you can become aware of the non-eternal nature of objects while living in Western society in the midst of so many temptations, you will be able to understand the hollowness of such pleasures. You will not succumb to the temptation of material pleasures. No matter what the circumstance, you will realize that such things cannot give inner happiness. Once you are able to exercise that principle, you will become stronger than the people here. But, children, you do not have to worry about it; you will get it by being with Mother and through your willingness to surrender."

This conversation occurred during a pause in the *darshan.* There were still a few more people to be blessed, so the Mother resumed giving *darshan,* as the brahmacharis chanted some slokas from the *Devi Mahatmyam*

O Devi, Who remove the sufferings
Of Your supplicants, be gracious,
Be propitious, O Mother of the world.
Be gracious, O Mother of the universe.

You, O Devi, are Ruler of all
That is moving and unmoving.
Salutations be unto You, O Devi Narayani.

O You Who abide as intelligence
In the hearts of all creatures,
Bestow enjoyment and liberation.

Salutations be unto You, O Narayani.
O You Who, in the form of minutes, moments
And other divisions of time,
Bring about change in things
And thus have the power to destroy the universe.

Salutations be unto You, O Narayani.
O You Who are the good of all good,

O Auspicious Devi,
Who accomplishes every objective,
O Giver of Refuge, O Three-eyed Gauri!

Salutations be unto You, O Narayani.
You Who have the power of creation, sustenance
And destruction. You are eternal,
You are the substratum and the embodiment
Of the three gunas.

One woman devotee came for the Mother's *darshan* and burst into tears as she reached the Mother's lap. Her husband, who had also been a devotee of the Mother's, had recently died. As Mother wiped her tears, the woman spoke, "Amma, my husband was lucky; he died a peaceful death. He had Amma's grace. Even when he breathed his last breath, my husband had Amma's picture clasped in his hand. He was courageous and confident until the end. Amma, by your grace, your daughter (referring to herself) was also very composed. I chanted the *Lalita Sahasranama* as I sat beside him and applied Amma's sacred ash on his forehead. All the while he was repeating his mantra. After he expired, I thought, as I was sitting next to his body, 'Why should I be sad? He has gone back to Amma. After all, he was Amma's son.' I felt very peaceful and tranquil. He is with you, isn't he, Amma?"

As the woman told her story, the devotees noticed the Mother also wiping Her tears. The Mother looked at the woman and said softly, "Yes, daughter, yes. He is with Mother." The lady now calmed down as if she had heard what she wanted to hear. She wiped her tears and was at ease.

Later the Mother explained, "She wanted a confirmation from Mother that her husband was with Mother. She felt worried before that. That is why she was crying."

Innocent faith and how to study the scriptures

When the *darshan* was over, the scholar again asked a question: "Amma, the scriptures say that a person who has attained the state of Brahman is beyond all dualities, like happiness and unhappiness, success and failure. But I saw Amma crying when that lady lamented her husband's death. I know that there must be a reason and a purpose for everything you do. Amma, be kind enough to give me an explanation for this."

Smiling at him, Mother gave this response, "Son, what you saw was only a reflection of her sadness. Mother could feel her pain. Mother's tears reflected her tears. If you stand in front of a mirror, whether you smile, laugh, or cry, everything will be reflected. But the mirror will remain unaffected. The mirror simply is; it simply reflects. The mirror does not do anything. It is actionless, feelingless. So, it is for the sake of their devotees that *Mahatmas* act and express feelings. Although that woman was sad and crying, her innocent attitude made Mother very happy. Therefore, Mother's tears were of happiness, too. Yet really they were neither; both the tears of sadness and those of joy were only reflections. Son, Mother has nothing of Her own. Everything depends on Her children. If they are happy, Mother is happy. If they are unhappy, Mother is unhappy. But She is neither of these."

Hearing the Mother's explanation, the scholar was very pleased. He prostrated in front of Her and said, "Now I see that I have been wasting my life immersed in the study of books. I am doing some kind of spiritual practice, but whatever I acquire through that is certainly spoiled by this study and constant inner talking. My head is full, but my heart is almost empty. Had I performed spiritual practices with the time and energy which I have spent in studying and learning the scriptures, I would at least have gained something. Amma, you have taught me a very important lesson. Your living example of love and compassion for others teaches me more than all those books. Now I see how stupid I have been to bury myself in books, foolishly telling myself, 'I am Brahman,' without giving any thought to real *sadhana*. "

"Son, don't talk like that," said Amma. "Study of the scriptures is also necessary. It will give you more clarity and understanding. It will also help you to discriminate properly when an obstacle arises. You have gained knowledge from the scriptures that has helped you understand Mother and Her words, haven't you?"

With palms joined, he immediately said, "No, Amma, no. Please don't say that I have understood you. No, I haven't understood Amma at all. My knowledge about you is nothing at all."

"Son," Amma explained, "what Mother means is that you now have a relatively clear vision. Children, those who have studied the scriptures properly and have understood their real meaning will not become egotistical. Such study will not be a waste of time or energy. On the contrary, it can very much help a person during times of difficulty, provided one uses discrimination.

"Theory can help, but there is a limit to its value. After a certain point, words or speech become a hindrance, a great hindrance. Eventually, you will have to drop the words. But this is not possible if you study them without the correct attitude. Don't be bound by the words of the scriptures. Study them with the attitude, "This is not the reality, and therefore, I should not feel attached to it. This is only the plan of the house; I cannot live in it. In order to build it and make it suitable to live in, I must work hard. Therefore, I must not get entangled in mere words." With this kind of attitude towards the scriptures, one can easily drop them when he wants to; otherwise, as pundit- mon puts it, the inner talking will not stop.

"It is a pity that most people who are in the field of scriptural study pursue intellectual learning without applying what they've learned in their own lives. They think that they have reached the goal, but as far as their actions are concerned, they are no better than a nonbeliever caught up in the world of likes and dislikes. They are full of ego. They don't know that the words which they have been studying and repeating in their heads have actually created a big wall between themselves and God.

"One should try to develop innocent faith. Innocence is of the heart. The head cannot be innocent. The head is full of questions and doubts. Shallow understanding of the scriptures is dangerous. A tendency to dispute is another problem seen in many who study the scriptures without understanding them properly."

This led to another question: "Amma, what do you mean by innocent faith?"

"Son, let Mother tell a story." Amma proceeded to illustrate the meaning of innocent faith with a story about Lord Shiva and His Consort, Parvati. "The Goddess Parvati had a serious concern. Although it was said that all those who take a dip in the Holy Ganges will be purified of their sins, She saw that this was not happening. 'Why not?' Parvati asked Lord Shiva.

"Her husband replied, 'Because they do it mechanically. None of them have innocent faith. They bathe in the Holy Ganges without believing in its purifying effects.'

"Parvati could not believe this, so the Lord made a suggestion, 'Let us go down to Earth and see for ourselves.' And so, together they left their heavenly abode and descended to Earth. Picking a spot near the Ganges River, they assumed the forms of an old woman and man. Having instructed Parvati on what to do, Shiva, in the form of an old man, then threw Himself into a deep, dark ditch.

"As instructed, the Goddess, in the form of an old woman, started beating Her chest and crying loudly for help. Many pilgrims passed their way after having bathed in the holy river, and Parvati pleaded with them, 'Look, good people, my husband has fallen into this hellish ditch because of a curse that befell him long ago. He will die there if he is not rescued before sunset. It is already late afternoon. For God's sake, save my husband!' She lamented like a madwoman.

"Taking pity on Her, some people came forward to save Her husband, who was crying loudly for help from the bottom of the ditch. But as if suddenly recalling something, the old woman went on, 'Only a pure and sinless person can save him. That is what was declared by the person who cursed him when I prayed for a remedy for the curse. If a sinner tries to save my husband, his head will break into a hundred pieces, and he too will die.' Hearing this, all those who had come forward to help retraced their steps and disappeared from the spot.

"But soon another person came forward volunteering to help Shiva out of the ditch. Parvati again stated the conditions of the curse. Without hesitation, this person answered, 'I am no more a sinner. I am pure and sinless as I have taken a dip in the holy waters of the Ganges. Mother Ganges has washed away all my sins.' There was not an iota of doubt in his mind as he spoke these words, yet he was not presumptuous in his confidence. From his innocent faith ensued fearlessness. There was no fear of death in him. His faith in the Ganges was so firm and unshakable that he really felt that all of his sins had been washed away and that he was now absolutely pure. He was totally unassuming. And so, due to his innocent faith, he really was absolutely pure.

"The others did not have faith; they doubted, and thus their sins were not washed away. The others bathed in the river simply out of respect for the words of the saints and sages that the waters of the Ganges are purifying and holy. But their belief was only in their heads. They had no faith in their hearts. They did it mechanically, out of respect for the *rishis* (sages). But this man alone was endowed with real and undivided faith in the purifying power of the Ganges.

"Children, innocent faith means doubtless faith. It means you have no doubts about what you feel and that you have no questions. You simply accept the Guru's words as truth. Just like a child. You tell a child as you point to a closed door, "There is a goddess in that room." The child will have no questions; he will accept it as one-hundred percent true. This kind of faith towards God or the Guru is innocent faith. Faith endowed with the innocence of a child is what we need.

"Innocence comes when there is love. Divine Love makes you like a child. Love makes you accept anything and everything. The lover does whatever the beloved says. We can see this even in ordinary love. When love is sincere, the lover will even jump from the top of a three-story building if the beloved asks him to. His love for her is so intense that he will act like a madman. When one really loves, one's intellect becomes empty; one stops thinking. No thoughts, no mind, nothing. Only love remains. This 'forgetting-all-else' kind of love culminates in innocence."

Mother sat with Her eyes closed for some time after talking about innocent faith. Then She opened Her eyes and chanted Her favorite mantra, "Shiva...Shiva..." Then She instructed everyone to meditate for a few minutes.

Since it was around 12:30 p.m. when She got up from the cot, She told everyone, "Children, do not go without eating lunch," and instructed one of the brahmacharis to take all the visitors to the dining hall and serve them food. But before leaving, the Mother noticed a bunch of bananas that a devotee had brought. Taking them and breaking them into little pieces, She fed each and every one of the devotees a piece with Her own hand. Everybody was happy, and one person remarked, "One little piece of banana from Amma's hands is enough to appease our hunger. Now we don't have to eat." Many agreed with him. The Mother left the hut and went to Her room.

At 4:30 p.m. the Mother came down to the meditation hall and sat for an hour with the brahmacharis. She then proceeded to the kitchen and upon entering, inquired, "What's new here?" Kunjumol, Gayatri and the other women and girls who worked in the kitchen all stood behind the Mother as another of Her surprise inspections began. They knew through past experience that She would catch them for even the slightest bit of disorder or lack of cleanliness that She found – and always She found something amiss. Although they fearfully awaited the Mother's discovery of their mistakes, they knew that along with any scolding, a beautiful *satsang*[10] would come.

The Mother went straight to the storeroom, where She looked into each container and inspected the shelves. When She came back into the kitchen, the women all heaved sighs of relief, thinking that everything was all right. But the Mother proceeded to look into every pot, scrutinized the plates, each cup and all the other utensils. She looked at a large pot that was sitting in one corner of the kitchen and gently rubbed it as She looked inside. Without mentioning a single word or revealing any hint of discontent, She tried to lift up the pot. Seeing the Mother's attempt, all the women came closer in order to give Her a hand. She stopped them with the words, "No, none of you should touch this. This pot has sat here unattended for more than two weeks. It was here in the same place when Mother visited the kitchen the last time. I wanted to see if anyone would clean it without being asked." She displayed Her palm which was black from the dirt on the pot.

---

[10] A spiritual discourse or advice given by a sage or religious scholar. Also, the company of the wise and virtuous.

"Look at this," She continued, "it's covered with dirt, both inside and out. This shows your lack of alertness. If any one of you had *sraddha*,[11] you would not have left this pot sitting here like this. Remember, doing service in the Ashram and taking care of the things which belong to the Ashram is equal to serving Mother. Such service shows your love for Mother. You should try to take care of these things with as much love as you have towards yourself, as if these things were your own. A careless person is not fit to be a spiritual seeker.

"External carelessness will lead to internal carelessness as well. God is beauty. He is purity. He is the harmony behind everything. There is a harmony behind every object, every place, no matter how insignificant it may look. The scriptures say that food is God. The kitchen is the place where food is cooked; therefore, it should be kept clean and tidy. There is a tendency to make the kitchen a mess. That is wrong. Do not allow yourselves to follow old habits. We are here to change, not to continue in the same old ways."

The Mother Herself then carried the big pot outside to the water tap. Again the women rushed forward, this time to do the cleaning, but the Mother would not allow it. She cleaned the pot all by Herself. After scrubbing and rinsing it, She brought it back into the kitchen and put it back in the same place, turning it upside down after having swept the floor. And thus, this incident served as a precious lesson for all the ladies and brahmacharinis who worked in the kitchen.

Even though the evening *bhajan* at 6:30 p.m. was a daily routine, one never tired of singing devotional songs with Mother. She had first begun singing and composing devotional songs to God when She was very young. Her singing was an out-pouring of supreme devotion and all-encompassing love, and every evening

---

[11] Faith. Amma uses this word with special emphasis on its aspect of alertness coupled with loving care of the work in hand as an offering to God or Guru.

those who gathered together for *bhajans* would always find Her presence an elevating experience. It was easy for one's mind to readily flow towards one's *Ishta Deva* (beloved deity) as one's heart overflowed with Divine Love. On this particular night Her whole being radiated with spiritual glory and splendor as She sang

Pakalantiyil

Time has reached the end of the day,
But my Mother has not yet arrived.

To sit alone, this one is afraid, O my Mother.
How long must this aching heart weep helplessly?

Who is there to give company to this one
Enveloped in darkness, O my Mother?

As Mother repeated some of the lines over and over again, She soared to a high, exalted mood. Tremendous vibrations of Her singing filled the evening twilight. At last, She continued the song with tears streaming down Her cheeks.

Do You take it as a play?
If so, I do not understand Your viewpoint.
Why such a fate? Is it because
I have not uttered Your Holy Name?

This one always searches with an aching heart
For Thy Lotus Feet.
Give me the taste of that sweet nectar
Of devotion in my heart.

Everyone present was deeply moved upon seeing Mother cry. Hardly anyone could control his tears and some even cried aloud like Her. Spiritual bliss prevailed everywhere as everyone was totally transported to an inner realm of joy. Suddenly Mother took a long, deep breath, and the crying stopped. Her body was absolutely still. Everyone became frightened to see Her holding Her breath for such a long time. She sat in a perfect meditation posture with Her eyes half-closed. The inner bliss manifested outwardly as Her face glowed like the full moon. There was still no sign of breathing as this state continued. Some brahmacharis felt that singing might help to bring Mother down to a normal state, so they sang, beginning with a slow tempo.

Sita Ram Sita Ram Sita Ram Bol
Radhe Shyam Radhe Shyam Radhe Shyam Bol

Gradually, step by step, the cadence increased until it reached a very fast tempo. All those present sang and sang with all their hearts. As the song continued in full swing, Mother let out a blissful laugh. She raised both Her hands, which held divine *mudras*, and at one point She placed both hands on top of Her head. Her eyes remained closed while the laughter of ecstasy continued. This divine mood of the Holy Mother lasted for a few minutes before it slowly subsided. The residents sang the *arati* as one brahmachari waved the camphor flame inside the shrine, and then the closing prayers were chanted.

The Mother continued to sit in the same place with Her eyes fixed skywards. After a while, She got up, but because She had not yet fully come out of the exalted state, Her steps faltered as She tried to walk. Assisted by two women devotees, Mother went to Her room.

Three hours had passed since the beginning of *bhajans*; it was 9:30 p.m. Everyone prostrated and stood up, looking at the Mother until She disappeared from sight. Then the residents dispersed. Some went to their huts and meditated. Some moved towards the backwaters at the edge of the coconut grove and did mantra *japa* as they walked to and fro along the banks. Some householder devotees remained seated on the verandah of the temple and meditated, while a few brahmacharis chose to sit inside the temple. Thus another unforgettable day with the Mother passed, granting us a vast treasure of experience to cherish as part of the eternal memory.

Chapter 6

Concentration and meditation

29 April 1984

Since this was Sunday, another *Devi Bhava* day, many people had arrived the previous evening in order to spend a full day at the Ashram and to receive the blessing of the Holy Mother in *Devi Bhava*. At seven o'clock in the morning, the Ashram was already crowded with devotees. The morning *puja* was being performed in the temple. One brahmachari chanted the *Lalita Sahasranama* and others chanted the responses. Some devotees had assembled on the temple verandah and were also chanting the responses.

When the chanting was finished an hour later, the Mother came to the meditation hall to observe the brahmacharis in meditation. As an expression of respect and reverence, they all stood up when the Mother arrived. When She took Her usual seat, they prostrated fully in front of Her and then returned to their seats. Upon sitting down, the Mother immediately closed Her eyes and began meditating. The residents followed Her example.

After some time, the Mother called out to one brahmachari by name. Startled, he opened his eyes. He was obviously a bit scared. A mischievous smile danced on the Mother's face. The brahmacharis, who had all opened their eyes upon hearing Mother's call, looked back and forth between Mother's smiling face and that of their frightened brother who now hung his head in guilt.

"Have you finished enacting the role?" She asked. "Yes, you have done it well. Now it is time to come out of your sweet reverie. Wake up."

The same mischievous smile still played on Her face, and everybody continued to listen and watch without understanding at all what was going on. Still, everyone sat with eyes wide open. Promptly came the following statements from the Mother, "Why did you others open your eyes? Did I call you? This shows your lack of concentration. If your minds were concentrated on the forms of your beloved deities, you would not have opened your eyes. You would not even have heard anyone call. This is a clear example of your lack of *sraddha*. How are you going to attain God-Realization if you are so outwardly oriented? Only a person endowed with strong determination can attain God. A single sound was enough to wake you up from meditation, and it was not even related to you in any way. A true spiritual seeker's concentration and determination should be such that he will be unshaken even if a mad elephant charges at him.

"Mother called one of you, but you all opened your eyes, so curious were you to see what was happening. Shame on you. Mother would have been happy if just one of you had remained unmoved, if one of you had continued to meditate. But no, that was too much to expect."

One brahmachari dared to say, "We opened our eyes because it was your voice. Had it been someone else's, we would not have paid any attention. After all, we all meditate on your form."

To this Amma responded, "Whether it is Mother's voice or somebody else's, if you were really absorbed in meditation, you would not have heard it. Once concentration is attained, you are in contact with the inner Mother, that means your own Self. Even when you meditate on the name or the form of a God or Goddess or Mother, you are, in fact, meditating on your own Self, not on some external object. In deep meditation there is no outside world. You will not hear, smell, taste, feel or see in that state of one-pointedness. Mother knows that none of you have reached that total state of Oneness. Yet, Mother would have been extremely happy if one of you had at least pretended to remain in meditation. Now, close your eyes and continue to meditate. Try not to let the mind wander. Imagine that the heart is full with your beloved deity's form."

When meditation was over and the Mother had returned to Her room, all gathered around the 'victim' brahmachari, eager for him to reveal what the morning's incident had been about. "While sitting in meditation," he explained, "I was carried away by thoughts of a drama in which I acted a role during my college days. My thoughts were on how beautifully I had presented the character." Everyone roared with laughter when they heard this confession.

Among the thousand names of the Divine Mother in the *Lalita Sahasranama*, which is chanted daily at the Ashram, one mantra is *Sadachara Pravrattikayai Namah*, meaning 'one who enforces good conduct.' After hearing this interesting experience of the 'actor brahmachari,' another fellow resident interpreted this mantra in a different way. In this mantra *Sadachara* is considered one word , but when divided in two, it takes on a different meaning, for *sada* means 'constant' and *chara* means 'spy.' *Pravrattika* means 'one who does them.' Thus, according to this brahmachari, the Mother is one who is constantly engaged in spy work. He said, "Dwelling within us, Amma always does spy work. She squeezes all information out of us, no matter what it is."

Around ten o'clock the Mother came to the hut and began giving *darshan*. The brahmacharis were asked to sing. Brahmachari Pai started with a few slokas from the *Sri Guru Paduka Panchakam, verses 4 and 5*

Salutations again and again to Sri Guru's sandals,
Which serve as the Garuda,
The mantra against poison,
To the multitude of serpents of desire and such
Which bestow the treasure of discrimination
And dispassion, which grant true knowledge,
And which give immediate liberation.

Salutations again and again to Sri Guru's sandals,
Which are the boat on which to cross
The endless ocean of the world,
Which bestow steadfast devotion,
And which are a raging fire
To dry the ocean of spiritual intensity.

Then he sang

Amme Ulakam

O Mother, this universe of Thine
Is verily a madhouse.
O Divine Mother, impossible it is for me
To describe Thy Divine Love.

Please feed me daily with Thine own beautiful hand
The nectar of Love, and thus remove my pride
Arising from the identification of the Self
With the body. Make me infatuated with that Love.

O Mother, Inner Core of the Scriptures,
If my eyes shed tears of devotion
When I utter the Name of Kali,
Then all the Scriptures would become secondary
Things fit only for the intellect.

Infinite masks of the Mother

To watch the Mother give *darshan* is always a fascinating experience. An infinite number of masks are at Her disposal, and She
goes on changing them from one moment to the next, as She
glides effortlessly between roles. This changing of masks goes on
and on, for none of these faces are really Hers. None of them is
Her real face, which is something far beyond the realm of forms.

The Mother is not at all attached to or identified with any of these different faces or roles. She wears each one for a particular purpose, and once that purpose is fulfilled, the mask is quickly removed. To each of Her children She shows a different mask, depending on the time and need. Even though She shows a mask, the fact remains that each one of these masks are not at all mere masks but a reality, a strong link to establish their personal relationship with Her, and thus feel that Mother is their own. Meaning, although for Mother these different faces are just like masks which can be removed and replaced at any time, in the hearts of Her children, She creates the feeling that She is their own and She is with them all the time. But while we become identified with and attached to this face and role, the Mother remains detached and unchanged. She can wear it or throw it away at any time.

On this day, like so many others, one lady was telling the Mother about the difficult situations she had to confront in her life. Her husband was very sick; he could not work due to his ill health. They had three daughters, all of whom were over twenty and not yet married. Such was her tale of woe. As the Mother listened intently to all that the lady had to say, one could clearly see how sad the Mother was. The anxiety She displayed on Her face when the woman was lamenting about her three unmarried daughters was evident. The Mother consoled the woman, wiped her tears and assured her that everything would be all right. Hearing this, the woman's face lit up, and by the time she left the Mother's presence, she appeared happy and relaxed.

Next came someone who looked very happy. "Amma, by Your grace I have gotten the promotion that I have been waiting for," he said. "I had been expecting and hoping it would come, but somehow it was delayed. I grew very disappointed, thinking that I would never get it. But all of a sudden yesterday the promotion notice came. It is Your grace, Amma." The man was exuberant with joy as he had the Mother's *darshan*, and the Mother, too, seemed very delighted and was wholly participating in his happiness. Joyfully, She told someone sitting near the cot, "Look, this son got a promotion. How long he's waited for it! He got it by God's grace." After this happy man moved aside, there came a young man who looked as if the burden of the entire world was on his shoulders. Two such different faces, one right after the other. Now the Mother's face changed to empathize with that of the sad young man.

Thus Her face goes on changing, but She is never identified with or bound by any of Her faces or moods. She is such a Master at this art of changing masks that She can even wear more than one at a time. With so many children all with different needs and demands, the Mother is an Adept at giving each one just what he needs.

It once happened that for three days the Mother did not so much as look at Brahmachari Balu, while She continued to converse with the other brahmacharis. For this reason, Balu had stopped eating. Upon learning about his fast, the Mother insisted that he eat, but Balu was stubborn and would not obey. In his early days with the Mother he used to be stubborn, demanding and disobedient at times. Again and again the Mother asked him to eat, but he would not. Thus when, on the third day of his hunger strike, Balu and Brahmachari Sreekumar were sitting beside the Mother, She was extremely loving towards Sreekumar, but displayed anger towards Balu. Out of one eye poured love, while anger darted from the other. While She may show infinite masks, infinite faces, infinite moods, deep down the Mother remains the same – unattached, undivided, totally One.

From *Ananda Srishti Vahini*, which is often chanted at the end of *Devi Bhava*, we have these lines which describe the Mother's infinite number of masks. Who is She, really? Numerous words can be written to try to describe Her, but the answer can only be found in one's heart.

Salutations to Thee, O Great Divine Goddess
Who art the support of all creation,
Of infinite states and infinite aspects
And ever in the state of supreme dance.

Salutations to Thee, O Ever-Effulgent One
The Mother of Immortal Bliss,
Ever-breaking the silence of the dead of night,
Thou art Protector of righteousness
And all that is wholesome in the world.

Salutations to Thee, in the form of Guru,
Thou art Goddess Shiva
Showing the path of dispassion
With a smile like the lotus flower.

Prostrations to Thee, O Bhadrakali,
Fierce form of Devi and cause of auspiciousness.
Permeating the whole of consciousness,
Thou art full of compassion and the cause
For the submergence of individuality in everything.

Prostrations to Thee, O Mother,
Ever-effulgent and wearing a crown,
Thou bestowest heaven and Liberation.
As the cause for everything in and beyond nature,
Thou art beyond time.

Chapter 7

Questions asked by Westerners: which path to follow

30 April 1984

The previous night's *Devi Bhava* ended at three o'clock in the morning. Since it was part of Mother's routine to go around among the devotees making sure that everyone had a place to sleep and a mat or a blanket to sleep on, it was a little after four o'clock when She finally went to Her room.

In the early afternoon came a group of Westerners who were spiritual aspirants traveling around India, visiting pilgrim centers and spiritual institutions. They had already been informed about the Mother's greatness by a friend and therefore requested to stay for a week. As they walked around the Ashram grounds they were impressed with the peaceful atmosphere. Brahmachari Balu led them to the northern side of the Ashram where they were given rooms in the guest house.

Mother came down around three o'clock in the afternoon. Immediately She went to the coconut grove. Presuming that She was going to sit there, Gayatri spread out a mat on a spot where there was good shade, and Mother came and sat there. She sent Gayatri to fetch the Westerners, and they all came running, exuberant with delight. After offering their prostrations to the Mother, they gathered around Her and sat. First of all, in Her usual manner Mother gave *darshan* to each one of them individually. The personal *darshan* they received was a totally overwhelming experience for them. Thus they sat entranced, gazing at the Holy Mother.

As Mother sat and looked at them, smiling, an inexplicable expression of compassion and love beamed from Her face. No one could speak as the moments passed in silence. Finally Mother inquired, as Balu translated, "Children, have you eaten?" Spellbound, they continued to gaze at the Mother. It was impossible for them to verbally reply, so they nodded their heads in the affirmative. Mother further asked, "Children, did you all get a room?" and again their response was non-verbal. Mother, being struck by a funny mood upon seeing them continue to sit like dumb mutes, grabbed the two closest ones and shook them vigorously. This finally awakened them, and they all roared with laughter. When that subsided, Mother said, "Mother is very happy to see Her children."

Light conversation followed for a brief while. Again came a pause, after which one of them asked a question, "Amma, which path is the best for Westerners? Most people in the West show a lot of interest in following the Path of *Jñana* (Path of Knowledge). Should this be encouraged? What is your opinion?"

"Children," Mother answered, "whether it is in the East or in the West, one's spiritual path can only be indicated according to one's inherited spiritual disposition and mental constitution. One path cannot be announced in a public address as the one and only path for all. To embark on a spiritual path involves personal guidance and disciplining. In the olden days, the spiritual masters always tested the competency of the disciple before giving advice. It was never general advice for all. That is why all the spiritual texts like the *Upanishads* and the *Bhagavad Gita* are in dialogue form. The advice given is particular to the individual. Each person is a patient with a different disease. Some people are in the beginning stages of a disease while others are in the middle stages. In addition, we find people with chronic diseases and still others who are half-cured. Therefore, the treatment for each person cannot be the same. The medicine will be different and the dosage will vary.

"Many problems will arise if only one path is prescribed for all. Real spiritual growth will not take place if a person who is supposed to follow the path of devotion is told to take the path of *Raja Yoga*. [12] It is like telling an asthma patient to take medicine for diabetes. Being advised to take a path not appropriate for them is a stumbling block for many people in their spiritual quest. Mother cannot say that one path alone is good enough for everyone in order to attain the goal.

"But generally speaking, the Path of Devotion is the easiest and the least complicated. While anybody can love, not all can do *pranayama* (breath control) or *Hatha Yoga* (yogic postures). Only certain people endowed with a certain mental and physical constitution can do these. But love has no prerequisites. Whoever has a heart can love, and everyone has a heart. To love is an innate tendency in human beings. However, we cannot say that *pranayama* or *Hatha Yoga* come naturally to human beings. *Bhakti* is love – loving God, loving your own Self, and loving all beings. The small heart should become bigger and bigger and, eventually, totally expansive. A spark can become a forest fire. So to have only a spark is enough, for the spark is also fire. Keep blowing on it, fanning it. Sooner or later it will burn like a forest fire, sending out long tongues of flame. At present, love is like a spark within us. Constantly blow on it, using the fan of the Divine Name, *japa* and meditation. You may perspire, sneeze and cough, but do not stop. Your body may become hot; tears may fill your eyes; you may want to faint. But do not stop. If you perspire, you sneeze and cough, persist in your efforts, and be assured then that you

---

[12] Mastery of the mind through the control and transformation of the psychic equipment.

are heading towards the goal. Soon you will become Love itself. This is the reward for your love.

"The Path of Love, otherwise known as the Path of Devotion, is the best one for Western children. Of course, this is a general statement. In the West, society is such that people, even from early childhood, are intellectual and take an intellectual approach to everything. It is the product of their 'modern' education. They are fed with all kinds of factual information about the empirical world, and the emphasis is on science and technology. So their analytical minds are well-developed, but their hearts are dry. In most cases, the hearts of people in the West remain under-developed and imperfect. The head is big, but the heart is shriveled up and dry.

"What is the cause for this dryness?" the Western man further asked.

Mother elaborated, "The social norm that prevails paves the way for this dryness of the heart. One gets one's first lessons in love from one's mother. But in the West, the roles of mother and father become confused. Mothers become fathers and thus lose the quality of motherly love. They have no real love for their children. The instability of married life is another factor. The husband-wife and the mother-father relationship is so weak and fragile. A child who lives in this kind of situation cannot be loving. He or she cannot be affectionate. Such children do not even learn the most basic lessons of love. Of course, love cannot be taught like one can be taught to read and write. What Mother means is that there are no proper circumstances created for them to develop love in their lives. They grow up seeing the conflicts, arguments, disputes, hatred, fighting and finally the separation of their parents. They never experience what love is, which is what they are supposed to learn from the mutual love between their father and mother. The parents are the two Gurus which the children see from birth until they come into contact with the world. If the seed of love is not sown at home, it cannot sprout or blossom.

"The Path of *Bhakti* teaches love. First, you develop one-pointed love towards God. When that love becomes the center of your life and as the devotional practices become more and more intense, your vision changes. You come to understand that God dwells as Pure Consciousness in all beings, including you. As this experience becomes stronger and stronger, the love in you also grows until at last you become That. The love within you expands and embraces the entire universe with all its beings. You become the personification of Love. This Love removes all dryness from you. This Love is the best cure for all emotional blocks and for all negative feelings. Therefore, Mother thinks that the Path of Love is the best for Western seekers."

Formation of qualities in children

One of the Western women responded in agreement, "What Mother recommends is really the perfect path for Westerners. I know from experience how much pain and tightness there is within me—and how little love. In our efforts to imitate men, we Western women have lost our essential femininity. This is really sad. A life based on love and patience is what we need."

Amma continued further, "Mother was just about to say that patience is another quality which is lacking in Western society. Children, a mother must have great patience in bringing up her children. A mother has to put into effect the molding of the child's character. The child learns his first lessons of love and patience through his mother. But she cannot simply talk about love and patience and expect her son or daughter to adopt those qualities. No, that is impossible. She has to set an example of love and patience by putting those qualities into practice in her dealings with her child.

"A child can be very adamant and uncompromising, of course. But that is the nature of most children since their minds are not fully developed. Caring only about their own needs, they can be very selfish and stubborn. But, that is permissible, for it is not contrary to nature or to the laws of nature. But if a mother becomes stubborn and impatient, that is something very bad. That will create hell. A mother must be patient—patient like the earth.

"A father is just as deeply involved in rearing the children as the mother. A father, too, must have patience. When a father grows impatient, that is the end of the child's innocent and trusting life. He or she will grow up to be impatient and adamant, never having experienced what it meant to be patient since nobody had shown them what it was. Socially, they will have a difficult time. Friends will not be patient with them. They cannot expect their girlfriends or boyfriends to have patience. Society is not going to be patient with an impatient boy or girl. Children will not have an opportunity to learn patience and love from anybody else if they do not learn these qualities from their parents. If the mother is patient and loving with her children, they, too, will grow up to be patient and loving. But if the Mother is not, the children are not going to be loving and patient because they will not know what it is to be so. We cannot blame them for that.

"Children express what is taught to them and what they have experienced while growing up. Therefore, you should be very careful and cautious for your children's sake. Be careful about what you say. Be careful about what you do, because each word that you utter and each deed you perform creates a deep impression in your child's mind. It goes deep into his heart because those are the first things that he sees and hears. They are the first impressions indelibly imprinted upon his or her mind. The mother is the first person with whom the child is in contact. Next comes the father. After that, the elder brothers and sisters. All other relationships come later in life. Therefore, in front of your children exercise good control over your mind. Create a good home environment for them in which they can grow up. Otherwise, you will have many worries in the future."

Family life as an ashram

"Amma, so you are saying that family life is not something to be taken lightly, that it is not just something that happens in the course of our lives. Should it be considered as another form of *tapas*?" asked another Western man.

"Children," Amma replied, "Mother does not like to use the word '*tapas*' because it scares many Western children. They think that *tapas* involves physical and mental torture. They are afraid that through *tapas* they will lose all their desires, and they do not want that to happen. They want to enjoy life. But the only problem is, they have the wrong idea of 'enjoying life.' Real enjoyment of life depends on relaxation, not on tension. Yet, most people, not only in the West but also in the East, are very tense almost all of the time. Men are not able to spend any peaceful moments with their wives and children. They are more worried about their work, their business, their status in society and about what others will think or say about them. They are always worried about one thing or another. They want a new house, a new car, a T.V., or a new relationship. A person engrossed with life in the world always wants some new thing. He is fed up and bored with old things. He can never be satisfied with what he has. He thinks that new things will make him happy. His mind is always set on what he does not have. He is always living either in the past or in the future, never in the present, and he runs after everything he craves. He goes on acquiring and possessing. He has no time to enjoy, to relax and be in the present. So finally, he collapses.

This is what happens to most people in this so-called 'modern society'—be it in the West or East.

"A family is not merely a group of individuals who live together. As they live together, this 'group' can learn to understand many things. It is another type of *gurukul* (the family of the Guru). Just like the spiritual Guru, who treats his disciples as his own children, the father and mother are the gurus in this case, and the children are the disciples. In the *gurukul* a very strong bond exists between the Guru and the disciple. The master is always like a father or a mother to his disciples. So there is nothing wrong in comparing family life to a *gurukul*. In the olden days in the Guru's hermitage, sometimes, if he was not married, the Guru was both the father and mother to his disciples. But if Guru had a wife, she was the mother of the Guru's disciples, exhibiting love and patience while the Guru took care of the teaching and the disciplining. That was how it used to be in the ancient Indian *gurukuls* where the master led a householder's life.

"In most families today, there is both a father and a mother. With the correct understanding about family life and about life as a whole, they can play their parts properly. The mother can try to impart in the child virtues like love, patience and forbearance, and the father can lovingly prevent the child from doing things which would do harm to society, his family and to his own life. The father can teach him obedience and respect for others. In some cases, a single parent becomes both the father and mother. It is possible if one tries. In all cases, the parents are the first ones to set an example, to show their children how they want them to be. If a good example isn't set, it is an impossible task to raise children properly. A father can also be a good mother and a mother can also be a good father. But this balance cannot be attained unless one does proper *sadhana*.

"So the family house should not be a place where a group of individuals live together in conflict, always fighting and arguing. It is not a place for just eating and sleeping, thinking that this is what life is and that this is what enjoyment is. That makes family life hell. It will cut your personality to pieces. Family life such as this is equal to death. A person who leads this kind of life in his family is nothing more than a corpse. This kind of family is like a prison where the inmates have no personal contact; they are just there, adjacent to one another. But you can turn your family into a haven, your house into a home, an abode of happiness and bliss, a place of peace and love. There definitely is effort involved; it can be a kind of *sadhana*. It is all right if you want to call it *tapas* if that helps you think of it as a serious matter.

"Nobody wants to be unhappy, nobody wants to suffer. Everybody wants to be happy at all times, if possible. But the way or the path they choose to accomplish this end is often wrong. The present way of living will only end up in greater distress and sorrow. The problem is you. It's within you, not outside. If you really want to enjoy life, try this path of mental disciplining and see what happens. There is no harm in putting forth some effort, doing some *tapas*, if it helps to bring more happiness. You want to enjoy life; of course, nobody wants to suffer. But remember that enjoyment depends on how you live life.

"A *griham* (house) is an ashram or hermitage. That is how the word *grihasthasrami* (householder) came into being. A *griham* can be converted into an *ashramam*. An ashram is a place where people devote all their time and energy to the remembrance of God, doing selfless service and developing qualities like love, patience and respect for others. They do spiritual practices to help them see unity in diversity. First, they fill their own hearts with love, and then whatever they do and wherever they go, this love is expressed in all that they do. They see beauty and harmony everywhere. This is what life in an ashram is intended to be. Family life can also be like this. It was like this before, in the olden days. If they did it, so can we. That is why a housholder devotee is known as a *grihasthasrami*, a person who leads an ashram life while remaining in his house. He is a person who tries hard to attain the supreme goal, bliss, even while living with his wife and children. This is possible if you sincerely try."

Fear of surrendering

Another question came from a Western man: "Amma, it seems that even though many Westerners are seeking spirituality, when it comes to renunciation, they have weak wills. I would even say that they are really frightened to give up possessions and surrender. Why is this?"

Mother said, "Son, this attitude is found in the people of India as well, but it is more apparent among Westerners. As Mother said before, people are afraid to give up their desires. They think that they cannot live without them. There is nothing to be afraid of because nobody is going to force you to give up your possessions and surrender your will to the Guru's will. No real Guru will press you or threaten you to do anything.

"Mother does not force anything. Her children have all the freedom they want. Mother has said, even to the children who live here, 'Children, you have the freedom to choose. If you have any strong worldly desires and if you find it difficult to continue as a brahmachari, you can frankly tell Mother about it. Mother Herself will find a girl for you and will arrange for your marriage. But if you are interested in continuing the path and if you truly feel that this alone is what you want, then you should try to live according to the rules and regulations of the Ashram. But you are to free to choose.'

"Furthermore, no real Guru will start disciplining you as soon as you move to his ashram. If you are interested in following the path, he will wait patiently until you become mature enough to be disciplined. There is no sense in instructing you to do things or not to do things if you are not truly willing to accept the Guru's words. This would be like talking to a rock. So the Guru is not going to force you or even instruct you to do something which you don't want to do. But he will make you become willing to surrender, not forcefully but slowly, patiently taking you to a point where you will have no other choice but to surrender. Therefore, the fear that the Guru will force you to surrender is meaningless.

"After all, why should the Guru press you to surrender? He is beyond all interest in anything. He is beyond desire and desirelessness. He has no selfish motives, for he is beyond everything. To force something onto somebody else is the nature of greedy people. The Guru is not at all greedy; so why would he do that? Surrender is not something which you do to somebody else. It is to your own Self that you surrender. The Guru does not want anything from you. He does not have any personal interest, nor does he have anything to gain from your surrender. He is ever full and complete. The Guru knows only how to give, and he goes on giving. The Guru does not need any of the external things that you might give him. The giving up is for your inner growth, for your own peace of mind and for your own bliss. It is for the unfolding of your little self into the big Self.

"Seeing only his body, people judge the Guru externally. They project their own ignorance onto him. This is what makes them afraid to surrender. They think that the Guru will control them or snatch everything from them. They are afraid that he will take away their individuality and make them suffer. Because they see only the human form of the Guru, they fear that they will be tricked by him. The Guru is beyond the body; he is beyond being human. He is the embodiment of pure consciousness. In realilty, he is formless and nameless. There is no person there. Only nothingness. How can the formless, nameless Guru snatch anything from you? How can he control you? He simply is, and you benefit from his presence. If you really want to use the Guru, then surrender to your own Self. Your Self is the same as the Guru's Self. Therefore, there is nobody who will claim, demand, argue or snatch. Surrendering to your own Self is for your own spiritual upliftment. It is not for the Guru, not for the Guru at all."

The group of Westerners listened intently to the Mother's words. They were clearly very happy to hear Her answers. The one who appeared to be the leader of the group expressed her gratitude to Mother, "Amma, You have really clarified some questions that have bothered us for a long time. This has been truly enlightening. We had many more questions, but you have answered them without our having to ask them. It is said that one cannot repay the Guru. Nevertheless, Amma, please accept our humble prostrations at Your Feet." They all prostrated in front of the Mother.

Mother called Brahmachari Sreekumar to bring the harmonium. When he brought it, She sang a few *namavalis* and the Westerners joined in the response. Their attention was completely focused on the Mother. Seeing Her God-intoxicated mood, they all sat gazing at Her with awe and reverence. Seeing these different moods of supreme devotion manifested in the Mother was a new experience for them. When She finished singing, Mother remained in a totally indrawn state for a short while. Then returning to the physical plane of awareness, She got up from Her seat and walked towards the southern edge, near the backwaters. The ripples of the water reflected the glow of the late afternoon light.

The incomprehensible Mother

Late in the evening, after the *bhajan*, Mother was lying down in the sand on the south side of the temple. Her head was on Gayatri's lap and Her feet rested on the lap of another woman devotee. Almost all of the brahmacharis and other Ashram residents were present. Mother was in a very playful mood. Like a child, She caught hold of Gayatri's hair and pulled. Gayatri bent her head down, but Mother kept pulling until Gayatri's head touched Mother's chest. Then She let go of the hair.

The next moment Mother closed Her eyes and with Her right hand outstretched, She went into *samadhi*. Everybody remained still. After a while, She came out of this mood, whirling Her right hand in circles and uttering a distinctive sound which She makes such times when She moves in and out of *samadhi*. Mother did not speak; neither did the brahmacharis ask any questions.

After a short while She placed Her right hand on the ground and began to dig a small hole. Suddenly She took a handful of sand, and threw it at one brahmachari's face. As he coughed and spat, struggling to remove the sand from his mouth, Mother roared with laughter. She rolled off Gayatri's lap onto the sand, laughing uncontrollably. After a few moments, She sat up and again grabbed another handful of sand. The brahmacharis watched this, and expecting a face-full of sand, some began to move quickly away. But She did not throw any. Seeing that Mother had stopped playing, the brahmacharis who had run away now returned. But as they sat down, the sand came flying. Mother's aim was perfect. The very same brahmacharis who had run away were now showered with sand. They rushed to the water tap to wash their faces and rinse their mouths, and when they returned, Mother was in Her normal mood.

Now one of the brahmacharis asked a question, "Shouldn't whatever a *Mahatma* gives be accepted with love and reverence?

"Yes, that's what the scriptures say," answered Amma. "There shouldn't be any question or doubt about it. Simply accept what is given and keep it as an object of worship. However insignificant the object may appear, we should not refuse it because we do not know what we are being given. In our eyes it may appear as a silly object. But it can be a rare blessing bestowed on you with a special *sankalpa*. *Mahatmas* can do this. A gift like this can be the fruit of your *sadhana*.

"You may think, 'Oh, I haven't done any spiritual practices in this lifetime; so how can this be the fruit of any *sadhana*?' If you have not performed any *sadhana* in this lifetime, you must have done something in your previous birth. That is why the Guru blesses you. You don't know anything about your previous life, but the Guru knows. Not only about your previous life, but He knows about all the births that you have gone through; He knows everything that you have done. He knows the past, present and the future. He knows what you have been, what you are and what you will become. Even a handful of sand is valuable and precious if a *Mahatma* gives it to you.

"Even if a person has not acquired any spiritual merits in previous lifetimes, a *Mahatma*, out of sheer compassion and love, can shower His grace on him or on whomever He wants. We do not know in what form this grace will come."

The Mother was clearly pointing out the mistake they had made to the brahmacharis who had run away. Full of remorse, one of them said, "Amma, we did not have enough discrimination to sit unmoved when You threw the sand on us. We simply thought that Amma was playfully throwing sand at us. We did not see the inner depth of Her game. Amma, please forgive us for our error." They each prostrated and sought forgiveness of the Mother.

Amma consoled them, "No, children, no. It is not your fault. It is Mother's mistake. Sometimes Mother becomes a little playful and does something like that. But, children, Mother simply does it. In fact, there is really no ego involved." She paused. Then all of a sudden, She burst into a song

Uyirai Oliyai

O Goddess Uma, where are You,
You Who are said to be the life, light
And firmness of the earth?

O artful One Who exists as the wind, sea
And fire, have You no mercy on me?
All wisdom has fled to a distant place,
Repeated births continue,
Unreality has become reality
And all defects are increasing
In the absence of You,
Who are Real Knowledge concealed.

The sound of the ocean waves served as background accompaniment to Mother's song, and soon She was again lost in a mood of divine rapture. She laughed and smiled as tears rolled down Her cheeks. Raising both Her hands, the Mother sang. As Mother Herself has said, Her mind is always spontaneously shooting up to the highest plane of consciousness. Within a split second She can switch off this world of plurality, this world of names and forms, and travel towards the unknown. Just like a child who can go to the kitchen and obtain the message needed for the stranger waiting in the sitting room, Mother can ascend and descend any time She wishes. Mother has free access to both worlds. We onlookers see only the closing and opening of Her eyes, the circling of Her hand, the uttering of *Namah Sivaya* or a blissful laughing, but we know nothing about the incomprehensible Supreme Reality where She is constantly established.

Mother's exalted mood cast a spell of charm and delight over all Her children, who sat unmoving, their eyes fixed on Her. The night was indeed enchanted, and all of nature seemed to respond to the Mother's divine bliss. After about ten minutes of this magical stillness, Mother's mood abruptly changed. She lay down in the sand and began rolling restlessly from side to side. All of a sudden, She said, "I want some roasted *katala*" (chick peas).

"O Narayana!" Gayatri exclaimed."We have no *katala*. How can we get any at this hour?" It was as if she knew that this request would not be quickly forgotten. Sure enough, just like a small child, Mother went on saying, "I want roasted *katala*, I want roasted *katala*." Immediately Gayatri jumped up and ran, first to the Mother's room, and then she ran to the kitchen and again back to the Mother's room. The Mother continued to ask for *katala*. Luckily, Gayatri could find some in her cabinet, so she brought it to the Mother. Sitting up, Mother popped a few pieces into Her mouth, and then proceeded to distribute a bit to everyone present. Noticing that two brahmacharis were missing, She sent someone to get them, but the messenger returned alone, reporting that both were meditating.

At this point, Mother Herself got up and strode towards the hut in which one of the missing brahmacharis lived. Everyone followed behind Her. Entering his room, She tip-toed up behind him as he sat in meditation, quickly grabbed his head, and stuffed the *katala* into his mouth. Jumping up from his seat, he was, needless to say, very startled. With an astonished look still on his face, he stood before the Mother, chewing a mouthful of food. As if this was just what She had wanted to see, Mother watched him and laughed.

Aroused from his meditation by Her loud laughter, the other brahmachari who had been sitting in an adjacent hut came to see what was going on. Having intended to play this same trick on him, when Mother saw Her second victim in the doorway, She said in a disappointed tone, "Oh, here he is! It would have been fun, but the chance is lost. Maybe another time." These words invoked yet another round of laughter. She gave this brahmachari a handful of *katala* and, making sure that everyone had received his share, She handed the bowl to a brahmachari, and followed by Gayatri and Kunjumol, She proceeded towards Her room.

Although each one is precious and unique, incidents of the Mother's playful and strange behaviour are not rare. In recounting these actions of the Mother, we find that first She wanted some fried *katala*. Yet when it was brought, She hardly ate any. Instead, She distributed it to everybody; thus it was a play for Her. As Mother has explained, Her playful and strange behavior often serves the very practical purpose of keeping Her mind fixed on the physical plane of consciousness. Her mind can easily rise up and dwell forever in divine union; therefore, out of benevolence for Her children She strives to remain on this physical plane. And for Her children who were lucky enough to be present on such occasions, these incidents are especially precious gifts. They provide unforgettable remembrances, memories to be cherished and contemplated for years to come. It is through these incidents and their memories that the Mother creates the most ideal conditions for cultivating in Her children the seed of Divine Love.

Aparigrahyam (incomprehensible) is the word used in the scriptures to indicate Brahman, the Supreme Truth. Brahman is incomprehensible. It cannot be comprehended through the limited faculties of the mind, intellect or the sense organs. This word is applicable to a person who has attained the Supreme State. The ordinary human intellect will search for the meaning of the actions of persons in the Supreme State, but that search is futile because the realm of the Supreme transcends everything. Stop searching for a meaning to their actions. Simply accept their actions as they are. Any attempt at explanation or interpretation will not reveal anything, for the meaning does not come via words. The search of the intellect or reason has to stop. Only in silence can one know and experience it. Once it is known, the knower 'keeps mum.'

A *Mahatma* is like a child. *Balavat* is the term used in the scriptures to describe this childlike nature. He neither has any regrets about the past nor does he have any anxieties about the future. He always lives in the present, totally unattached. To an ordinary human being, who is burdened with all kinds of pre-conceived ideas and prejudices, a *Mahatma* might appear unreasonable or crazy. The scriptures call this aspect *bhrantavat*. The fact is, he cannot be comprehended by human intellect. To get a glimpse of his real nature, one should drop his reasoning. Until one's reasoning is dropped, the *Mahatma* remains inexplicable, incomprehensible and indescribable.

Chapter 8

A profound teaching illustrated in everyday cooking

1 May 1984

On this morning Mother came downstairs even before eight o'clock and headed towards the east, away from the Ashram, followed by Gayatri and Kunjumol. As She passed a few brahmacharis sitting in front of the meditation hall, the Mother glanced at them and asked, "What are you talking about? Is it worthwhile?" Not waiting for an answer, She continued on and passed 'Unni's hut,' which was only a few yards away from the Ashram. (This hut belonged to a fisherman's family who were devotees of the Mother. It was situated just east of the Ashram temple. On this spot now stands the new seven-story temple building; its construction was begun in 1986).

Wondering where She was going at this early hour, two of the brahmacharis decided to follow Her. But they did not follow too closely, knowing from experience that the Mother did not always like them to go with Her when She went out. Mother had Her own reasons for this. Sometimes when She was about to leave She would specifically tell them not to come and would often give reasons why. And other times She would simply go without saying anything. On those occasions, like this morning, when nothing was definitely said, the brahmacharis took it as an indication that they could come if they wanted, and always some of them would follow behind. Because they could never be sure about what the Mother would say or do from one moment to the next, whether it was all right for them to come along, or whether She might suddenly turn around and tell them to go back, the young men followed at a distance, hoping She would not send them away.

When Mother reached the edge of the backwaters, She turned towards the south, still accompanied by the two girls. Pausing at the water's edge, She turned and looked at the brahmacharis, shouting to them, "Hey, you little thieves, no problem! Come along!"

Thus getting a green signal, the two boys ran and joined Her. They walked together, and along the way She pointed out a public water tap and recalled, "This is the spot where the windmill pipe was. Mother used to wait here for long hours to fetch water for the household needs. But She never wasted time. If there was a long queue Mother would go and cut grass for the cows. Whether Mother was standing in the queue waiting for Her turn or cutting grass for the cows, She would never cease to remember God and to repeat His Name."

After a brief pause, She continued, "The villagers were very kind to Mother. They tried to help Her whenever they could. They knew that Mother worked day and night, attending to all the household chores. The difficulties that She had to undergo and Her devotion to God were also well-known throughout the village. Therefore, even if Mother left Her empty water pot near the tap and went off to cut grass for the cows, one of the villagers would always fill it and keep it aside for Mother."

At this point they reached the house of Pushpavati Amma, an ardent devotee of the Mother. She was, in fact, standing in front of Her picture when Mother entered the house. The very small hut with one bedroom and a kitchen was filled with household utensils. Half the space in the small bedroom was occupied by a large wooden box, the kind used to store rice in traditional Kerala homes. Seeing this small hut, one wondered where all the family members slept.

Hearing people entering her house, the middle-aged lady, who was standing in front of the altar, woke up from her prayerful mood. When She saw the Mother with a big smile on Her face standing in front of her, the lady's pent-up emotions gave way. Tears streamed down her face as she fell at the Mother's Feet. All her children came out of the kitchen and prostrated. Mother lifted Pushpavati Amma from the floor where she was still lying in prostration, shedding copious tears at the Mother's feet. She rose to her knees, but continued to cry, as she embraced the Mother's waist. Most compassionately, Mother stroked her and kissed her on the cheek. Then Mother hugged and kissed each of the daughters, who were also crying. Sobbing like a child, Pushpavati Amma said through her tears, "It has been such a long time since You've visited our house. When I woke up this morning, I felt so sad. I even said to my children that You must have forgotten us. When You walked through the door, I was praying, 'O Amma, if only You would come, then I would be happy.' I prayed and prayed and now You have come." Again she was caught up with emotion.

Amma turned to the brahmacharis and explained, "Previously, Mother used to visit here frequently, but that was before there were so many people at the Ashram. Now Mother's *prarabdha* (usually meaning 'past actions which are bearing fruit in the present', but here the term is used to mean 'responsibilities or burdens') has also increased.

Turning back to the woman, Mother told her, "Just as you have responsibilities to take care of, Mother also has the burden of so many children who have renounced everything and sur-rendered their lives to Her. What can one do? Years ago, before these children came, Mother had more time to spend with you. But now Her time is slowly being divided among so many other matters. Anyhow, Mother has come when you really had the longing, hasn't She? The fact is, Mother was going to remain in Her room today, but suddenly She felt like coming here. Without even mentioning one word to Gayatri, Mother just walked down the stairs. Maybe it was your innocent desire that brought Mother here."

Mother went on, "You say that you wanted Mother to visit your house, but you never told Her. Even though you always come to the *Bhava Darshan*, you never said anything to Mother." Since Mother had sat down on the floor, one of the daughters brought a mat and requested Her to sit on it. Mother lovingly refused it, "No, daughter. This is fine." Then She continued as before, "How am I supposed to know your desire if you do not tell me?"

The woman smiled and said in an innocent way, "O *Kalli Amme* (O Mother, You little Thief)! Why do You play tricks on us? You know everything. That is why You come here even without my verbal request. I always wanted to tell You but I simply couldn't say anything whenever I came near You. Anyhow, You heard my prayers. You saw my anguish and pain, didn't You? I know that You know everything, and I had faith that You would hear my prayers."

Mother laughed and rejoiced at Pushpavati Amma's innocent remark. She turned around and told the brahmacharis, "Look at her innocence. Learn to be innocent like this." With these words the brahmacharis now thought they understood why Mother had allowed them to come along. It seemed to them that She wanted them to witness this incident, and they learned an important lesson. She further advised the brahmacharis, "Do not drown your innocence in the letters of the scriptures."

One of the daughters brought some *puttu* and *katala*[13] to Mother and Her party. She served tea for the Mother and *palum*

---

[13] Ground rice flour and ground coconut mixed together and steamed in an iron or wooden cylinder, served with cooked garbanzo beans and usually eaten for breakfast.

vellam (hot milk diluted with water) for the others. Mother drank the tea and ate a little of the food as She told the brahmacharis to drink their milk. The Mother fed each of the family members with Her own hands and then a little was given to each of the those who came with Her. She said, "It is too early for them have this heavy breakfast. *Mol* (daughter), pack it up. They will eat it later, after their meditation."

Mother now went into the kitchen and looked around a little. She sat down near the fire on which an iron cylinder of *puttu* was being cooked in a pitcher of water. Mother removed the tube from the pitcher and tested it to see whether it was done. Seeing that it was still raw, She put the tube back on top of the pitcher, and not wasting an opportunity to dispense a bit of spiritual wisdom, the Mother gave this analogy, "The pitcher is the body, and the water in the pitcher is the mind. The fire is *tapas*. The fire boils the water and steam is produced. The steam cooks the raw mixture of rice flour and coconut into a delicious food, *puttu*. People can appease their hunger by eating this good food. Similarly, we are raw and uncooked now. We are a bunch of useless things called the body, mind and intellect. Yet we carry them around with great pride. We are full of selfishness and egotism. These raw, useless faculties should be cooked in the heat of *tapas* to transform them into something useful. For this to happen the water of the mind, the ego and thoughts, should disappear in the intense heat of *tapas*. *Tapas* makes the mind subtler and subtler, pure and more expansive. And thus you become a good and useful person for the world. When you can love and serve humanity, you become food for the world."

After it was cooked, She removed the *puttu* from the tube. While refilling the cylinder with the mixture of rice flour and coconut, She further elaborated on this same theme: "Look, now we are like this, raw like this rice flour. Uncooked, nobody can eat it, for it will cause stomach problems. Not only is it useless, it is harmful. This is how we are now." She held up and displayed the tube as She continued: "We should enter into this dark prison-like tube of *tapas* to get cooked and thereby become freed so that we can be of some use to others. One may feel that the period of spiritual practice is a period full of strict rules and regulations, a period of control. We may feel that *tapas* and renunciation imprison us, that they make us lose all freedom. But know that this prison-like feeling is temporary and that it will soon take you to eternal freedom. Just like the *puttu*, we become food for the world once we are cooked in the fire of *tapas*.

"A real *tapasvi* (one engaged in austere spiritual practices) lives for the world. He remains in his body only for the world. He sacrifices himself for the good of the world. He becomes the inner food for those who approach him, seeking to quench their inner thirst and to appease their inner hunger. He is the food for those who thirst for the Truth. Sri Krishna became food for the world. Jesus and Buddha also willingly served as food for the world. But to become this food, one should cook oneself in the fire of *tapas*. The Gopis of Brindavan cooked themselves in the fire of their love for Sri Krishna. One may think that they did not perform any severe penance, like sitting long hours absorbed in meditation, fasting or torturing the body. But through their intense love for the "Butter Thief" who also stole their hearts, they too, were doing *tapas*. This is what is meant by His stealing butter from their homes; He was stealing their hearts. The excruciating pain of separation from the beloved makes one extremely heated up. In that heat, the ego melts away and finally there is union. In this state of union, a cooling down takes place, and one becomes totally peaceful and full of bliss."

The Holy Mother returned the tube of *puttu* to the pitcher on the open fire pit and got up. Everyone relaxed. While listening to

Her words, they had been transfixed. A simple, everyday household job of making a breakfast food had just been the subject for a most profound spiritual talk. Who could have drawn out such great spiritual principles hidden in simple cooking? Pushpavati Amma remarked, "There is nothing that Ammachi does not know."

Although she was an ordinary-looking village woman, Pushpavati Amma was quite familiar with spiritual principles. Her husband, also a devotee of the Holy Mother, was highly respected and loved by everyone in the village as an outstanding *Bhagavata* reader.[14]

The *Lalita Sahasranama* glorifies the Divine Mother as *tattvartha svarupini*, meaning 'the embodiment of all spiritual principles and their meaning.' Such incidents and occasions make one feel that the Mother is the personification of all Vedic dictums and wisdom.

Before leaving their house, the Mother performed a short *puja* at the family altar. On the way back to the Ashram, the Mother spoke more about this family. "Pushpavati Amma is a pious lady. During the days when Mother was ill-treated by Her elder brother, she used to take Mother to her house. Mother would sit in her front yard and cry, praying to the Divine Mother. Sometimes Mother would get so absorbed in meditation that She would not come out of it for many, many hours. Pushpavati Amma revealed that she used to get very worried and frightened on such occasions, thinking that Devi would take Ammachi's body away. She used to cry and pray to the Divine Mother, requesting Her not to take Ammachi away. She is very innocent. Most of these villagers have innocent faith; but they have no spiritual understanding.

---

[14] In India there continues the tradition of the 'poet-singer' who reads or chants the tales of the ancient gods and heroes, just as in the Greek tradition, Homer sang about the adventures of Ulysses.

They believe God is different from man and that man cannot become God. If they had spiritual understanding in addition to their innocent faith, it would be very easy for them to progress."

Upon reaching the Ashram, the Mother at once told the two brahmacharis to go and meditate, since it was past their regular meditation time. On the way to Her room, She peeked into the hall through a window and, seeing that all Her children were there, She climbed the stairs to Her room.

Householders and spiritual life

By ten o'clock quite a few people had already come to see the Holy Mother. They were waiting, some in the *darshan* hut and some on the temple verandah. The Mother came to the *darshan* hut in an hour's time as the devotees were singing

Amritanandamayi

To Mata Amritanandamayi, Immortal Goddess
Salutations again and again.
May You rise like the dawn in my inner mind,
O Mata Amritanandamayi!

O Mother, I know not how to sing
Your sinless praises.
O Pure One, Your holy words
Are nectar to Your children
As the cooling clouds are to life.

O Detached One, Bestower of destiny,
Universal Enchantress, continue Your dance,
O Ambrosial One, by the radiance
Of Your gentle smile
My heart is overflowing with sweet nectar.

As an expression of their love and reverence for Her, the devotees all stood when She entered the hut. Utterly humble, the Mother prostrated as She always did, and everybody prostrated in deference to Her example. The singing continued as She sat on the cot, where She remained throughout the *darshan*. Before receiving the waiting devotees, She called the little children who came to Her one by one. In their innocent attraction to Her, some of the young children did not want to leave the Mother's lap, so the Mother had them sit beside Her on the cot. But often they did not want to move away from there either, and finally their mother or father had to carry them away.

When each of the children had been seen, the devotees went for *darshan*. As this proceeded, a male devotee asked a question about how a householder should live in the world and still maintain a spiritual life.

The Mother gave him this reply: "A householder who wishes to lead a spiritual life after completing his responsibilities in the world should exercise renunciation from the very beginning, because it won't come easily. Renunciation demands constant and long-term practice. He may not be able to relinquish everything externally; therefore, he should try to be detached from within. His mind should not get too involved in things. In order to keep this spirit of inner detachment, *lakshya bodha* is very important. Whatever happens in the home or outside, one should always contemplate and pray in this manner: 'My goal is far beyond all these silly and trivial worldly problems. O Lord, please do not push me into these conflicts and arguments. Give me the strength and courage to be in the midst of these problems and still remember You and remain detached. Let me try to work through them as part of my duty, but let me be untouched by their vibrations.'

"A good householder should be a *sannyasin* internally. Mother does not say that a man should run away from his duties. No, he shouldn't. He should perform his duties as best he can. It is not good to run away from life. That is cowardice. A person who runs away from life is not fit to be a spiritual seeker. That is why Krishna did not let Arjuna run away from the battlefield. Life is a battle. It is not something to be avoided. Furthermore, you cannot avoid it. What will you do to avoid it? You may run to the Himalayas, or to a forest, or to an Ashram in order to escape from life. But life will follow you there as well. Just as you cannot run away from death, you cannot run away from life. Wherever you go, death follows. Wherever you go, life also follows. You cannot avoid either; you can only transcend them. Therefore, an intelligent person does not try to escape from life, but lives it sensibly, giving proper attention to his affairs.

"The intelligent way of living life is to have a good foundation in spirituality. Children, do not try to run away from your duties. If you are a householder, perform your duties properly, but try to be detached as much as possible, so that you can prepare yourself for total renunciation. If you are a spiritual seeker or a *sannyasin*, you are still living in the world, aren't you? Therefore, you have certain duties towards society. Of course, nothing binds a true *sannyasin*. But since most people are not *sannyasins*, they should play their part well in the world. Do some good and beneficial things for society, but try to be detached. As a person who leads a spiritual life while leading a family life, prepare yourself for the final letting go."

"Amma, how is this possible?" asked the same devotee.

The Mother continued to explain, "Whether one is a *grihasthasrami* or a *sannyasin*, renunciation is the means to the end. Internally, a householder should be a *sannyasin*. Externally he should be active, performing his duties neatly and well. Externally he has desires and needs to fulfill. He may need acquisitions and possessions, but at the same time he should prepare himself to drop everything at any time. A *sannyasin* who lives in the world should also be like this. He should be dynamic in his actions, but untouched and totally detached within. That is the secret.

"A *sannyasin* is one who has dedicated his entire life, both external and internal, for others, for the good of the world. Whereas, a real *grihasthasrami* is one who still leads a family life externally, but a *sannyasin's* life internally.

"In order to set an example, a *sannyasin* also should perform actions while living in the world. He should not sit idle saying, 'I have attained the state of actionlessness, therefore I don't have to do any work.' This will set the wrong example that others will follow. Even after attaining the state of perfection, a true *sannyasin* who lives in this world of pluralities will be very dynamic, active and creative on the outside. But he will be totally silent within.

"Once a *sannyasin* was traveling in a train. Many other passengers were in the compartment with him, and everybody had several pieces of luggage with them. Noticing that the *sannyasin* had by his side a cloth bag stuffed with things, one of the passengers observed, 'We are worldly people. We have many possessions. But you, too, have a bag full of things. Is there any difference between you and me, other than the color of our clothes?' The *sannyasin* smiled and kept quiet. A few minutes later, the train was crossing a bridge over a river. All of a sudden, with a beaming smile on his face, the *sannyasin* took the cloth bag and a few other things he had with him and threw all of them out the window into the river below. With the same expression on his face, the *sannyasin* turned towards the passenger and asked, 'Dear brother, can you do that?' The passenger exclaimed, 'What! What are you saying? All our valuables are in our bags. How can we throw them away?' The *sannyasin* smiled and replied, 'I, too, had my so-called valuables in that bundle, but I could easily renounce them without any feeling of pain or attachment. Whereas, you cannot do this since you are attached to your things. That is the difference between us.' Realizing his impertinence, the passenger hung his head and kept silent.

"Children, a real *sannyasin* is like this. He is totally dispassionate. Even the things that he may seem to possess cannot bind him. He is free, eternally free and untainted. Such a being can easily renounce all things.

"A householder, on the other hand, may not be able to renounce things so easily, but he should try to quiet his mind. A householder's mind tends to be noisy with all the problems which disturb him from every direction. He is always worried about his personal problems, his wife's complaints, his children's needs, social demands, and so on. He cannot keep quiet. Both internally and externally he will be running around, wandering to and fro, talking and discussing, calculating and solving, disputing and fighting, and finally collapsing again and again. Mother knows that it is very difficult to overcome these problems which make thunderous noises both in your head and in your minds. But it is not impossible to learn to obtain silence within. Most of our ancient masters were householders. They could do it. They were also human beings. So if they did it, we can do it. If they had the power to do it, we also have the power. To give an example of how a real householder should be, Mother will tell you a story."

The Mother proceeded to tell the story about the golden mongoose, one of the tales from the *Mahabharata*: The eldest Pandava, Yudhisthira, who was the king of the city of Hastinapura, once performed a great *yagña*.[15] This *yagña* was praised by all as he distributed rich presents to the lame, the blind and the poor as well as to the priests and learned men. Food was served and distributed in abundance to all.

---

[15] Vedic ritual followed by the distribution of wealth, both to the brahmins and to the poor and needy.

While the ceremonial rituals and distribution of gifts were in progress, amidst the cheering praises in glorification of the great King Yudhisthira, a mongoose appeared on the scene and began rolling on the very spot where the ceremony was being conducted. This was a strange mongoose, for half of his body was golden in color. The mongoose rolled and rolled around for a while. Finally it stopped. Looking at the assembly of learned men, the mongoose said, "This sacrifice, O learned ones, is not as great as that of the brahmin family." The learned men reacted, "How dare you try to belittle this great sacrifice which is being performed exactly as prescribed by the scriptures! We are all well-versed in the ancient scriptures, and we are sure that these ceremonies are being performed exactly as prescribed. Yet as you have apparently found something amiss, we would like to know what wisdom you have to share. Please tell us about the greater sacrifice that you seem to have witnessed."

The mongoose then narrated his story. "In Kurukshetra there once lived a brahmin family. The family consisted of four members—the brahmin, his wife, their son and daughter-in- law. They led a simple and austere life. Even in the best of times, the brahmin ate only one meal a day, and that consisted of only a few grains of corn. But a time came when a great famine descended upon the land. No crops could grow and even the weeds dried up. At last the family could not find anything to eat, and the entire household went hungry for several days. Then one morning the brahmin found some barley. His wife and daughter-in-law pounded the barley and divided it into four equal portions. They were about to eat when suddenly a guest arrived.

"Even in this time of hardship, the brahmin welcomed the guest with all humility and love. He offered water for the guest to wash his feet and brought a seat for him to sit on. After inviting the guest to partake of some food, the brahmin went into the kitchen and returned with his portion of the barley. Offering the simple food to the guest, the brahmin said, 'Sir, forgive me, this is all I can offer to you.' The guest gulped it down and wanted more. The brahmin felt very troubled, thinking that he would have to do the unthinkable thing of sending his guest away hungry. But the wife happily offered her portion of food. The guest ate that and still he wanted more.

"The brahmin did not feel any impatience or anger towards the guest, but again he was worried that he would have to send the guest away hungry. Then the brahmin's son came forth offering his portion of the food. Again, after that was eaten, the guest looked at the brahmin with a dissatisfied look of hunger on his face. The brahmin once again wondered how he could please his guest. This time, the daughter-in-law persuaded him to give away her share too. The brahmin graciously offered that to the guest, saying, 'Here, sir, please have some more.'

"But this time the guest's response was different. 'No, that is enough,' he said. 'You have passed the test. I am very pleased with all of you. You were prepared to sacrifice everything, even your lives, in order to fulfill your *dharma* (right action, righteousness). Hunger deprives a person of all righteous thoughts and actions. But your renunciation and steadfastness have impressed even the *devas* (demi-gods). One who conquers hunger has won an abode in heaven. Now all of you come with me to the abode of the immortals.'

"Thereupon, the guest revealed his true form to the brahmin family. A *deva* stood shining before them, and with a golden chariot, he took the brahmin and his family to heaven. I was witness to all these events. Soon after the *deva* took the brahmin family up to heaven, I went over to the spot where the brahmin had been standing while serving the guest. A few grains of barley flour were scattered on the floor. I rolled over it. To my amazement one half of my body turned golden! Since then I have been visiting every place where a sacrifice has been peformed in order to see if, by rolling over the sacrificial ground, the other half of my body will also turn gold. But all my attempts have ended up in failure. No sacrifice has equaled that of the brahmin. Great indeed was the brahmin's sacrifice."

After Mother had finished telling the story, She spoke about how its meaning could be applied to spiritual life: "Children, a *grihasthasrami* should be like this brahmin family. In both the story about the *sannyasin* who threw away his bag and the story about the brahmin family, there is one thing in common. It is renunciation.

"This potential is in everyone. It may be in seed form, but it is in everyone. If you keep the seed in your pocket, it will not sprout. The seedling will not germinate by itself. You need to sow it, fence it in to guard it from stray animals, protect it from too much sun and too much rain, apply fertilizer at the proper time, remove the weeds, water it appropriately, and thus care for it well. It will then grow into a tree, a huge, shade-giving fruit tree. It will yield an abundance of blossoms and fruit. This kind of effort is needed to attain the goal. The saints and sages did *tapas*, and thus they attained the goal. We should also try to attain the goal with steadfastness.

"Sri Krishna was a householder. He had many responsibilities, but He was the embodiment of detachment. Sri Rama was also a householder and in addition to that, a king. He was the embodiment of *dharma*. King Janaka (father of Sita, the holy consort of Lord Sri Rama) was a king and a householder. He, too, was a *jivanmukta* or liberated soul. They all found enough time to do *tapas* and to lead a spiritual life even in the midst of all their court duties and other problems.

"If we say that we have no time due to our problems and family responsibilities, that is simply an escape. That means that we have no desire to follow the path of spirituality. We are lazy and want to avoid work. So immersed in *maya*, so trapped in its net, we do not even realize that there is a reality higher than the body and the external world around us. We have no eyes to see it, no ears to hear it and no heart to feel it.

"If we want to be more honest and sincere with ourselves, it would be better if we were bold enough to admit, "I'm not interested in spiritual matters," rather than twisting the truth by saying, "I have no time." When we really have the desire to do something, time and the proper conditions will be at our disposal. Time and circumstance follow desire."

Another question about how to conduct one's spiritual life while living in the world was asked: "Amma, suppose somebody is a businessman, and he is spiritual as well. His Guru is in town, but he has some business crisis and cannot leave his work. What should he do when such a challenge arises, when he has to choose between his Guru and his business?"

"Son," the Mother replied, "you said the businessman is spiritual. Has he surrendered everything to his Guru? This is the question to be asked. There are businessmen who want to give up their business and take up spiritual life; however, the Guru may ask them to continue the work as a *sadhana*. If this is the case, the man should remain at his office and attend to his work and not leave if there is a crisis. If the Guru has asked him to continue to work in his business, it is no longer his own work but the Guru's work. So if he chooses to leave at a time of crisis in order to go see the Guru, that is not right. His business is in service to the Guru; therefore, he must remain and settle the problems as part of his *sadhana*. That is what the Guru wants him to do. Such a person should constantly remember his Guru while he is doing his work. His mind should revolve around the Guru at all times.

"However, when the intensity of one's concentration on and love for the Guru is so strong that he is totally absorbed in that alone, then he cannot continue to do any external job. External work spontaneously falls away just as a ripe fruit falls off a tree. All this depends on the amount of surrender one has. There are people who leave their work to go see the Guru even if there are problems that need to be settled. In such cases, faith will protect them. But remember that this faith should be a pure and taintless faith without even one iota of doubt. Doubt will spoil its intensity and interfere with faith. It will create an obstruction to the flow of the Guru's grace. If you have faith, you can leave everything in the hands of the Guru, whatever the situation may be. You can go see him or anyone at any place, for the Guru's hands will be there to protect you. That faith arises when you no longer have any doubt about the omniscience, omnipotence and all-pervasive nature of the Guru.

"How many people have this kind of unshakable faith? Sometimes a certain amount of faith comes even to ordinary people, to people who have not given up all their attachments. But this will not last long, for it arises in a particular situation and disappears after some time. They will not be able to sustain this faith. Yet while it lasts, this faith will prompt them to act without fear, so they will be benefitted by it.

"Then there are the kinds of people who will give their own reasons on whether to go see the Guru or not. They are in between the two categories already mentioned. They do not have complete faith and have not surrendered fully to the Guru. These people stick to their work due to over-attachment, but the reason they give will be something else, they will try to give a more 'noble' reason. They may have reverence for the Master, but their faith in him is not very strong; it is divided. They stick to their work because of excessive attachment and lack of spiritual aspiration.

"There are also those who leave their work because they are incapable of dealing with problems that arise. They do not have the strength or courage to confront problems. In the name of wanting to be with the Guru they escape from their work, but they do not really go to be with the Guru. They may go to see the Guru, but it is only to run away from the problems at work. They will not gain anything. Even while sitting in the physical presence of the master, they will be brooding over something else. Such people have weak wills and are unstable. They neither lead a healthy life in the world nor a good spiritual life.

"Some people are attached to the Guru's form, which is very good, especially in the beginning. Attachment to the Guru will help make the roots of spirituality go deeper. Such people may lose their power of discrimination when they hear that the Guru is in town. They will become over-excited. In this excitement, there is the possibility of doing things with lack of discretion or of neglecting responsibilities. If they can't help but go to the Guru, then they should entrust their work and responsibilities to a capable and trustworthy person who can handle them. Such people should at least have enough discrimination to choose a substitute for themselves."

Darshan continued. The brahmacharis sang

Arikil Undenkilum

O Mother, even though You are near,
I wander about, unable to know You.
Even though I have eyes,
I search, unable to see You.

Are You the beautiful moon
That blooms forth in the blue winter night?

Unable to reach the sky, I am a wave
That beats its head against the shore.

As I come to understand the truth
That all worldly comforts are worthless,
I long to know You,
As I shed tears day and night.

Oneness with God through Love

"How does love for God culminate in Oneness?" a devotee asked the Mother.

She answered, "Son, as the mind becomes more and more one-pointed through spiritual practices, thought waves gradually decrease. And the mind, along with the thoughts, disappear and dissolve into the total mind. Our mind is nothing but a part of the universal mind, the cosmic mind. Thoughts are like a wall which stands between our own minds and the one cosmic mind. It is like two rooms separated by a wall. Demolish and remove the wall, and the rooms become one.

"In pure innocent love there is no wall. The wall of thoughts disappears. The lover's mind becomes one with the beloved's. In selfless love the lover forgets everything. Past and future drop away and love alone remains. There are no motives behind this love, except the desire to become one with the beloved. Remembrance of God becomes constant. The constant and one-pointed remembrance of one's beloved makes one forget all about the world.

"When Krishna left Brindavan, the Gopis became mad with love for Him. They thought that He would return, but He did not. Remembering Krishna and His Divine Music, the Gopis became oblivious to the external world. Slowly it disappeared from their sight. In their perception everything turned into Krishna. Whatever they saw was Krishna's enchanting form. Whatever they heard was the melodious music of His flute. They did not see cows as cows, but as their Beloved. They did not see their husband or friends, but instead, they beheld Krishna's form. The blowing of the wind and the trickling of the water in the river sounded to them like the Divine Music of His flute. Love rose to its supreme heights, and they became truly mad with Love.

"Once a Gopi saw two deep footprints under a flowering tree. She immediately thought, 'These must be His, my beloved Krishna's Feet.' She continued to imagine, 'Why are the footprints so deep? I know! Some lucky Gopi was with Him. She must have asked for some flowers from this tree. Since the branches were too high for her to reach, Krishna carried her on His shoulders in order for her to reach the flowers. And that is why the footprints are so deep. Oh, how fortunate that Gopi is! She is the luckiest among women to have been carried by Krishna.'

"Such was the condition of the Gopis. Whatever they saw, they somehow related it to Krishna. Their burning love for Him was so great that their individuality disappeared. Their minds were consumed by this burning love. The inhalation and exhalation of their breaths, the throbbing of their hearts and the pulsation of their blood—everything moved with the thought of Krishna. The all-consuming flames of love destroyed the world of thoughts, the world of diversity. There were no more thoughts; only Krishna. They forgot to eat or sleep. They forgot everything, as they became totally identified with their beloved Lord. Mad with love, the Gopis used to say to one another, 'Dear friend, look at me. I am Krishna. Look at the peacock feather which adorns my head. Look at the way I walk. Look at my hands and the flute I am holding. Look at my dark blue complexion.' Thus the Gopis, intoxicated with love, forgot themselves and merged into Krishna.

"In this merging with the beloved deity the small 'I' disappears, for the mind stops functioning. Through constant remembrance of the Beloved you become Him. He becomes your food and you eat Him. Now the food that we all take in is a variety of objects. Through the sense organs we partake of pleasurable objects—seeing desirable things with the eyes, hearing nice sounds or flattering words with the ears, smelling exotic fragrances with the nose, tasting delicious food with the tongue in the mouth, and touching and being touched or caressed, which is felt by the skin. All of these are a form of eating, eating which makes one's ego puffed up. But this kind of eating, this partaking of sense pleasures, stops when you eat your Beloved. Then, the feeding of the mind with sense pleasures gushing in through the sense organs automatically stops. A constant process of spiritual purification takes place within you via another simultaneous process of giving up what you claim as 'I' and 'mine.' Those pleasurable objects cease being separate objects when you eat your Krishna, Rama, Devi, Jesus or Buddha. When you stop partaking of sense plea-sures but start eating Him through those objects, diversity ends. Your Beloved becomes your food; no matter what you partake, it is your Beloved, and thus you become One with Him. Only Oneness exists.

"Only when you are not so attached to the world will it be possible to remember God. Holding onto the world will obstruct the remembrance of God. But once you become established in this remembrance, you will see and think of everything as God. Life in the world cannot be an obstacle once God is enshrined in your heart. So bind Him with the rope of love. If you forget all about yourself, then all that you see, smell, taste, and touch will be Him. Thus you become one with Him. Your little world of ego disappears and you become the Pure Self.

"Children, do you know the story of Vidura's wife? Vidura was the brother of the blind King Dhritharasthra and served as the prime minister in his court. Lord Krishna was going to visit Vidura's house, so they made all the preparations to receive Him. Vidura's wife was, of course, very excited. She made all the arrangements necessary for an elaborate welcoming ceremony, and when everything was ready, she went to take a bath. Being unpredictable, Krishna arrived earlier than expected, and Vidura's wife was informed.

"Hearing that Her Lord had arrived, she forgot everything; she could only think of Krishna. Her mind became completely absorbed in Her Lord. In that divinely intoxicated mood, she took a banana, peeled it and threw away the fruit, feeding Krishna with the peel. Forgetting herself and becoming totally oblivious to the circumstances, she did this again and again. The Lord, however, relished the peels with great joy and happiness.

"Love makes one forget all things. Our selfless, innocent love is the greatest offering that we can give to the Lord. It is the most delicious food for God. This story reveals the essence of pure love. Pure love makes one forget everything, even one's physical existence. That forgetting about oneself culminates in Oneness. The little 'I' disappears as you become identified with the Beloved. Pure love is Oneness."

The Mother stopped talking and continued giving *darshan* to people. The residents sang a *bhajan*

Adi Parashakti

O Primal Supreme Power,
Please bless us, rid us of distress.

O Goddess with eighteen arms,
Mounted on a lion,
Thine eyes are worshipped by lotus petals,
O Thou Who hast a gentle smile.

O Goddess of the Universe,
Dance in my heart always;
Granting me all boons,
Please consider this supplicant with kindness.

As they sang the concluding verses of the song, Mother was transported to another world. She closed Her eyes and sat still. Her hands showed two different divine *mudras*. The chanting reached its heights with everybody singing, and the *darshan* hut reverberated with "Om Shakti, Om Shakti, Om Shakti, Om."

The Mother slowly came down to the normal plane of consciousness. The song gradually subsided, then there was silence. She resumed receiving people as there were only a few more who had not been blessed by Her. Mother blessed the last person, and getting up from the cot, She prostrated on the floor as is Her usual manner to set an example for us, and proceeded to walk out of the hut. She continued walking to the edge of the backwaters where She spent a little time before returning to Her room. Having relished the Mother's spiritual food, the devotees now went to the dining hall to have their lunch.

Chapter 9

Young man from Rishikesh

2 May 1984

Soon after the morning meditation one of the brahmacharis noticed a young man sitting in front of the temple. He had a long beard and long hair, and there was a calm, quiet manner about him. The brahmachari was very impressed by the young man's meditative posture and serene look. After the usual breakfast of rice gruel, served to residents and visitors alike, the brahmachari once again came to the temple verandah to see if the young man had stirred from his meditation, but he found him still deeply absorbed. Half an hour passed, and the young man was still sitting on the verandah, but his eyes were open now. The brahmachari asked him, "Have you had your breakfast? If not, please come and have some." Very politely he answered, "No, I have not, but I do not want to eat before I see Amma."

Sitting down next to him, the brahmachari inquired, "Where do you come from and how did you come to know about Amma?"

The young man revealed that he was from Rishikesh and proceeded to share his experience of how he came to know about the Mother. "I am also a *sadhak*. By God's grace I have been on the spiritual path for the last fifteen years. I live in an ashram in Rishikesh with the Ganges River only a few yards away. Every day I spend some time on the banks of the river, chanting my mantra and meditating.

"Of course, this holy river is most conducive for meditation, but recently I began to have problems in concentration due to some mental agitation. Two weeks ago while trying to meditate, I heard someone calling my name, not only once, but several times.

I did not open my eyes, thinking it was only my imagination. So I continued to sit with my eyes closed and tried to concentate on the flowing sound of the Ganges. Again came the voice calling me. It was a female voice, calling me again and again. The sound was so clear that I had no doubt that someone was calling me, so I opened my eyes. I looked all around, and as I was doing this, the voice came again, "Here, look here." The voice seemed as if it was coming from the Ganges Herself. I sat gazing at the water and as I held my gaze, a form slowly began to take shape on the waters.

"This form became clearer and clearer, revealing itself as a woman in pure white clothes. Around Her stood many saintly-looking people who clearly showed great reverence and devotion to Her. Rubbing my eyes, I looked again and again. It was not a dream. It was a reality. My eyes were wide open. I could see this woman and all those who were standing around Her, but I could recognize none of them. A divine aura surrrounded Her, and I could not take my eyes off Her.

"Radiating peace and bliss, She smiled graciously at me. Slowly I became totally unaware of the external world. The saintly-looking people who were around Her also disappeared. All that existed was the lady in white and myself. Time and space did not exist. I was all alone in Her presence. Gradually She grew bigger and bigger. She became as big as the universe, and there was nothing but Her. A strong effulgence emanated from Her whole being, and I was totally enveloped in that light. Then all of a sudden, the form disappeared and there was only pure light filling the entire universe. And then, in a split-second of a moment the light suddenly became a pin-point. That is all I could remember. I was aroused to normal awareness hearing a constant ringing in my ears. It was the same voice, "Come to Me. Come to Me. Come to Me."

"Gradually regaining my ordinary consciousness, I looked around. I was stunned to see that it was already dark. I looked at my watch which registered 8:30 p.m. Since I had begun sitting for meditation that afternoon at around five o'clock, this meant that nearly three and a half hours had passed. The flowing sound of the Ganges filled the air. Everything else was silent.

"I returned to the ashram. The residents wanted to know where I had been all that time since it was not my normal routine to spend such long hours outside of the ashram. My daily visit to the Ganges was usually around an hour, never more than an hour and a quarter. From the look on my face and my sudden indrawn manner, the residents suspected that something had happened to me. But I kept quiet. I did not feel like talking. The experience was so overwhelming and full. I could not sleep that night. I was haunted by the vision of that form which had appeared in front of me, and my heart and soul were totally immersed in it.

"That day marked a great transformation in my life. The next morning found me a completely changed person. The fellow ashram residents noticed this change in me and were very inquisitive, asking questions of me constantly. But my thoughts always revelled in that enchanting form of the lady whom I saw in the vision, and my heart continued to overflow with the bliss of that experience. It is not that I wanted to avoid the others, but I remained unable to speak.

"Finally the news of my behavior reached the ears of one swami who also lived in the ashram. He was a *sadhak* himself and a good soul. Summoning me, he lovingly inquired about the reason for the change in me, and for some reason, I felt that I wanted to disclose everything about the experience to him. I related it all to him, and I also told him that my mind was now completely absorbed in the vision of that form. I asked whether he knew anything about this lady in white. I could easily give him a description of Her since the vision was so clear. He listened to me carefully and told me that he would try to discover who She was.

"Days went by and my longing became more and more intense. I was like one gone mad. I was unable to sleep and I gave up eating. After a few days, the swami called me to see him again. He had a big smile on his face, and without any introductory remarks, he pulled out a picture from his pocket and asked if this was the lady whom I had seen. I jumped up and danced with joy because that was a picture of Her! He gave it to me and told me who She was and where Her ashram was located. He also revealed that while he had listened to me relate my experience to him, he had felt tremendous inner peace and a strong feeling that this must be a Great Soul. This caused him to immediately begin inquiring about Her, and finally he met another swami living in Rishikesh who was from Kerala. From this swami he learned about Amma."

The young man showed the picture to the brahmachari. Full of emotion and his eyes swelling with tears, he asked, "Will I be able to see Amma today?"

The brahmachari assured him that he would certainly be able to see the Mother, telling him that She is always available for Her children. Again he invited the young man to have some food.

He replied, "My brother, I have not been eating for many days now. I do not feel like eating. I am not hungry. Anyhow, let me see Amma first. If She asks me to eat I will do so. Until then, please do not insist that I take any food."

The brahmachari was about to leave when he saw the Mother coming down the stairs. "Here comes Amma," he said in a soft voice.

The young man jumped up and looked around. Just as a hornbill bird waiting for water runs to catch falling raindrops, he ran towards the Mother and fell into full prostration at Her Feet.

The Mother lovingly lifted him up, and holding his hands, She brought him back to the verandah of the temple. He sobbed like a little child, while She expressed tremendous love and compassion to him by patting his back and rubbing his chest. Wiping his tears, She laid his head on Her shoulder and consoled him, "My son, why do you cry now? You have come to your Mother, haven't you? Son, don't cry. Mother is here for you." These sweet and loving words soothed him and gradually he could somewhat control his emotions.

In a short while he calmed down and the Mother proceeded to reveal to him something only he could understand, "Son, Mother did not want you to jump into that 'other thing' which disturbed your mind. Do you understand 'the other thing'?"

The young man looked at the Mother's face in astonishment and nodded his head, saying softly, "Yes, Amma, I understand."

The Mother continued, "Mother wanted to sharpen your *vairagya* (detachment) and determination. She also thought that such an experience would help you to deepen your faith and devotion, and thus to give up that idea totally. Son, your fate would be totally different if you had not received that vision. Sincere *sadhaks* should not stray from their path, no matter where they might be in this world. Mother knows that you are very sincere in your spiritual practice and She did not want you to go astray. That experience you had was to awaken devotion in you. It was to intensify your longing. Mother repeats, a sincere *sadhak* should not go astray. Son, do you understand what Mother is saying?"

The young man gazed at the Mother's face in amazement. He couldn't speak and therefore nodded his head in affirmation. While the others who were present wondered what this 'other thing' was, the young man once again wept like an innocent child.

Through tears he said, "Now it is very clear to me that it was you who appeared before me. You came to save me from a pitfall.

Amma, now I know why you bestowed such a wonderful vision on me. You wanted to change my mind. You wanted to create a transformation in my life. Yes, Amma, you are right. If I had not had this vision, I would not have changed my decision. Amma, you have protected me; you have kept me from wasting my life, from getting entangled in *maya*. Amma, Amma, you have revealed everything to me."

None of the residents witnessing this scene understood the meaning of the Mother's words and were curious to know about what Amma had said. But before leaving the Ashram, the young man spoke to the brahmachari whom he had first met. "I did not want to tell this part of my story before having Amma's *darshan*. Now, however, I feel that this would be a good lesson for all sincere seekers to let them know that the Guru's protection is always with them if their desire to attain the goal is sincere."

The young man related the rest of the story. It involved the conflict that he was having with his family concerning marriage. Although he had two other brothers, as well as two sisters, he was the eldest son, and everybody in the family, parents and siblings alike, were insisting that he marry. Even though he was living in an ashram, having dedicated his life to *brahmacharya* (celibacy) and spirituality, he visited his family regularly. His family was not very keen on his desire to be a monk and continually urged him to marry. They told him about different girls whom he could meet to select a wife.

While he had been quite confident in his determination to lead a spiritual life away from the affairs of the world, his self-confidence began to weaken as his family became more and more insistent. So powerful were their appeals and entreaties that he began to consider that it might not be such a bad idea to lead a spiritual life while simultaneously leading a householder's life. One day upon returning to the ashram after being amidst the worldly vibrations of his family home, he began to rationalize that even the ancient saints and sages were married and had children. He even began to daydream about different girls whom he might choose as a bride.

At the same time, he was also crying and praying within, begging God to help him and protect him. He realized that he was not able to remain steadfast in his resolve to be a monk since his fantasies and desires kept gnawing at him. They became so overwhelming that he could not even find solace on the banks of the Ganges. So agitated was he and unable to find peace of mind, he was on the verge of committing suicide, thinking of jumping into the river, when the vision of Amma came to him.

He finished his story: "That experience helped reinstill my courage and self-confidence. It gave me such spiritual bliss that I could easily overcome my mental agitation and instability. That is what Amma meant when She said those words to me. She did not want me to get enmeshed in worldly bondage. That is why She gave me such a rare gift that has transformed me completely."

Thus the young man from Rishikesh concluded his story. Taking leave of the brahmachari, he was full of joy and enthusiasm as he left the Ashram.

The nature of the Guru

The Holy Mother was still sitting in front of the temple at 11:30 a.m. Almost all of the residents were there. One of the brahmacharis asked a question about sincere seekers: "Amma, there are many sincere *sadhaks* in this world, aren't there? But it seems that God or the Guru helps only a few from such dangers."

Amma replied, "Son, first of all, a sincere *sadhak* has no dangers, for he takes everything as God's will. For him everything is *prasad*, both negative and positive. The word 'danger' has no meaning in his life. He is always optimistic, not at all pessimistic.

185

Secondly, how do you know that God helps only a few? This young man is the only one that you have seen. Sincere *sadhaks* will always find a way to overcome difficult situations in life, for they depend on divine grace. God will go in search of them to help them and uplift them.

"Sincere *sadhaks* will undoubtedly receive grace. Mother says this unconditionally out of Her own experience. Sincerity springs forth from the deepest recesses of your heart. It cannot be superficial. Some people are sincere only in words but not in deeds. They will not receive the benevolence of Providence or have divine hands to help them because they are shallow. No sincere *sadhak* will stray from the path; Mother can guarantee this. Somehow or other, he or she will be saved. God or the Guru cannot abandon such *sadhaks*. Just as a brood of little chicks is protected under the wings of the mother hen, sincere *sadhaks* will always be under the care and grace of the Guru or God. No matter where they are, they will always be under the protective wings of the Supreme Being.

"Mother does not say that the less sincere *sadhaks* will be completely abandoned by the Guru. That will not happen. They will also be taken care of. But just to teach them a lesson, the Guru or God might let them fall, only to save them later.

"Look at that son from Rishikesh. Of course he had desires. But Mother knows how much pain he endured to overcome them. He tried hard; his heart was aching. He really wanted to rid himself of the desires which were interfering with his desire to realize God. He did not sit idle. He prayed and cried to God to show him a way out of his confusion and doubt. Therefore, God had to help him. God must help a true devotee. It is His responsibility to do so. When all are plunged into the quagmire of illusion and desire, a true *sadhak* is the one who tries to emerge from it and know God. He is the one who offers his own life at

His feet. He wants to sacrifice his body and mind for his own spiritual evolution and for the upliftment of the world. God is with him or her who is willing to do this. That is why that son had that vision. Children, this is a very good lesson for you."

Another brahmachari made this remark: "Who gave him the vision? I don't think that it was God who gave that vision to him. It was you, Amma. You bestowed that rare blessing on him. He saw your form in the vision, not some god's."

"It was the fruit of his prayers," Amma explained. "That vision was the result of the tears he shed. And it was the outcome of his innocent faith, determination and intense longing."

She further elaborated on the nature of the Guru, "The Guru is like the sun. He just shines. He cannot be otherwise. He just shines and whoever keeps the doors of his heart open receives the light. God simply is. He has no conditions and no limits. He gives unconditionally. If the door of your heart is closed, He will not come in. He will wait outside, but He will not break in. He is not aggressive because He is love. Love is not aggressive. Love is a constant, uninterrupted and unbreakable flow. Compassion is like a stream, a never-ending stream. It never hurts anyone. Hurting is the nature of human beings. Love never hurts. Compassion never hurts. But we hurt people because we have egos. The ego is happy to see others' unhappiness. The ego is happy to see others struggling and suffering.

"The Guru is neither an ego nor is He egoless; He is beyond these. Neither the clouds nor the sky, the Guru is beyond them. He simply is. You can see your suffering reflected in the Guru, and you can see your happiness reflected in Him. He, however, is neither happy nor unhappy. He is like a mirror. The ego, on the other hand, cannot reflect anybody's feelings. An ego is clouded, unclear and dusty. It cannot see anything; it is blind. The ego cannot see others. The ego sees only you, the little you alone.

"The Guru is not an ego. He is the universe. He is everything. He can accommodate anything and everything. You can see His external form but not what's inside. Internally, He is inaccessible. The Guru is unpredictable. You cannot say that He is like 'this' or like 'that.' You really can't even say what an ordinary human being is like, let alone a Guru, who is extraordinary. Yet while He is extraordinary, He is ordinary too. He is both. Don't try to label or judge Him. And don't expect Him to be a certain way or to fit into a particular kind of mold. He cannot be stereotyped. He cannot be judged with your limited intellect. Whatever you say about Him will be wrong because the Guru cannot be explained. His being cannot be reduced to words. Again, whatever you may say about Him will also be correct because He is everything. He is night as well as day. He is darkness as well as light.

"Sri Krishna was a great Master. He was a person who enacted all roles. He had hundreds and thousands of masks. People mistook the masks for Him. Whatever they said about Him was wrong, for He was beyond all judgements. The Kauravas made many statements about Him and the Pandavas, too, said many things about Him. But they were all wrong. Those who understood at least a little about Krishna kept quiet, because they knew that whenever they spoke about Him, they missed the mark. Even His own wives could not understand Krishna. His friend and disciple, Arjuna, saw a tiny part of Him, as did Bhishma, Uddhava, and Vidura (devotees of Krishna in the ancient classics). Others, too, saw Him in a similarly limited way. But still He was far beyond what they could understand. What Arjuna saw was His cosmic form, but he could not experience His formless aspect. Many scholars have tried to explain Krishna. Many are still trying to interpret Krishna and to depict what He is, but these interpretations and depictions do not really reveal anything about Him. Even Vyasa, who wrote about His life in the *Srimad Bhagavatam*, could not explain Krishna fully because all his explanations and descriptions were dependent upon words. Words come from the intellect and from the mind, both of which are limited. But the Guru is far beyond mind and words. Such is the nature of a truly great Master."

Everyone sat fully absorbed in the Mother's talk as if he had just received a taste of that nature of the Guru. The Mother's words were full of authenticity. There was so much power in them. Everyone felt that the Mother was talking about Herself even though She had not referred to Herself specifically. Some of the brahmacharis had the feeling that the Mother was saying to them, "You speak a lot about 'Me,' but that is not 'Me.' You continue speaking and you always miss the mark, my children. You always miss 'Me.'"

No one spoke. There was a majestic expression on the Mother's face clearly displaying spiritual splendor and glory. As She sat in the midst of the residents and devotees, She appeared to be detached from Her surroundings. She might have been reminded of Her own real nature. Her eyes were fixed on a particular point, but it was difficult to say where. Even though wide open, the Mother's eyes were completely unmoving, not even blinking for five or six minutes. Her spine was erect. It seemed as if She were not even breathing. Her hands were on Her lap with palms up. It took a few more minutes for the Mother to come back from that mood. Uttering Her favorite mantra, "Shiva...Shiva," and whirling Her right hand in the air, She returned to Her usual state.

A brahmachari requested further clarification: "Amma, You said that the Guru neither has an ego nor is He egoless, that He is neither the clouds nor the sky. We are trying to become ego-less, aren't we? So why did you say that the Guru is not without an ego either? In the analogy 'neither the clouds nor the sky,' if the sky is expansiveness, then are You saying that the Guru is not expansive? But our understanding is that expansiveness is the final state. These seem to be contradictions. Amma, will you please explain?"

Amma proceeded with an explanation, "Children, one quality cannot exist without its opposite. When you say, "He is good," the concept of 'bad' is also there. Without bad, good cannot exist. When we say 'dark,' the idea of 'not dark' or light is implied. If there were only darkness or only light, we could not describe either because there would be no contrast. When we say 'the flower is beautiful,' we definitely have an idea of something being 'not beautiful' or ugly. All the statements that we make are like this. To say 'beautiful,' the opposite must also exist. To say 'good', 'bad,' its opposite, must exist as a concept. Otherwise, there is no comparison. In this world of names and forms, in this world of duality, we can only think and speak in terms of the concept of opposites and contrasts.

"Similarly, when we say the Guru has no ego nor is He egoless, we are indicating that He is beyond the world of duality. There are no words to describe the state in which the Guru is established. When we say 'neither the clouds nor the sky,' these are still words which indicate forms. No matter what words we use, words will always be limiting. This means there is a boundary. We might use the image of the sky as 'expansive,' but this is only relative, that is a cloudless sky as compared to a cloudy sky. But still, the concept of 'sky' indicates a limit. Even to say the Guru is 'egoless' indicates a limit. Any description implies a limit, and where there is a limit, contrast is possible. The opposite must exist.

"To say the word 'expansiveness' also brings an idea of 'non-expansiveness'; whereas, the Supreme State where the Guru dwells is far beyond all comparison and contrast. In reality, it cannot be expressed in words. But for us who are only familiar with names and forms, there is no other way to get an idea about this inexpressible state except through comparisons, contrasts and analogies. Yet this state of Supreme Oneness is far beyond them all.

"In the Supreme State where the Guru is permanently established, duality does not exist. There are no contrasts and there are no opposites. That Supreme State is beyond limits. You cannot say, 'This is where it ends.' It is endless. Now, you might say *maya* or ignorance is the opposite. But *maya* or the world or ignorance is only a projection of the Supreme Reality. It cannot exist without Brahman. Nothing can exist without Brahman, the Absolute. Brahman is totally independent; whereas, the world depends on Brahman for its existence. Brahman alone is. Therefore, in the One, the Whole, all comparisons and contrasts of opposites cease to exist. What we are speaking of is far beyond human comprehension. We cannot say anything about it, for it transcends everything. There is an apparent contradiction, but that contradiction is in your head. Drop the reasoning, and you will see that there is no contradiction at all."

Another brahmachari raised this query: "Amma, You said that the Guru never hurts anyone, but You scold us sometimes and we feel hurt."

Amma explored this question, "Son, you say Mother scolds you, but you do not say why. Does Mother scold you for a little mistake that you have committed just once? No. She points out and corrects for repeated errors, mistakes that are serious impediments to your growth. You may call this scolding. So if Mother scolds you, it is in order to make you strong. Mother's children should have the strength to confront all difficulties of life no matter where they are. This Ashram is a real *kalari*, a place where warriors train for martial arts with sword and shield. You should become real warriors, really courageous ones.

"Mother only loves you. She has only compassion for you, and She is very patient with you. But that external expression of love, compassion, affection and patience does not always help you grow. You remain selfish. You forget the goal and start acting indiscriminately. You children become jealous and start fighting one another for Mother's love. She has never scolded you. On the contrary, She only tries to remind you about what to do, how to do it and when to do it. Mother only tries to make you be more careful and alert. This comes as an expression of Her love for you.

"Now, about scolding. She will say something when you repeat the same mistakes again and again. She might say something to correct you if She sees you repeatedly doing something which hinders your growth. But She does not scold just for the sake of scolding. If Mother thinks that to say something firmly to you is the only way to make you aware of your goal, then She will say it firmly to create an impression in you. Otherwise, what is the use of living here if you are not going to change your habits and attitudes in order to expand your vision about life? The very purpose of being here will be defeated if you want to remain always the same without growing spiritually.

"Children, do you know how much scolding, how many trials and tribulations Mother had to undergo in the past? Damayanti Amma observed all of Mother's actions minutely. If there was any little bit of trash left over in the courtyard after it had been swept, she beat Mother. When all the vessels were washed, she scrutinized them, and if there was even a slight trace of dirt, she scolded Mother. While Mother was sweeping the ground, if even a single stick of the broom happened to fall out inadvertently, she would not spare Mother. If one speck of dust or ash happened to fall into the pot while cooking, punishment followed. When Mother plucked grass for the cows, Damayanti Amma watched from a distance to see if Mother indulged in gossip with others. She beat Mother if Mother stood around to talk with someone. Mother did not feel hurt because of the scoldings, not even from the physical beatings, because Mother took all these experiences as the benevolence of Providence. Mother's mind did not become bitter or resentful; instead Her mind turned inwards.

"Children, the pain that you feel upon being reprimanded for an error is not the fault of the person who scolds you. Pleasure and pain belong to the ego. Your ego is hurt, that is why you feel pain. You want to do something the way you like, but somebody is against it and they tell you. That is why you feel sad or experience pain. You do not think that what you want to do may be wrong. Failing to consider the problems it might create if you act the way you want to, you do not think of the consequences of your improper conduct. You are not considerate of others and how they might feel as a result of your selfish actions, that you might cause them pain. You think only about your pain. You feel hurt; your ego is hurt.

"Somebody pointed a finger at your ego, and you cannot bear it. You feel hurt because your ego is questioned. Feeling that your self-importance is being diminished, you react negatively because you cannot tolerate it. You cannot see anything but your own little selfish self and the small world created by your ego. If somebody puts a little dent in your tiny little world by trying to correct you, you get angry at him. You abuse him, criticize him and place all the blame on him. You think you are innocent. You think you are trying to be a good boy, clean, pure and flawless. Then you say that the other person hurt you, that he scolded you and that it was all his fault.

"Just what do you think of yourself? Do you think that you are a perfect soul? No, you are not. You are just a limited ego. You can attain perfection, but for that to happen, you need guidance. You need to be corrected. You need to be disciplined. That is what a disciple must undergo. If you do not allow somebody, and this 'somebody' means a Guru, to work on you, then it is difficult for you to be transformed.

"The Guru's scoldings are not to be taken as mere verbal jugglery. They are blessings. When the Guru starts scolding you, that means His grace and compassion have started flowing towards you. He has set His eyes on you. He wants to save you. He wishes to free you eternally. The Guru cannot hurt anyone. The river cannot hurt you; the wind cannot hurt you, and the sun cannot hurt you. They simply are. They are just present. The river cannot change its nature. The wind and the sun cannot change their natures. In a similar manner, the Guru cannot change His nature.

"The Guru sheds light. Just as wind cannot stop blowing, the river cannot stop flowing, or the sun cannot stop shining, the Guru cannot stop being what He is. A person can hurt you because he has an ego. A person, who has an ego, sees you as different from him. He has the feeling of 'the other.' His ego and your ego will conflict. But the Guru sees no differences. He is beyond all differences. He does not have the feeling of 'the other.' He has no ego, for He is not a person. In fact, there is no person there at all. There is only Consciousness. Consciousness cannot hurt anyone. Whatever comes out of the Guru is for your good. You are the one who perceives it as something that causes pain, and then you complain that it is the Guru's doing.

"Human beings cultivate fragrant flowers and trample common weeds. They grow beneficial and useful trees and cut down useless ones. Human beings kill wild, ferocious animals and breed gentle, useful ones. They have a whole history of exploitation. Such killing is exploitation. It comes from selfishness; it does not come from love. They cultivate flowers and fruit trees, but the reason is to exploit them for their own selfish purposes. Fruit is used to appease their hunger and quench their thirst. Flowers are used to decorate their hair, their homes and gardens. If the flowering plants stop blossoming or if the fruit trees stop producing, they cut them down or pull them out and throw them away.

"The same thing happens in their domestication of animals. They need milk to nourish their bodies, so they raise cows. No sooner does the cow stop giving milk, than it becomes beef. If it no longer serves one selfish purpose, they kill it to serve another selfish purpose. They exploit the cow and then destroy it. Cats and dogs are raised for their own enjoyment, not because they have tremendous love for them. On the contrary, it is because the animals love them, and they need that love from the animal. If their dog bites them or the cat steals their food, their love for the animals disappears, and they start hating them. It is the same among family members. Yes, the same thing happens. People exploit each other. The father and the mother become a burden when they are old and weak, and they are sent to an old age home. Children love their parents when they are dependent on them for their food, clothing and shelter. Once they become independent the love disappears. In its place come conflicts and arguments. Children, this is the situation in the world. This is how human beings live, depending on others, exploiting them for their own gratification, and finally destroying them once their needs are met. That is the nature of the world.

"But *Mahatmas* are not like that. *Mahatmas* are like the wind. While human beings enjoy the aroma of fragrant flowers but trample down the weeds, the wind gently blows and caresses both the flowers and the weeds. The wind never pauses to smell the sweet fragrance of the rose or the jasmine flower, nor does it stop blowing on putrid-smelling excreta. It has no preference and knows no difference. It is beyond all differences. The same is true of a *Mahatma*. He loves all and accepts everything, both what we call 'good' and 'bad.' He is beyond all likes and dislikes. He simply is. Whoever wants to benefit by a *Mahatma's* presence can do so. Those who do not want to come to him do not have to. They can criticize him, abuse him, insult him or scandalize him if they like. But do not think that his attitude towards them will be any different. He will remain the same. He will always be the same, for he sees no differences. He sees everybody and everything as Pure Consciousness. However, you are different. You see differences. But remember, your being different and your seeing differences belong only to you. They have nothing to do with the Guru, for He remains the same. You cannot divide Him by projecting your own state of seeing differences onto Him."

All those present listening to this, the brahmacharis, house-holder devotees and visitors, were tremendously inspired by the Mother's enlightening talk. They were all spellbound. It was an incessant flow of pure knowledge, like the flow of the Holy Ganges. It was so clear and spontaneous and it dispelled all their doubts. Everyone felt that the Mother was talking about Herself when She was talking about the Guru. It was Her own experience that She was sharing with the listeners. Devotees have hundreds of experiences they can share about the Mother's limitless compassion and love. They can relate numerous incidents to show how She is beyond all differences.

When the Mother stopped, that particular brahmachari who had made the retort about feeling hurt when he was scolded felt very ashamed of himself. He said in a voice full of remorse, "Amma, I seek your forgiveness for making that comment. I was not protesting. I did not mean that your reprimands are unnecessary." He paused for his throat was choked up. With tears in his eyes, he continued, "Amma, please do not stop correcting me. Please continue doing that. I just wanted to tell you that even though I knew that your reproofs were for my spiritual upliftment, they caused a little pain due to my ego. Forgive me for my faults, forgive me, my Amma." Filled with remorse, the brahmachari could not control his emotions as he tried to wipe his tears.

What followed was another display of the Mother's over-flowing compassion for Her child. His innocence also filled the Mother's eyes with tears. Her all-enveloping love was showered upon him as She put him on Her lap and patted his back with great affection. The Mother wiped his tears, and slowly lifted him up from Her lap and put his head on Her shoulders. Keeping his head there, She spoke to him soothingly, "Son, there was nothing wrong in your question. In fact, Mother liked your frankness. It is said that one should present questions to the Guru like confronting a cobra. A cobra keeps its hood folded most of the time. But if you hit it, immediately it will unfold its hood. The more you provoke it, the more it will unfold its hood. In a similar manner, when you ask the Guru questions, be demanding of him. By asking provocative questions, you will get more profound answers.

"A sincere, inquisitive seeker will spontaneously ask questions. One should not fabricate arduous questions just for the sake of asking. If questions are asked just for the sake of asking, you may not get the proper answers for them. The determining factor is the inner thirst of the questioner in his desire to know. That will invoke the Guru as well, because the Guru, by nature, prefers to abide in the Self, in the inner silence. To come to the level of the physical body and have to communicate is a struggle for Him. To speak about the Supreme Truth is something which He does not want to do. Speech distorts Truth. He does not want to distort Truth because His speech and mind are established in the inner experience of the Truth. To speak requires an ego. In the case of a Perfect Master, He has to create an ego to speak and to teach. But when the Guru speaks, He speaks out of His own experience; that is what He puts into words. His words do not distort the Truth. To make the Guru speak, the disciple, the devotee or whatever questioner, should put forth sincere questions. They should be guided by the quest to know. Before a serious seeker, the Guru cannot remain silent. He must speak."

The brahmachari's head still rested on the Mother's shoulder. As She gently lifted his head, She eased his mind further by clarifying what She was saying, "Therefore, son, you don't have to worry about the question you put forth. That was a sincere and spontaneous question. A well thought-out question can be lacking in sincerity, for it loses its spontaneity. Sincere and spontaneous questions are often true questions that just come out with no effort. Don't be sad."

The Mother's soothing words consoled the brahmachari. Then another brahmachari made a remark, "If one can lie on Mother's shoulder for such a long time, I would also like to ask a sincere question." Everybody laughed and the Mother also burst into delightful laughter. She kept on laughing for a while as the atmosphere began to lighten up.

❧ ☙

Chapter 10

Work as worship

3 May 1984

At 6:30 a.m. Mother was sweeping the Ashram premises. When they saw this, Gayatri, Kunjumol and some of the brahmacharis rushed towards Her and tried to take the broom away. "Amma," they insisted, "please stop, we will do it." Bent over the short reed broom, She went on intently sweeping the ground. She did not look up at all, despite the persistent pleas for Her to stop. Some went to fetch more brooms, hoping that they could help Her by sweeping another side of the compound. When Mother saw them coming with brooms, She said, "No, no. No help needed. Take the brooms back." They continued to pester Her until finally She stopped and stood up straight to admonish them, "Stop talking. Do not make any noise. When Mother works, She wants to do it with concentration. Mother considers this worship. Mother sees God in the work, not just the act of sweeping."

With those words, Mother continued to sweep. Still everyone followed Her, but they did not say anything further. Her sweeping was done quickly and efficiently. Not only was the ground clean but the marks left by the reed bristles of the broom left a pleasing pattern in the sand. Mother surpassed all others in doing this work. Since it was a daily custom, the residents usually took turns to sweep the compound, and usually it took at least forty-five minutes to do it. Mother swept the entire Ashram premises within twenty minutes, less than half the time.

After completing the work, Mother sat down on the south side of the temple. Although perspiring after such vigorous sweeping,

She was not at all tired. The group that had been following Her now gathered around, but not too closely, for they were a bit afraid. Mother did not say anything. She wiped Her face and hands with a towel offered by Gayatri. Kunjumol brought a glass of tea for Her, but she simply stood holding it, afraid to ask the Mother to drink. Finally, overcoming her fear, Kunjumol said, "Amma, tea." She replied, "No, I do not want any. I am not going to eat or drink today."

Now came the real *satsang* as She proceeded to talk about the matter on hand: "You children have no real *sraddha*. It was 6:30 a.m. and nobody had swept the Ashram grounds. Don't you know that it should be completed before dawn? Don't you know that this is an Ashram, a place of worship? How many brahmacharis are here? How many? And these girls have also become careless. It is your duty to keep the place clean and tidy. None of you had the common sense or discrimination to do it. Can you sit and meditate in an untidy, dirty and ugly place ? No, you cannot. You need a clean and orderly place for that. If the place is untidy and dirty, it will affect your mind. You will not be able to concentrate. If you do not keep the Ashram environment clean, visitors will think that those who dwell here are of the same dirty, disorderly nature.

"People use every opportunity to judge Mother. They will think that the Mother is not bringing up Her children properly. It is for your own benefit that Mother is concerned about how people judge the Ashram. What they say will not affect Mother. She can live anywhere, regardless of what people say. Mother is used to that. She has trained Her mind very well. During Her *sadhana* period, Mother spent Her days and nights outside in the open air, rain or shine. She has lain down in the sand, in the muddy backwaters and amidst the rubbish. Mother has eaten pieces of glass, used coffee grounds, and even human waste. She did these things in order to transcend everything. She had that much *vairagya*. Children, do not think that the things that Mother says or does are for Her own benefit. They are all for your benefit. Mother has nothing to gain or lose. For Her everything is the same. For you, however, everything is not the same; you still see things as different from one another. You have a long way to go.

"Furthermore, none of you has ever experienced sorrow in your lives. Never having toiled or sweated in your life, you do not know the difficulties that other people have. Most of you come from well-to-do families. With nothing to worry about, you simply sat down at the dining table and food was there waiting for you. No chores were required of you; you did not even have to wash clothes. You grew up accustomed to having your parents fulfill all your wishes.

"But spiritual life is not for such people. To lead a genuine spiritual life one must know through experience what suffering is and what sorrow is. A person who grows up in the midst of plenty cannot easily lead a true spiritual life. He needs to come down to the ground. He must be willing to go through real life, a life of strenuous work. He has to be given an opportunity to taste and smell the odor of his own sweat. You children do not know the value of work. Do you know, work is God. Mother used to always pray to the Lord, 'O Lord, give me work. Give me Your work.'"

A brahmachari spoke up, trying to explain that the person who was supposed to sweep had left the Ashram early in the morning to go on an errand. But Mother interrupted, saying, "Children, do you know that beginning at age nine Mother had to be up at three o'clock in the morning to start Her day's work? The whole day She was constantly engaged in different tasks. She began by cleaning the house and sweeping the premises. Then She had to attend to a hundred other chores: fetching water, cooking three times a day, cleaning and feeding the cows, milking them, scrubbing the cooking vessels, washing clothes for the entire family and beating coconut husk with a wooden pestle to make coir (rope made from coconut husk fiber). Sometimes Mother had to beat raw husk which is even more difficult. Due to constantly carrying jugs of water and pots of hot *kanji* (rice gruel) on Her head, a bald spot appeared. The hair fell out, but Mother was not bothered by this.

"Throughout the entire day Mother's own simple garment was never dry. She had to wade through the backwaters in order to collect grass for the cows. Fetching water and washing the family's clothes, She was always drenched. Mother would have liked to have seen Her own clothes dry, but She never murmured a single word of complaint. Even though She had so much work, Mother would pray to God for more so that She would always be busy in dedicating Her every action to Him. Mother was scolded harshly and even beaten physically, but She used this adverse treatment to turn Her mind inward instead of becoming bitter or resentful.

"In addition to Her duties at home, Mother was sent to Her relatives' homes in order to render service to them. At Her grandmother's place, Mother was engaged in every kind of work, sometimes even having to act as a boatman to ferry Her cousins across the backwaters to school."

Amma paused for a while as everyone sat still. Then She continued, "Children, Mother was constantly busy from the time She was five years old until She was twenty. Even today Mother does not like to sit idle. She simply cannot.

"If a *sadhak* does not work, he is cheating the world and cheating God in the name of spirituality. None of you has had to suffer like Mother. Even today you have no difficulties or vexations. You do not have to think or worry about anything. Look at Mother. She does not have to do any work, but still She does. She works, but the work is not for Herself, not to earn wages, not for name or fame, not to please anyone. Still, doing the work gives Her happiness and bliss. Mother does not expect anything from anyone. She simply works because She feels like doing it.

"Children, there were other family members whom Mother could have asked to help Her during those years in the early period of Her life when She was working so much. She could even have said, "I cannot do all this work. There are other children. Ask them to do some of it." But no, She never uttered a word of complaint nor did She seek anybody else's help. The Mother accepted everything as the benevolence of Providence. She never thought of Her work as a burden. On the contrary, She was only happy to do it because She considered it as God's work, as work coming from God's Will. The work was Her *sadhana*.

"When someone says, 'It was the responsibility of so-and-so to sweep today, but because he was not here, the work was not done,' that is the attitude of a person who is insincere and not conscientious. Especially since you are spiritual aspirants, you should not have this kind of attitude. You would not have said that if it were your own house. 'If it is mine, I will do it. But if it is someone else's, I don't care. I'm not going to do it for someone else.' That is the attitude of a selfish person who thinks only of 'I' and 'mine.' 'It is none of my business to poke my nose into somebody else's affair,' is always the attitude of selfish people. Children, we are trying to get out of this narrow vision. The attitude we want to cultivate is 'Everything is mine; everything is God's. I am just an instrument in His hands here to do His work.'

"You are the ones who have to soar high into the vast sky of spirituality. And to do that, you need the wings of selflessness and love. We should be able to do everything with love and sincerity. The opportunity to love and serve others should be considered a rare gift, a blessing from God. We should be happy and thank Him for providing such opportunities. A spiritual seeker should always be positive in his attitude. He should never harbor any negative feelings or negative attitudes. To be positive requires strength and courage. It requires a daring mind to give up old habits and to develop and cultivate new ones based on spiritual principles. It is possible. This is the purpose of *sadhana*.

"Ordinary people choose and do only work which they like. Spiritual seekers should not have that attitude. Discarding likes and dislikes, they should be able to do any work at any time. Therein lies greatness."

Without another word, Mother got up and left. Since it was now nearly time for morning meditation, everyone rose to go, their minds full of regret yet inspired by the Mother's words.

Two Mothers

During *darshan*, one of the householder devotees asked the Mother a question: "Amma, I once heard You say that there are two Mothers, the outer Mother and the inner Mother. I do not understand what you mean by that. Will you please tell why there is this division?"

This reply came from the Mother: "Son, there are two different aspects of Mother, the *maya rupam* (the illusory form) and the Mother of the 'Mind of minds'. [16] The *maya rupam* is the external form, the body. You consider this body as Mother and you call this form Mother. But in the depths of the 'Mind of minds,' there is another Mother. You do not visually see the Mother which is in the 'Mind of minds.' You only see the external Mother.

"The outer Mother, the *maya rupam*, will laugh, play, speak, eat, sleep and do everthing that ordinary human beings do. This form mingles with you and communicates with you. This form changes. This form gets older. It was born and therefore, it must

---

[16] From the *Kenopanishad*, 'manaso manah,' or 'Mind of minds,' meaning the Supreme Purusha, the Absolute Consciousness, the Witness Consciousness.

perish. It has a beginning and an end. Through close association with this body, you can understand this Mother, the outer Mother, to a certain extent. You can speak to this Mother. You can ask Her questions. The children love this form, and the Mother also loves Her children. You can sometimes please the external Mother. You make Her happy and you can make Her cry. You can feed Her, serve Her and make Her rest. She will enjoy playing jokes. She will worry about Her children. She will sometimes show attachment. She will sometimes express likes and dislikes. The external Mother will sometimes 'dance' according to your whims and fancies. This external Mother is important. The outer Mother is just as important as the Inner Mother, for without it you will not be able to have any idea about the Inner Mother.

"The Inner Mother, whose true nature is infinitude and silence, manifests visibly through this body so that Her children can have a glimpse of the Mother who is deep within. This body is powerful; it has the power to express the infinite inner power. The reason this external Mother exists is to help you reach the Inner Mother, the Mother of the 'Mind of minds.' The Inner Mother has none of the external qualities. It is totally silent and attributeless in the 'Mind of minds.' Silence is the language of this Inner Mother. All spiritual practices are done to please that Mother. Whatever service you do for the external Mother, the *maya rupam*, is done to please the Inner Mother. You actually cannot use the word 'please' in the case of the Inner Mother. When you open up through spiritual practices, the experience of grace just flows into you. Then it is there within you. It was always there.

"You cannot even call the silent Inner Mother 'Mother,' because 'Mother' is a name, and there are no names or forms in the 'Mind of minds' where the Inner Mother is. That Inner Mother is completely detached; She has no likes or dislikes. Neither excitement nor worry exists for that Mother. She doesn't sleep or eat; She doesn't love nor hate anyone. She simply is. Whatever is expressed through this body is for you, for your spiritual growth. Without the body you cannot even get a glimpse of the Inner Mother. The fact is this external Mother does not exist as you think you are seeing Her. That Inner Mother alone exists. That Inner Mother is still, silent, changeless, immovable."

She did not complete that sentence. Before She could say anything else, the Mother suddenly burst into blissful laughter. The laughter was loud, but it did not last long, for Mother immediately took a long, deep breath and became absolutely still. She sat in perfect meditation posture with Her eyes closed and head slightly raised. After an initial deep breath, there appeared to be no exhalation. Time passed. Everyone grew tense and worried. It was as if their breath had stopped as well. Some people suggested shaking the Mother vigorously, but this idea was forgotten, when Brahmachari Pai chanted a Sanskrit *sloka* from the *Soundarya Lahari*

> *United with Shakti, Shiva is endowed*
> *With the power to create the universe.*
> *Otherwise, He is incapable even of movement.*
> *Therefore, who except those endowed*
> *With great merits acquired in the past*
> *Can be fortunate enough*
> *To salute or praise Thee, O Mother Divine,*
> *Thou Who art adored even by*
> *Vishnu, Shiva and Brahma.*

This was followed by the *Karunalaye Devi* chant in which everybody participated wholeheartedly.

Karunalaye Devi

O Goddess, Abode of Compassion,
Giver of all things desired,
O Katyayani, Gauri, Sambhavi, Shankari...

O Essence of OM, O Mother...Mother...Mother,
Thou art the Essence of OM,
Lover of the sound 'OM,'
When Thou hearest the mantra 'OM Shakti,'
O Mother, Thou wilt come running, O Great Maya.

Creation, preservation and destruction
Of the universe are all Thy doings,
O Mother, all is Thyself, Thou Thyself art all.
There is none other than Thee, O Mother,
This suppliant has no other support except Thee,
The Self of Bliss. O Blissful Self,
Grant me a good boon.

Hearts were filled with exhilaration, and most people were sobbing, unable to hold back their tears. As they sang they held their palms together in reverence as they fixed their eyes on the Mother. The momentum of the chanting ascended to its climax when the lead singer chanted, "Amme... Amme... Amme..." As the chorus resounded, it was almost as if a dam had burst, and inspired by the Mother, the waters of love and devotion poured forth. Everyone was transported to heights of emotion no words can describe.

Hearing this loud singing mixed with crying at such an odd hour of the day, some of the villagers came over to the Ashram to investigate what was happening. They stood a short distance away and watched the Mother and the devotees, who were sitting on the front verandah of the temple. The chanting continued with more *slokas* from the *Soundarya Lahari*

> *The dust of Thy Feet is the island city*
> *Whence comes the luminous sunrise*
> *Of spiritual illumination,*
> *Driving away the darkness of ignorance*
> *From the hearts of devotees.*

> *It forms the cluster of flower buds*
> *From which pours forth the nectar of intelligence,*
> *Enlivening the dull-witted;*
> *It is a veritable necklace of wish-yielding gems*
> *For the poverty-stricken. For those immersed*
> *In the ocean of samsara, it becomes their uplifter*
> *Like the tusk of Vishnu (which raised the earth*
> *From submergence in the pralaya waters*
> *When He incarnated as the cosmic boar).*

> *O Consort of Parabrahman! Scholars who know*
> *The real meaning of the* agamas *(scriptures)*
> *Describe Thee as Saraswati, Goddess of Learning,*
> *And the Consort of Brahma. Furthermore,*
> *They speak of Thee as the lotus-born Lakshmi,*
> *Consort of Vishnu; also as Parvati,*
> *The Daughter of the the mountain*
> *And Consort of Shiva.*

> *Yet Thou art, however, the Fourth—*
> *That unique Power which is the Source*
> *Of the three deities mentioned—*
> *Of inconceivable and limitless majesty,*
> *The indeterminable Mahamaya*
> *Who revolves the Wheel of this world.*

O Mother! The crest of the Vedas
Bear Thy Feet as its crown.
May Thou condescend to place those Feet
On my head as well – the Feet, the water—
Offerings of which form the Ganga
In the matted locks of Shiva,
And the bright red dye which gives
Brilliance to the jewels on the diadem of Vishnu.

At last, people noticed a slight movement in the Mother's body. Their eyes were riveted on Her with great anxiety and fear, and they took note of every single movement She made. First Her hands slowly moved, then Her feet started gently swaying back and forth. Next came a visible movement of Her lips as if She were murmuring something. Gradually the rise and fall of Her chest indicated that Her breathing had returned. Everyone heaved a sigh of relief and their anxious looks disappeared. It was perhaps over ten minutes since the Mother had entered into *samadhi*, and now as She was coming out of it, the singing continued in full swing. When the song was over, She opened Her eyes. Then came the familiar but inexplicable circular gesture of Her right palm while She softly chanted the mantra, "Shiva... Shiva." Within seconds everybody found the Mother back in Her normal mood. No one had been aware of the passage of time as it was already one o'clock, even though three hours had passed since the beginning of *darshan*.

Time always passes quickly whenever one is in the presence of the Mother. One becomes so enraptured that one loses sense of both time and place. The scriptures say that one who attains the State of Perfection is not bound by time and space. It is a truism that a person has the same experience of not being aware of time or space when one is in the presence of a Self- Realized Soul. Perfect Masters can easily steal the minds of people who come to see them. Once the mind disappears, the world also disappears. The concept of time and space exists only when there is mind and when one is conscious of the outer world. Thus, when one transcends this outer world consciousness, time and space also disappear.

It is an innate quality of a *Mahatma* to attract people's attention to Himself and to make people forget the world outside. All genuine *Mahatmas* do this, and so does the Holy Mother. Her spontaneous expressions, Her words and deeds, and Her all-consuming love make one feel fully relaxed and peaceful. In Her presence the concept of time disappears. People have the feeling that they have spent only a few minutes with the Mother, only to realize afterwards that they have spent many hours with Her. That is what happened that day.

Only a few people were left in the queue as *darshan* was drawing to a close. Nobody had thought about lunch, so when *darshan* was over, the Mother exclaimed, "Oh, none of my children has had their lunch. Such a pity! What a cruel Mother I am." She ran to the kitchen and after putting the rice and curry dishes in the appropriate containers, She brought the food to the dining hall and proceeded to serve each person with Her own hands.

First spiritual food had come from the Mother's words; now there was food for the body from Her own hands! Joy brightened the faces of all as they partook of this special repast.

When asked if She would eat, the Mother replied, "Mother's stomach gets filled by serving food to all Her children and seeing them eat together." Flashing a bright smile to everyone in the dining hall, She then went to Her room.

Chapter 11

Spiritual Love and worldly love

7 May 1984

Today in response to a question put forth by a devotee about the difference between spiritual love and worldly love, Mother gave the following answer:

"Son, love is love, but the intensity is different and the depth is different. Spiritual love is as deep as a bottomless pit. How deep and how expansive it is cannot be measured. Spiritual love is without limits or boundaries while worldly love is superficial and not very deep. The spirit of worldly love is not constant. Its rhythm fluctuates; it comes and goes. The beginning is always beautiful and enthusiastic, but slowly it gets less beautiful and less exciting until it ends up being shallow. In most cases, it ends up finally in upset, hatred and deep sorrow.

"Spiritual love is different. The beginning is beautiful and peaceful. Shortly after this peaceful beginning comes the agony of longing. Through the middle period, the agony will continue to grow stronger and stronger, more and more unbearable. Excruciating pain will ensue, and this pain of love will prevail until just before it leads up to unity with the beloved. This unity is beautiful, even more inexpressibly beautiful than the beginning of love. The beauty and peace of this unity in love remains forever and ever. Love of this kind never dries up or diminishes. Always alive, both within and without, it is constant, and each moment you live in love. Love will swallow you, eat you up completely until there is no 'you,' only Love. Your whole being will be transformed into Love. Spiritual love culminates in unity, in oneness. Sometimes a relationship between two people, if it is pure, can reach that union. Mother will tell a story."

Mother proceeded to relate a story about pure love between two people named Manohari and Arun. The daughter of a king named Shaktivarman, Manohari was a beautiful princess and a paragon of virtue. Her mother, the queen, had many servants. One of them was a pious lady named Arundhati, who had a son named Arun. Since Arundhati's husband had died, Arun was her constant companion. When she came to the palace to serve the queen, Arun naturally came with her. Princess Manohari and Arun became childhood playmates.

Since they were children, no one attached much importance to the amount of time they spent playing together. The years rolled by, and their close friendship continued as they grew up. They confided in each other what they did and how they felt. Whenever Arun came to the palace, Manohari was eager to share with him everything about herself and about life in the palace. "Ah, my dearest friend, the queen has given orders to have made for me a beautiful bed inlaid with precious gemstones. This golden gown I am wearing was presented to me by the king. Do you know, soon the queen is going to have a beautiful garden made for me? We will play together in that garden." Such were the things she told him. Arun always listened keenly to the princess' stories, and he, in turn, talked about how his mother strained and toiled day in and day out, in order to bring him up. Manohari, being the model of all good qualities, had great sympathy and compassion for Arun's situation and for his hard life.

Time passed and as they became young adults, their relationship was stronger than ever. They were bound to one another by an unbreakable chain of love. Their love was not a shallow, superficial love, but one of great depth. It became very difficult for them to be away from one another as they each began to feel the agony of separation. At the same time, it was very difficult for them to see each other as freely and constantly as before since they were no longer children but young man and young woman. Yet they managed to meet secretly and pour out their hearts to one another. Silently gazing deep into each other's eyes, they would forget about the world outside.

Even while physically apart from each other, Manohari and Arun would be lost in thoughts about each other. Their minds always revolved around thoughts of where the other was and what the other was doing. The excruciating pain of separation burned in their hearts. When they could meet and be together, their encounter became like meditation. They sat facing each other, looking in each other's eyes. Verbal communication almost ceased as their hearts communicated through their eyes. There was no physical contact, yet they experienced the warmth and depth of pure love."

Mother paused and then made some comments about pure love: "Children, where there is pure love, there is no lust. Where Rama is, Ravana cannot thrive. That is, where there is pure, taint-less love (Rama), lust (Ravana) will not exist. Mother remembers another story.

"Having kidnapped Sita, the holy consort of Rama, and taken Her to Lanka, Ravana, the demon king, tried different ways to win Sita's heart. But all his efforts failed. Sita constantly chanted Rama's name. She was always thinking of Rama and Her heart was one with Her Lord's.

"Although Ravana was demonic, his wife was a virtuous and honorable woman. Wanting to please her husband, she suggested a way to win Sita's heart. 'Look, my lord,' she said, 'you have many magical powers. You can assume any form you want. Take the form of Rama and approach Sita that way. Surely, She will be yours.'

"Ravana immediately replied, 'Once I become Rama, then there is no *kama* (lust) in me. What sense is there in approaching Sita that way?'

"Pure love transcends the body. It is between hearts. It has nothing to do with bodies."

Mother continued with the story of Manohari and Arun. "The two lovers lost all their interest in other things. Manohari spent all her time in her private chambers experiencing the agonizing pain of separation. Arun wandered around, feeling torment at being away from his beloved. The flame of love burned and consumed them. Their hearts were like burning tapers. The king and queen noticed the change in their daughter. They wondered what was happening to her, so they appointed some spies to discover what she did and whom she saw. Before long, the whole story of the relationship between Manohari and Arun was exposed. It became the scandal of the palace.

Immediately the king sent Arun in exile to a remote island. He further ordered his soldiers to kill Arun by poisoning his food and then to bury him. The soldiers did as they were ordered. Hoping to avoid suspicion, they did not use a coffin to bury Arun. Instead they put Arun in a simple wooden box and buried him in the dead of night."

Pausing from the story for a few moments, the Mother closed Her eyes and sat absorbed in Her own Self. She laughed blissfully every now and then. After a few more moments, the Mother opened Her eyes, and twirling Her right hand in the air, She chanted, "Shiva, Shiva. Shiva, Shiva."

Silence prevailed until someone reminded Her about the story. Mother continued, "Okay. Where were we? Oh yes. The soldiers buried Arun on a certain spot on the island."

The story continued: Unknown to the soldiers, two robbers were hiding in the bushes closely watching everything. Since it was dark, the robbers could not see what the soldiers were burying. All they had seen was a large box which the soldiers carried on their shoulders. Thinking that it was some treasure, they immediately dug it up when the soldiers had gone some distance away. The robbers were excited and happy, thinking that God had bestowed some great fortune upon them. In their excitement and wishful anticipation of digging up buried treasure, they were shocked when they opened the box. It was no buried treasure but a man.

At first they thought it was a corpse, but noticing movement in Arun's chest, the robbers realized that he was still alive. Though he was unconscious, Arun was still breathing. Taking pity on this man who was buried alive, they sprinkled some water on his face and took him out of the box. When Arun regained consciousness, they give him some water to drink. Immediately upon drinking, Arun started to vomit. He continued to vomit for some time until cleansed of all the poison.

Arun looked around and was puzzled to see that he was still alive. Although the robbers asked him many, many questions, he gave no answers. He did not speak; he simply looked at them. Both robbers became overpowered by an unknown and mysterious sympathy and compassion for this man. Being so moved by this strange compassion, they stopped asking questions and let him go. Regaining his physical composure, Arun walked away into the dark like one transported to another world.

The king had kept his orders of the exile and execution of Arun a secret. The soldiers and the queen were sworn to secrecy. Even though Manohari knew nothing about Arun's fate, she immediately became restless and experienced severe and excruciating inner pain the moment Arun was banished. This pain reached its climax when Arun was buried alive, and her suffering plunged to agonizing depths. She received no news from Arun. It had been a long time since they had seen each other, a long, long time since lover and beloved had been together.

Day after day, languishing in tumultuous waves of pain, she became thinner and thinner. Forgoing food and sleep, she thought only of the one she loved. The entire royal family became very worried. Her health quickly deteriorated until finally the princess was completely bed-ridden. Many eminent physicians were called. They tried all different types of medicine and treatments to no avail. Nothing could restore Manohari's health. Her face was gaunt and pale, but her eyes remained wide open all the time, glowing with love even though she was in deep pain, wanting to be with her love, Arun.

Mysteriously, every now and then strange wounds, bruises and cuts appeared on her body. There was no explanation for this since there were no dangerous instruments lying about her room. It was truly puzzling to the doctors. Sometimes she fell out of her bed as if she had been thrown off. At other times she was found crawling on all fours on the bed. Occasionally she would murmur strange sounds that appeared to have no meaning. But as much as these disturbing, unexplained things happened, there were also times when she was completely peaceful and calm. Maintaining the poise of the princess that she was, she appeared to be totally normal, except that she would not say anything or even acknowledge the presence of other people who came to her room. Nobody could figure out what all these things meant and it remained a great mystery for everybody at the palace.

Meanwhile, Arun was all alone without anybody to whom he could pour out his heart. He wandered over hills and plains, across rivers and through forests in search of his beloved Manohari. Sometimes he would dash about in a frenzy like a mad man. His external appearance was that of a crazy, deranged man with long matted hair and a long beard. He became thin and gaunt like a skeleton. His eyes sank deep into their sockets, but even though hollow, they still glowed with burning love. He neither ate nor slept. Constantly on his lips was the name of his beloved, Manohari. Even though he looked like someone who had escaped from an insane asylum, there was something special about him. The islanders became used to Arun and his strange ways, and they grew very fond of him.

As the days went by, Arun's love became much increasingly intense. He sometimes called out loudly, "Manohari!" He even started asking the people he met, "Where is she, my heart's beloved? Have you seen her?" Since he spent most of his time in the forest, he would also ask the animals, birds, trees, creepers, bushes and even particles of sand, had they seen his beloved?

Suddenly the Mother once again went into an intoxicated mood. Her eyes were shut and tears ran down Her cheeks. The way the Mother was narrating the story was so touching that all the listeners were also moved to tears. Whenever the Mother mentions something about pure love, She drifts away from this world. Love is Her real nature; thus, occasions on which She must talk about love must be a real 'test' for the Mother to keep Her mind in a lower level of consciousness.

After some time Mother came back to the normal plane of consciousness and She continued the narration: Arun's burning love for Manohari prevailed, so much so, that even the ferocious wild animals became calm and quiet in front of him. The lions and tigers became his friends. They were so tamed by love that they lay down peacefully next to the deer and the rabbits. They sensed his sadness and also shed tears when he cried. They joined in his ecstatic dancing when he twirled about in the bliss of love. Then when the excruciating pain of separation struck him, he fell unconscious.

Sometimes when he fell or stumbled about, he injured himself on a sharp stone or a branch, or ran into a tree. Rain or shine, he was always out in the open air, totally oblivious to the condition of his body. So identified were the two lovers that whatever happened to Arun manifested on his beloved's body. That was the mystery behind the injuries, cuts and bruises which manifested on Manohari's body.

Since the princess Manohari was completely bed-ridden and had fallen into a coma, her body was wasting away. She lay like a corpse. Sometimes her lips moved slightly, and if someone paid close attention and listened carefully, he could hear her say, "Arun... Arun... Arun..." Other than that, she hardly breathed. Her parents were drowned in deep sorrow for their daughter. The gave up all hope for her recovery. The princess's attendants, who loved her dearly, gathered around her bed lamenting. The entire kingdom was plunged in gloom. Even crops failed to yield a good harvest.

At this point a saintly man appeared one day at the palace. He carried about himself an aura of serenity and profound peace. When he saw the sorrowful state of the king and the queen suffering in their concern for their daughter's strange malady, he requested to see Manohari. He entered the princess's chambers and saw the girl lying in a coma. Looking silently at her pitiful form for a few minutes, he sat down and went into meditation. Opening his eyes, the saint called for the king and queen. He told them, "Your daughter can be saved, but..." He stopped.

The king quickly entreated, "O Reverend One, tell us. Whatever it is, I will do it. Please tell us what it is."

The saint revealed, "Your daughter is deeply in love with a man. He alone can save her. There is absolutely no other way. Otherwise, she will soon be dead. Call the man here and let him touch the princess. He will bring her back to life."

The king was stunned and fell down at the saint's feet. He confessed the whole story about how he had exiled Arun to a remote island and ordered his soldiers to poison and bury him. Remorse struck the king's conscience and tears came from his eyes as he sat in repentance at the feet of the saint.

Upon assessing what he had just heard, the saint again sat in meditation. Coming out of his meditative trance, he smiled as he assured the king, "Don't worry, the boy is still alive on the same island where he was exiled." Before the saint left the room, he gently and affectionately caressed the princess as if blessing her that soon all would be well.

There was another pause. During this short interval, one of the new brahmacharis was about to ask a question, but he did not, remembering that it was improper to interrupt when the Guru was speaking. Realizing his wish, the Mother inquired, "Son, come on, don't hesitate. What is it that you were going to ask?"

"Amma," the brahmachari said, "you said that Arun even asked the animals and birds about his beloved Manohari. That doesn't make any sense to me. One would be mad to do something like that."

To this, Amma replied, "You are right, son. He was mad, mad with love. When a person is mad with love, he doesn't see objects in their many forms, but he beholds his beloved in whatever he sees. He sees all-pervasive life pulsating in all objects. He becomes one-pointed. He becomes alert and aware. His mind flows only to one object, his beloved. Everything else ceases to exist in this kind of madness.

"In ordinary mental craziness the person loses all concentration, and he turns both the mind and the world into a hellish mess of confusion. But in this madness which ensues from pure love, one becomes totally one-pointed. His whole being, every pore of his body, becomes totally concentrated. Here the madness becomes divine and divinely purifying.

"Children, what did the Gopis of Brindavan do? They, too, found messengers in all objects, both animate and inanimate things. The pain of their separation from Lord Krishna was so unbearable that they even thought that a bee would be a good messenger to intercede to the Lord on their behalf. One Gopi's message was this, 'O bee, pray to my Lord to please wear the garland of my adoration.' Another Gopi said, 'Tell my Beloved to come and illumine the darkness of my heart.' Radha's message was, 'Supplicate my Beloved Lord to make the desert sands of Radha's heart sprout into green grass, so that His Feet may tread thereon, light and soft.'

"What did Rama do when Sita was kidnapped by Ravana? He too inquired about His beloved of the trees, creepers, birds and animals. Let us finish the story now."

Mother continued: The king immediately sent a troop of soldiers off to the island to find Arun. The soldiers who had performed the burial led them to the spot where they had buried the box. Digging at this same spot, they found nothing. No trace of anything that had been buried there could be detected and certainly no sign of any body. The soldiers were then divided into small groups and sent to scour the countryside in search of Arun. Wherever they went they asked the local people if they had seen the young man. Eventually they heard about a crazy wanderer who had a special air about him.

Continuing in their search, they finally came to the forest where Arun was living. They were astounded to see a man dancing, singing, laughing and crying amidst lions, tigers, deer, squirrels, birds and other forest animals. The animals neither did any harm to the soldiers nor did they run away in fear, but they remained very calm, quiet and friendly. The soldiers wanted to find out if this strange man was indeed Arun. They really did not think that this could be the same person they used to see at the palace. How could they find out? Finally, one person had a good idea. The best way to discover if this was Arun was to repeat the name of the princess loudly for him to hear. So one man was appointed to approach the crazy man and call out, "Manohari... Manohari... Manohari..."

Upon hearing this most pleasurable sound and feeling ambrosial nectar flooding his heart, Arun turned and followed the sound. His eyes were filled with ecstatic love as he ran towards the sound of his beloved's name and fell at the spot where the soldiers were standing. Now they were sure that this was Arun. So they lifted him up onto their shoulders to carry him away. The animals and the birds silently stood by, watching the whole scene, shedding tears as they witnessed their dear friend and kindred spirit being taken from their midst.

Arun was brought back to the kingdom. As he stood by Manohari's bedside, a radiance emitted from his entire being. His mere presence brought life and vitality back into her body. He touched her, and like one awaking from a deep sleep, she was gently aroused. She felt as if she were in a trance as she beheld her lover. She smiled at him and he at her, their eyes drinking in deep draughts of love. It was as if they had never been separated, and in a sense, they never were.

The king and queen were filled with joy and gratitude that their daughter had returned to life, and all the court attendants rushed about with beaming smiles on their faces to tell everybody that the princess was awake and well. But the world of the court was not what these lovers wanted. They wanted nothing of the world. Their hearts had already been united long before the exile, and their world was the world of love. Both of them chose to follow a spiritual life, so they renounced the world to become *sannyasins* as their hearts remained in union forever.

Thus Mother ended the story of the two lovers, Manohari and Arun. It was a tale of enchantment that stirred the hearts of all. Everyone remained silent. Moved with emotion, each person sat still and watched the Mother. Within the hearts of the devotees, there was the feeling that they were seeing before their eyes the embodiment of Love itself. Sometimes they felt that if they stared intently at Her they would detect the secret of what they were searching for, but that, of course, was always elusive. The silence was finally broken by the Mother singing

Nin Premam

O Mother, make me mad with Thy Love!
What need have I of knowledge or reason?
Make me drunk with Thy Love's Wine!

O Thou who steals Thy devotees' hearts
Drown me deep in the Sea of Thy Love.
Here in this world, in this madhouse of Thine,
Some laugh, some weep, some dance for joy.

Gauranga, Buddha, Jesus and Moses
All are drunk with the wine of Thy Love.
O Mother, when will I be so blessed
To join their blissful company?

Everyone felt that the Mother was expressing the beauty and fragrance of pure love through Her words and through the song. She stopped for a while. Again there was a deep silence. All eyes were fixed on the Mother because Her eyes remained closed for some time. The impact of the story was so touching that it seemed that everybody present was experiencing the silent depths of pure love. The cool sea breeze which blew from the west gently removed the cloth covering the Mother's head. A few strands of Her hair danced in the cool air. The Mother opened Her eyes as She put the head cloth back in position.

One of the brahmacharis took this opportunity to ask a question, "Amma, what is the conclusion?"

"Children," Amma replied, "whether it is spiritual love or worldly love, love remains love. The difference is only in depth and degree. Even if love has a worldly touch in the beginning, it can reach the highest peak of purity if it becomes one-pointed and selfless. Pure love has nothing to do with the body. It binds and unites the soul of the lover with the soul of the beloved. But as Mother said before, pure love does involve a tremendous amount of self-sacrifice. At certain points it may cause great pain, but pure love always culminates in everlasting bliss.

"In that ultimate state of oneness, even if the lover and beloved retain their bodies, that is, even if they exist as two bodies, deep in the depths of their love they are one whole. It is like two banks of the river. The banks are different; they are two as we see from the outside, but deep down they are one, one united in the depths. The same is the case with genuine lovers. Though they appear as two persons externally, deep within they are one, united in love."

A devotee then asked, "Amma, why is there so much pain and suffering in pure love?"

Mother explained, "Because what is impure should become pure. All impurity should melt and disappear in the heat of the pain of separation and longing. This suffering is known as *tapas*. The Gopis became totally identified with Krishna through this pain. Their pain was so excruciating and intense that their individuality disappeared completely and they merged with their beloved Krishna. The impurity is the feeling of 'I' and 'mine,' the ego. The ego cannot be eradicated unless one puts it in this furnace of love. Love is heat and cold at the same time. It consumes you first. That consuming is a bit painful. But if you have the power to withstand the pain, you can relax and experience the heart's soothing coolness and the oneness of love.

"Let Mother give you the example of the Gopi Neeraja. Originally, she was from another province, but she was married to a Gopa from Brindavan. Before coming to Brindavan, she had been warned about Krishna. But when this Gopi first saw Krishna during the Govardhana festival, she was completely drawn to Him and she fully surrendered her heart to the Lord. This spiritual attachment made Neeraja pass through severe ordeals, but she endured them with great courage. When she first met Krishna, the Lord was playing sweetly on His Divine Flute as He stood at the foot of Govardhana Hill. Thereafter, Neeraja would often visit that bower where she first saw Him just to inhale the holy air.

"When Krishna left Brindavan for Mathura, the separation from her Beloved Lord Krishna was unbearable for Neeraja. Yet she suffered silently for years and years. Like all the other Gopis she thought that Krishna would come back some day. Neeraja waited and waited, spending her days and nights in the bower.

"Years rolled by and Krishna never returned. For Neeraja the pain of separation was excruciating. Her agony grew unbearable, and finally one day she collapsed, unable to withstand any more. As she lay in the bower about to die, Krishna appeared before her. "I have always longed to again hear Your Divine Flute," she told Krishna. The Lord replied, "I did not bring it." But just to fulfill her wish, Krishna broke a length of reed from the bower and made it into a flute on which He played a melody that melted Neeraja's heart. As she listened to that tune while lying on the lap of her Beloved Lord, Neeraja, the true lover and true devotee, finally merged into Krishna forever and ever.

"Pure love removes all negative feelings. Destroying all selfishness, it expects nothing but gives everything. Pure love is a constant giving up – giving up of everything that belongs to you. What really belongs to you? Only the ego. Love consumes in its flames all preconceived ideas, prejudices and judgements, all those things which stem from the ego. Pure love is nothing but the emptying of the mind of all its fears and the tearing off of all masks. It exposes the Self as it is.

"For the lover to wholeheartedly receive and welcome the beloved, pure love prepares the mind by chasing away all the enemies of love. This results in a constant flow of the lover's heart towards the beloved. There is an unquenchable thirst to drink in the beloved, an unappeasable hunger to eat him up and an immeasurable intensity to become love. It is the death of the ego to live in love. But once you attain unity with the beloved, then there is only peace, love, light and silence. All conflicts end and you shine forth in the radiance of Supreme Love. In order to attain this highest kind of love one has to undergo some pain. But that pain is not pain when you consider the unending flow of bliss which you are going to gain when you reach the goal.

"To reach the destination you must travel, and you may have to endure some hardships along the way. You may have to travel for many, many hours in an airplane or for several days on a train without proper sleep or food. Once you reach your destination, however, you can lie down, rest and relax. A river has to flow many miles in order to reach the sea. Profit comes after losses. Likewise, the eternal peace of love comes after some trials and tribulations. In order to gain the highest form of bliss one has to undergo purification. Purification is heating up the mind in order to remove all impurities, and this process inevitably involves pain. Even to attain something material, a certain amount of sacrifice is involved.

"While momentary happiness obtained from the world ulti-mately pushes you into the throes of never-ending sorrow, spiritual pain uplifts you to the abode of everlasting bliss and peace. It is up to us to choose between temporary happiness, which will culminate in never-ending unhappiness, or temporary pain which will culminate in everlasting peace."

A devotee added, "Pure and innocent love is capable of eradicating everyone's problems, both mental and physical. That is what Mother's life is all about. Her universal love bestows peace and tranquility to all those who come to Her."

Amma continued, "Children, love can accomplish anything and everything. Love can cure diseases. Love can heal wounded hearts and transform human minds. Through love one can overcome all obstacles. Love can help us renounce all physical, mental and intellectual tension and thereby bring peace and happiness. Love is the ambrosia which adds beauty and charm to life. Love can create another world in which you are immortal and deathless.

"Pure love is the best medicine for the modern world. This is what is lacking in all societies. The root cause of all problems, from personal problems to global problems, is the absence of love. Love is the binding factor, the unifying factor. Love creates the feeling of oneness among people. It unifies a nation and its people. Love creates a sense of unity while hatred causes division. Egotism and hatred cut people's minds into pieces. Love should rule. There is no problem which love cannot solve.

"In the modern age, human minds are dry. Too much reasoning has spoiled the contemporary mind. People use their intellects for everything. They have lost their hearts and their faith. Beauty lies in the heart. Beauty lies in faith and faith dwells in the heart. Intellect or reasoning is necessary, but we should not let it swallow the faith in us. We should not allow the intellect to eat up our heart. Intellect is knowledge, and knowledge is ego. Too much knowledge means nothing but a big ego. The ego is a burden, and a big ego is a big burden.

"If a person's intellect predominates, he will not be able to enjoy sweetness and beauty. Unable to penetrate the surface of things or dive deep within, he will perceive only exteriors. While sitting on the seashore, instead of enjoying the beauty of the waves and the vastness of the ocean, he will think about how the ocean came into existence. Filled with such thoughts, he will even fail to notice the gentle caress of the breeze from the sea, its expansiveness and vastness. A predominantly intellectual person will not be able to imbibe and experience the magic and enchantment of a moonlit night. He cannot simply appreciate something for what it is but must engage in analysis. He will try to analyze the moon as a luminous body, attempt to give a scientific explanation of the moon and how it shines. He cannot think in other terms.

"While drinking a cup of coffee or tea, his thoughts will be on how to breed a new species of coffee beans or tea leaves. He will not be able to enjoy the flavor of the tea or coffee. Thus the intellectual person who has no love in him will always miss the beauty and charm of everything that comes to him. Think of the life of such a person. Can we call it life? It is death, nothing but death. We want to live life as well as we can. We do not want to make life a mess. Therefore, we want everything in perfect proportions, without too much or too little of anything. Presently, the intellect predominates and there is not enough love. Therefore, we must strive to empty the intellect of useless thoughts and fill the heart with love. That is the solution for all the distress and confusion of modern society."

Another question arose about love and war, "Amma, you state that love should rule and that there is no problem which love cannot solve. But is this applicable to the modern world where each country is intent on increasing its military force to attack and conquer other countries? How can a nation hold on to the theory of love and practice it when enemies are lining up artillery at its borders?

"Children, in pure love there is no attachment," explained the Mother. "One has to transcend all petty human feelings to attain Supreme Love. In other words, love dawns only when detachment arises. All attachments to all other things, whatever they may be, should fall off, and the mind should become fully one-pointed. Here, love alone is the subject and the object. Such love will not arise from attachment; it is a product of total detachment. Therefore, when a challenge confronts the nation you must fight for the good of the country, if it is a good cause, but with detachment.

"In order to fight without attachment, the battle must be waged not against the evil-doer but against the evil. The fighting is not against an egotistic person in the opposite army but against the ego, the destructive force. It is not out of hate that you fight but out of detachment and love – that is, detached love or love without attachment.

"All wars and all conquests arise from the ego, in most cases the national egos, the collective egos of a nation. Rarely is it personal egos. Whenever there is a conflict, it is between two big collective egos. Each side may shout at the top of their lungs that they are fighting for the commom good, for the protection of the nation's freedom, for the peace of all of humanity, and so on. But if you penetrate to the real cause, you will find that it is their egos fighting. If some country or leader poses a threat to a country or to the world, threatening all nations and all of humanity, you may fight, but fight with love. If you go to war, fight with love for humanity; fight against evil and against unrighteousness. Fight with detachment, for real love arises from detachment.

"Real love arises only when all attachments to individuals, objects and personal interests drop away. Then the battle becomes a beautiful play. It becomes selfless service extended toward the entire human race out of love and compassion. In that fighting your ego will not fight, but love will fight to consume the ego and transform it into love.

"Lord Krishna was 'love incarnate,' even while He fought in the epic battle described in the *Mahabharata*. Although He sided with the righteous Pandavas, He did not hate the evil Kauravas. He still loved them, but he did hate the evil that motivated them. For righteousness' sake He wanted to save the country from total destruction. The cause He stood for was universal. Had it been the Pandavas who had acted in an unrighteous manner, Krishna would definitely have taken the side of the Kauravas. He was not attached to individuals. On the contrary, He was support-ing *dharma*. He was fully detached from everything, even from His own abode. That is why He could smile even when His city, Dwaraka, was swallowed up by the ocean.

"Krishna fought in the battle with complete detachment because His love was not divided. His love was whole. Pure love is undivided. Pure love sees oneness; it sees no caste, creed, sect or religion. Pure love can fight, kill or destroy; yet there is no hatred in it, only love. When pure love fights, it is not one person fighting with another. It is the higher nature fighting against the lower nature. Pure love has no form. Even if there is a form, that form is only for the sake of having a name to identify it, such as Krishna. Behind that form is the formless love because love has consumed the form in its flames.

"What opposes pure love is the ego. It is ignorant, limited individuals fighting for an evil cause. But love does not see the form or persons. Love sees through the form and wants to burn the ego in its all-consuming flame. There is no hatred involved on the part of love, for pure love has no ego. When only love is involved, it can fight and kill, but at the same time, it can love and even walk away untouched because that person who is the embodiment of love is the embodiment of detachment as well. That is why Krishna could fight and still love. Rama could fight with Ravana and still love him. Jesus could whip the corrupt merchants and still love them. That is why Krishna could bestow the highest form of blessing, salvation, upon the hunter who shot Him with an arrow, causing Him to cast off His human form. That is why Jesus could forgive and pray for those who tortured His body. Krishna, Rama and Jesus were detached and undivided. Being whole and pure, Their love transcended all forms of attachments and aversions. In Them there was nothing but love and compassion. For Them there were no individuals, no separate entities. Everything was a whole.

"Children, we should take Them as examples. Follow Their footsteps and fight if society calls for it, provided it is for a good cause. Discharge your duty properly, but be detached. Have love and compassion for the entire human race.

"In this modern age, to be detached while at war is quite difficult because almost all nations have their own vested interests. Therefore, Mother knows that it would be an almost impossible task to observe the principles just mentioned. Most soldiers are bound to obey the commands issued to them. Even then, a person who is truly devoted to *dharma* will not fight for an evil cause. He will have a universal outlook. But if one is helplessly pushed into such a situation, he should fight, taking it as his duty towards his country, and sincerely pray to the Lord for cleansing him of all sins which he might incur. He should not have any personal envy or selfishness towards the other nation."

The western sky over the Arabian Sea glowed with a brilliant red and golden hue as the sun sank on the horizon marking the end of another day. From the southwestern corner of the Ashram premises, one could take in a panoramic vista of the dark blue waters and the setting sun. High waves rose and fell upon the shores of the black sand with a thunderous crash. Big fishing trawlers lined the seashore, waiting to set out to sea at the turning of the tide. The constant roar of the ocean echoed through the Ashram. The Holy Mother was sitting on the south side of the temple, facing west. The Mother sat in a perfect lotus posture with eyes opened; She was unmoving and transfixed, revealing a visible depth. She radiated an extraordinary aura of divinity.

The Holy Mother slowly glided into a state of rapture. With Her eyes half-closed She sat motionless. Her sister Kasturi's son, Shivan, came running and stood in front of the Mother, gazing at Her face. After a few moments, he squatted down beside Her. His eyes were still fixed on the Mother's face. Perhaps inspired by the Mother's ecstatic mood, he also sat like a little yogi and started meditating. With eyes closed he began chanting 'OM.'

The Mother continued in Her exalted mood for a while longer. As the tide turned, the waves lapped on the shore while the fishermen pushed their long boats into the sea. Excited that the weather was most favorable for a good evening catch, they were in a merry mood as they chanted their rhythmic, traditional songs, creating an ancient setting for the timeless quality of the Mother's mood.

As the Mother slowly opened Her eyes, She remained facing the western horizon. Then She turned and looked at Shivan, who was still repeating 'OM.' Very pleased with him, the Mother called, "Shivan-*mon*... Shivan-*mon*" He opened his eyes and immediately asked in his own innocent way, "Ammachi, why did you call me? I was meditating." His innocence deeply touched the Mother, and She smiled with delight as She moved closer to him. Gently caressing his head with Her right hand, the Mother said, "Good boy, you meditated for a long time. That is enough for the time being, okay?" Shivan nodded his head in agreement. Taking him by the hand, the Mother said, "Now, get up, son. Come along with Mother." Pointing to the banks of the backwaters, She continued, "We will go and sit there for a while." Holding hands, they walked together to the southern edge of the Ashram. The Mother sat there for some time with Shivan at Her side.

The evening *bhajan* began at the regular time with the brahmacharis and resident devotees singing. In the middle of the *bhajan*, the Holy Mother joined in as they sang

Idamilla

Here I am a wanderer with no hearth or home.
O Mother, give me refuge, lead me towards Thee,
Let me not get tossed about in deep waters
But extend Thy helping hand, take me to the shore.

Like butter poured in fire
My mind is being burned in this world,
A bird can at least fall to the earth
But for a human being,
Who but Thee art the Support?

After this song there was a short pause. Everyone waited for the Mother to start the next *kirtan*. She sang

Kali Maheshwari

I salute Kali, the Holy Consort of Lord Shiva,
Who is verily the Mother of the Universe.
O Mother, what a great magical power
This world has,
Which completely blocks the mind to think
And contemplate Thy Divine Form and Name.

O Great Goddess Kali,
It has been declared that You are
The Root Cause of this world,
Having neither head nor tail,
Neither alpha nor omega,
Thus mixing up truth and untruth.
O Mother, crazy indeed is what You have done.

O Kali, O Great Illusive Power,
Can one find any reason
In this universal play performed by Thee?
Crazy indeed is this play,
O Thou Who art intoxicated
By drinking the bliss of eternity.

O Kali, One Who causes the final dissolution,
Being the One who weaves heaps and heaps
Of the beginningless cloth of maya,
It is such a strange sight
To see Thee wearing the severed hands
Of Thy enemies around Thy waist.

The Mother sometimes would cry, and at other times, She would burst into ecstatic laughter. At a certain point She drew within and became totally absorbed while the brahmacharis took over the lead singing. Next Her gestures were like those of an innocent child in supplication to its mother. With both hands raised, She called out, "Amma...Amma... Where are You?" or "Hey, Kali... Kali! Come here."

With this kind of supreme devotion, different aspects and different layers of the Supreme Consciousness appeared, disappeared and reappeared in the manifestations of the Mother's body. Perched on those wings of divinity, everyone present passed beyond the ordinary to the blissful world of supreme love and devotion. As She sang, one could see the Mother wiping tears every now and then.

Whenever She talks about the path of devotion, Amma says, "Look, children, Mother knows very well that all names and forms are limited and that God is nameless, formless and attributeless. Still, the sweet and blissful feeling that one has from singing the glories of the Lord is an incomparable and inexpressible experience. While singing to the Lord, it is very difficult for Mother to control the mind and bring it down. On such occasions She may become mad with Divine Love. It is a real struggle to keep the mind down. Therefore, Mother puts on a temporary veil which can be removed at any time. It is this veil which helps the mind to remain in this physical plane. This veil can be removed by mere will whenever Mother wants. Children, innocent love can easily take us to that inexpressible experience. Therefore, try to develop that love in your heart."

The bhajan ended at 8:30 p.m. Even after the arati the Mother still sat in the same place, Her gaze fixed beyond. Her right hand rested on the right cheek with the elbows resting on the knee of the right leg which was kept in a bent upright position. Her eyes were still and did not blink. The Mother remained in that absorbed mood for about a half hour and did not leave to go to Her room until nine o'clock.

Chapter 12

A devotee's experience of Kali

11 May 1984

A devotee who had a wonderful vision the night before during *Devi Bhava* was sharing it with one of the residents. He was very excited and wanted some clarification about the vision. He related what had taken place. While the residents were immersed in singing *bhajans*, his mind was overflowing with love and devotion for the Mother. They sang a song about the Mother

Entinanamme Hara

O Mother, Why do You stand
Keeping Your Foot on Lord Shiva?
Also what have You relished
For Your tongue to stick out?

O All-Knowing One, You always walk around
Like an ordinary girl who knows nothing;
But I know within me that this is how You are,
O Omniscient One.

Though fierce, how pleasant and compassionate
Is Your countenance, O Mother.
My longing to sleep on Your lap
Is becoming more and more intense.

O Kali, the Enchantress,
People say that You walk around intoxicated,
Having fully drunk.

O Eternal Truth, Who knows
What You drink is the Nectar of Immortality?

By placing Your Foot on Your Father's chest,
O Mother, You show us that Your Holy Feet
Can only be attained through the quality of Sattva,
By filling the mind with sattvic qualities.
O Mother, kindly bestow that quality
Upon this humble devotee as well.

His eyes were fixed on the Mother's face. All of a sudden everything disappeared from his sight. In a whirlpool everything seemed to dematerialize while his eyes were wide open. The temple, the people and the surroundings vanished from his sight. No singing reached his ears. The entire universe with its duality and diverse nature disappeared. He lost his own individuality, and even the Mother's form vanished from his sight. Though he wanted to call or shout aloud, he could not move or speak. He felt as if he were moving out of his body. He experienced that he was different from his body. Then he beheld the entire universe flooded with effulgence. His eyes could not stand the light.

Slowly the light solidified into a form. While he was experiencing great difficulty in seeing, the effulgence evolved into the fierce yet enchanting form of Mother Kali dancing on the chest of Lord Shiva. There was the Great Mother's infinite spiritual glory and splendor, Her protruding tongue, big red bulging eyes, and the divine weapons which She held in Her numerous hands. Awesome as She was, the devotee was so relaxed and blissful that all the fears he had before dissolved. He expressed it this way: "Her form was such that even Lord Shiva would be afraid to go near Her, but the compassion, love and spiritual bliss which I experienced were like ambrosia, so soothing to the heart that they removed my fear and delusion."

Gradually everything returned to normal, and the devotee was thrown back into the realm of time and space. Coming back to his normal consciousness, the devotee fainted and fell backwards from his sitting position. Some other devotees who attended to him found him perspiring profusely and breathing irregularly. After taking a few gasps of air, he remained breathless for a while. As time passed people became worried, not knowing what was happening to him.

Mother, who had been watching the whole scene with a mischievous smile on Her face, sent a rose that She took from the garland She was wearing with instructions that it be held close to his nose. As soon as the rose was placed near him, he began to breathe normally. Then he opened his eyes and sat upright. The expression on his face revealed much serenity and bliss. As if returned from another world, the devotee looked around to re-orient himself. Finally, he kept his gaze on the Mother's countenance. A special, sweet smile of inexpressible joy lit his face as he sat in deep meditation throughout the night until the *Devi Bhava Darshan* was over.

The next morning he was still full of bliss and peace. He confessed, "I am unable to control the spiritual bliss I am experiencing which comes from deep within. It is a rare experience that Amma has bestowed upon me." The brahmachari to whom this experience was being told felt envious of this middle-aged man who had been given the rare blessing to behold the vision of Mother Kali.

Later in the *darshan* hut the devotee once again saw the Holy Mother while She was giving *darshan* to people. He begged the Mother, "Amma, I have no doubt that you are none other than Mother Kali. It is also very clear to me that it was you who appeared as Kali in front of me. Who else could give me the *darshan* of Kali other than you? But, Amma, maybe it is my ignorance, but still I have the desire to hear from your own lips, 'I am Kali. It is I who gave you the *darshan*.' As my Guru and *Ishta Devata*, you must tell me that. Please, Amma, please..."

The Mother kept looking at him. There was an expression of tremendous motherly love and compassion on Her face. A few moments passed as the Mother kept quiet, yet not turning Her face away from this devotee. He began sobbing like a little child. He covered his face with both hands and fell on the Mother's lap. With great love the Mother rubbed his back and tried to console him, saying, "Son... son... don't cry, don't cry." But he couldn't help crying. Then She lovingly put him on Her shoulder and whispered something into his ear. As soon as She did this, he burst into a sudden stream of blissful laughter. He jumped up and started dancing. Laughing and crying at the same time with tears of joy rolling down his cheeks, he shouted, "Kali! Kali! Mahakali... Kali has come as my Guru and *Ishta Devata*. Kali! Kali! Kali..." He kept on repeating this until the Mother finally laid Her right palm on his chest to calm him down, and he returned to a normal state.

Later he related that this blissful mood lasted for about two weeks. He revealed that indeed the Holy Mother had whispered in his ears that She was the one who had given him the *darshan* and that She was Kali. That was the reason for his rapturous joy.

Do not judge others

While the Mother gave *darshan* to people, one of the devotees mentioned the name of another person and asked the Mother about him, "Amma, why do you let him come here? He is a very unpleasant person; he has bad character."

Mother said in reply to this devotee's remark, "Son, God descends to the earth for the sake of people in ignorance. They need to be transformed. How can you judge someone when you yourself are plunged in ignorance? Do you know how much that son has changed? Do you know how much he regrets and repents his past? It is people like him that need the most attention. When someone like that changes for the better, it is of great benefit to society.

"One needs only a little stain remover to remove a small spot, but more has to be applied if it is a bigger and denser spot. Likewise, a person who is already spiritually inclined may not need much attention and care, but a person who has spoiled his life without having any real principles to live by needs greater attention and personal care in order to be re-educated and to lead a worthwhile life. Light coffee needs only a little milk. Strong coffee needs more milk. Mother is ready to take any number of births to help such people. How can Mother abandon them? Who else would take care of them?

"If that son is to be prevented from visiting Mother on account of your judgement, then you need to be driven away. You should get the same treatment. You are more ignorant than he. He, at least, openly admits his mistakes and expresses remorse, whereas you do not even know how much negativity you carry within you. Are you a perfect soul? No, you are not.

"Are you asking Mother to abandon people who are in ignorance? Is the body not a product of ignorance? We do not give it up, do we? This whole world is nothing but ignorance, *maya*. Why do we try to acquire and possess more and more, even after knowing that all this is illusion? Each one thinks that he himself is good and that others are bad. This is wrong. If you are good, if there is goodness in you, you should be able to see goodness in everything. You see the bad in others because there is bad in you. Children, try to realize this truth. Do not point at the faults and errors of others. Realize your own mistakes and try to correct them. Let your own errors, your own ego, become a burden to yourself, not to other people.

"Only when we become aware of the burden of our own ego will we be able to remove our faults. At present, we cannot bear someone else's ego or mistakes, but ours is all right. "My ego is beautiful, but his is ugly." This is our present attitude, and this attitude should go.

"Children, try to be humble. We are here to see God in others, not the evil or ignorance in them. That is what our practice should be. We don't need a Guru or an ashram to see evil in others. Children, why do you come here? What is the purpose? What is the goal? Undoubtedly, it is to remove your old habits and tendencies. It is to lead a higher life based on spiritual principles. Do not forget that. Do not forget your goal. By seeing ignorance and evil in others, the very purpose of coming here is defeated.

"The feeling of 'other' should go. That feeling is due to the ego. Try to see oneness, the whole. Seeing the parts is ego, but seeing the whole is egoless. Seeing the branches, leaves, fruits and flowers as separate, we forget the tree. To perceive the branches, leaves, fruits and flowers as separate is ego. To see the tree as tree, as a whole, is perfection. Seeing only the hands, legs, eyes, nose and ears as different parts is ego. When we see the body as a whole, that is perfection. But the problem is, we cannot see the whole. We pay attention only to the parts. We concern ourselves with division, 'the other,' separate from us. Mother does not see parts. Mother sees only the whole. Mother sees only God, the Supreme Atman. Mother cannot do otherwise. Children, seeing 'the other' will divide us, but seeing the whole will lift us to the undivided state. Therefore, try to be egoless; try to be humble."

The devotee felt guilty for his thoughtless comment. He said regretfully, "Amma, I am sorry for making that comment. Amma, please forgive me for my ignorance. You know what is best for everyone. My ignorance is so dense that I forgot all about your omniscience and made that thoughtless comment."

Ever-compassionate, the Mother affectionately patted him on the back and said, "No problem, son. It happens. That is the nature of the mind. Think how many times a child falls down and injures his body before he learns to walk properly! Committing mistakes is quite human, but try to refrain from doing it again and again. Try to learn a lesson from every mistake you make and try not to repeat it. If it happens accidentally, no problem. Don't worry. But consciously making the same mistake again and again is a tendency of the lower instincts. Don't do that. Try to overcome that weakness. If you persist in that weakness, it will ultimately push you into darkness from which there is no escape."

Mother got up and walked towards the coconut grove. She started walking around under the trees with Her hands held behind Her back. After a while She sat down in the shade with Her eyes fixed on the vast expansive sky. Seeing Mother sitting alone and thinking that She might like to be away from people for a while, Brahmachari Nealu put a sign up on a coconut tree not far from where Mother was sitting. It read, "Please do not disturb. Amma wants to be alone for a while."

Out of his love for Her, Nealu always felt that Mother was working too hard and that She needed a lot of solitude and rest. He was very concerned about Mother's health. Thus, whenever he had the opportunity, he attempted to serve Her in this manner. Sometimes when Mother was resting, Nealu guarded the door to Her room and let absolutely no one go inside. However, if Mother found out about his efforts to give Her 'peace and quiet,' She would invariably see to it that his plans were spoiled. Still, all the past attempts and failures on his part did not change Nealu's attitude. He was ingenious at implementing new ideas in order to give Mother some rest. Now he was trying again.

Having posted the sign on a tree, Nealu sat a few yards away, ready to prevent anyone who might dare trespass. After a short time and for no apparent reason, Mother called a brahmachari to Her and started conversing with him. In no time Mother was again surrounded by devotees, brahmacharis and householder residents. Poor Nealu did not know what to do. With a discouraged and frustrated look on his face, he removed the sign, muttering to himself, "What to do! Amma doesn't want solitude or rest."

Sitting in the coconut grove surrounded by devotees and residents, Mother sang a song

Hamsa Vahini

O Goddess Who rides the Swan
Mother Saraswati (Goddess of Wisdom),
Who is the Moon to the entire Universe
Who resides on Sringeri Mountain
Who plays in the bliss of music.

Mother has Her own way of doing things. Trying to do something against Her wish and will is foolish. One cannot set any limits on *Mahatmas* like the Mother. They are beyond all limitations. One cannot fit them into a frame of rules and regulations or set conditions for them. Such boundaries are for ordinary mortals. But once we transcend the world of duality, our words and deeds become the law. Then we will not be bound by anything.

❧ ❧

Chapter 13

Inevitability of death

22 June 1984

A reception for the Mother, followed by a *bhajan* program was being held in Alleppy, a town forty miles north of the Ashram. As the van carrying Mother and Her children drove on the highway, they passed the corpse of a boy who had been hit by a car. Mother advised, "Do not look on that side of the road. The sight might haunt you during meditation." Silence prevailed as the van drove by the accident.

Then Mother continued, "We will understand how silly this life is if we realize that we are next. To really have the awareness that we will die will help increase detachment. Death always follows us like a shadow. Knowing and understanding the inevitability of death, one should strive hard to realize the eternal truth before the body falls off. Nobody knows who is next. Nobody can predict it."

One of the brahmacharis quoted a great scholar and a Realized Soul, who wrote the *Srimad Bhagavatam* in Malayalam based on the Sanskrit original: "Even when people see their own loved ones dying right in front of their eyes, they are full of hopes and expectations about life. Alas! Never do they think that death will come to them one day. Even if they do think about it, their conviction is that it will not happen for the next hundred years."

Amma's responded in this manner, "That Great Being was right. Mother has heard a story. There once was a king who wanted to know when he would die. He summoned an eminent astrologer who could predict the future. In studying the king's horoscope, he made some astrological calculations and found that the king was going to die that very evening at dusk. One can easily imagine the great dismay of the king when he heard this, for naturally he did not want to die. He wondered how he could escape death. Now, this is not surprising. Who wouldn't try to save his own life if it were threatened or if he learned that he were to die at a particular time? The king acted quickly. He immediately summoned all the great scholars in his land and ordered them to find a way to overcome death.

"The scholars convened and began discussing and disputing. They searched many different scriptural texts to find a way to save the king's life. When one learned being suggested something – a way, a ritual or a mantra – another scholar would refute it and recommend another method. Thus it went on and on without reaching any conclusion. Afternoon fell and still no conclusion had been reached. The king became very restless. He yelled at the scholars, 'Hurry up, hurry up! Quick! It is getting late.' But the scholars, as usual, were caught up in the words of the scriptures. They could not move beyond the rhetoric and their dispute. Finally a wise elderly man of the court whispered to the king, 'Sire, do not rely on these people. They will not find a solution. If you want to save your own life, take the fastest horse you have and go as far as you can away from the palace before dusk falls. Don't waste any time. Start right now. Go!'

"To the desperate king this sounded like a good idea. Soon he was flying on the best horse from the royal stables. Before dusk fell he had traveled hundreds of miles away from the palace. Exhausted, the king wanted to rest, so he dismounted and lay down under a tree. Lying there on his back, he began thinking about the events of the day and was feeling happy that he had tricked death by leaving the court before nightfall. Since he felt safe, he glided into sleep. Soon dusk fell and all of a sudden, death jumped out from nowhere. His thirsty eyes fell on the king as he declared victoriously, 'I knew you would come here. I have been waiting for you here by this tree. I was beginning to get worried, thinking that you would not make it in time. Anyhow, you got here just in time. Thank you.' In no time the helpless king was in the grip of death."

Thus Mother finished the story. The van continued along the road for a while, and again She spoke: "Children, who can run away from death? When you are born, death also comes with you. Each moment of your life you are getting closer to death. People are not aware of this. They are so enmeshed in pleasures of the world that they totally forget this. There is no time when death does not exist. In fact, we lie always between the jaws of death. The wise ones are aware of the inevitability of death and try to transcend it.

"While living 'in life,' a wise person acquires the mental and spiritual strength to live also 'in death' or to live in eternity beyond death. He dies to his ego. Once one dies to the ego, there is no person, and thus there is no one to die. Such people are so full with life that they do not know death. Having transcended death, they know only life, ever-pulsating life everywhere. They become the very essence of life. Death is an unknown phenomenon; it does not exist for them. The death that we know about – the perishing of the body – might happen to them, but that death is only a change for them. They do not fear death of the body. But in life and through death they will remain as the essence of life which will assume another form if they so wish.

"The waves are nothing but the water. After one wave rises and falls, the same ocean waters take the form of another wave in another place. Whatever form or shape they may take, they are nothing but the ocean waters. In a similar manner, the body of a perfected soul may also die like the body of an ordinary human being. The difference is that while a mortal human being considers

245

himself a separate entity—a part, different from the Supreme Consciousness like a single wave isolated from the ocean—a perfected soul is fully aware of his oneness with the Absolute. He knows he is not an isolated wave but the ocean itself, even if he has taken human form. Therefore, he does not have any fear of death. He knows that it is a natural phenomenon, only a change. He knows very clearly that just as a wave rises up, dies away and rises up again in another shape at another place, the body too must pass through birth, death and birth again. *Mahatmas* know that they are the ocean, not the wave. They are the *Atman*, not the body. But an ordinary person thinks that he is the body, an isolated wave, and that he is finished forever when the body dies. This fills him with fear because he does not want to die. Thus he grieves when he thinks of death. He wants to run away from death."

A devotee who was traveling in the van with Mother quoted from the *Bhagavad Gita* in which Krishna tells Arjuna not to grieve about death. He paraphrased in his own words: "Arjuna, death must happen after birth and birth must follow death. Therefore, do not grieve, thinking of this inevitable phenomenon. There is no meaning in it." [17] What Amma had just said was a beautiful interpretation of Krishna's words.

One swami, author of a very popular spiritual book, was also traveling in the van. He sat in the seat just in front of Mother. The whole time they were traveling, the swami was looking at Mother's image reflected in the rear-view mirror of the van. He remarked like a child, "I can see Amma's image in the mirror." Mother laughed and gave a retort, "You will be able to see God everywhere when the mind is cleansed of all its impurities and made into a clear mirror."

---

[17] Chapter 2, Verse 27: "Death is certain of that which is born; birth is certain of that which is dead. You should not, therefore, lament over the inevitable."

A brahmachari, still remembering what they had passed on the road previously, asked Mother a question, "Amma, you said that those who did not have enough mental strength should not look at the corpse of the boy hit by the car because that would haunt them during meditation. Why did you say that?"

"Son," Amma said smiling to him, "that is the nature of the mind. Whatever we do not want to think about will come first. Let Mother explain this with another story. A king who was completely bald-headed had an intense desire to have his head full of thick, black hair. So sensitive was he about his baldness that he always wore a turban. He tried many different kinds of medicine and underwent various types of treatments, but nothing worked. Feeling very sad and desperate, he finally summoned the most renowned and eminent physician of the land and ordered him to invent a medicine to produce the growth of hair. 'If you fail,' the king threatened, 'you will be beheaded.'

"Such an order from the king threw the physician into a great dilemma. Although he knew clearly that there was no such medicine for baldness, he could not tell the king that. For if he did, that would be the end of his life. Therefore, the physician decided to tackle the problem in a diplomatic way, hoping that he would somehow be able to save his own life. Bowing low with all humility in front of the king, he replied, 'Your Highness, I consider it a great privilege to make the medicine for you. I am honored. But, Sire, please be kind enough to grant me two weeks time to make this very rare medicine.' Since two weeks did not seem too long a time to wait, the king agreed.

"Two weeks later the physician appeared with the specially prepared medicine. In the private royal apartments, he presented the medicine to the king. The king was exuberant. He felt that his dream of having a head of thick, dark hair was coming true at last. The physician cleared his throat and said, 'Sir, this is an oil which is very rare and precious. I have especially prepared it for Your Highness. I have no doubt that it will take effect in a very short period of time, but...' The doctor stopped in hesitation. His curiosity aroused, the king jumped up from his seat and asked, 'But...what? Speak out!' The physician continued, 'Nothing, nothing serious. It is only a very minor point. While applying the medicine on your head, don't think of rats, that's all. That's all, nothing else, and everything will be fine.'

"The king sat back and relaxed. He thought, 'That is nothing. Not to think of rats while applying the oil.' He sent the physician away after having given him the promised reward.

"The next day a happy king got up early in the morning and took out the medicine from the closet with reverence. After chanting a prayer, he poured a little on his right palm and was about to apply it on his head, and what came rushing into his mind? Rats, big rats, marching in a long procession!" A roar of laughter filled the bus. When that calmed down, Amma completed the story, "The king was shocked and poured the oil back into the bottle. Yet he was not ready to give up so easily. He tried again and again, at different times of the day, outside the palace and in his garden, but each time the number of rats increased. He became so exasperated that ultimately he threw the bottle of oil out the window."

The story ended with more laughter, and when that finally subsided, Mother continued with these comments: "Children, this is the nature of the mind. Whatever incident, object or idea we want to forget will follow us and haunt us wherever we go, no matter what time of day or what we try to do to forget it. *Sraddha* and devotion are the only ropes with which we can bind this mind.

"We have been living a totally uncontrolled life for so many years. Now whatever we hear or see will easily get imprinted in us. It just rushes into the mind without being invited. It will take time to bring the mind under control. Practice coupled with patience is needed to attain that."

Mother glanced at everyone in the van with a bright smile on Her face and then started to sing *Sri Chakram* as everybody joined in on the response.

Sri Chakram

*In the mystical wheel Sri Chakram
Dwells the Goddess Sri Vidya,
That Devi, who is the nature of motion,
The one Power that moves the wheel of the Universe.*

*Sometimes riding on a lion,
Manifesting as the Power of the Creator,
Sometimes mounted on a swan,
O Mother who leads and controls
The Divine Trinity,
Is not the Goddess Katyayani
Yet another of Thy forms?*

*These devotees pay obeisance to Thy Forms
For the alleviation of their miseries.
O Mother, who among human beings
Captivated by Maya understands the truth
That this human body is most despicable?*

*O Mother, Thou who sports riding on a tiger,
How can one in ignorance hope to extol
Thy most exalted majesty?*

Now the van was getting closer to the program site. Mother stopped singing and sat with eyes closed for the rest of the time, deeply absorbed in Her own Self. Most of the brahmacharis also meditated or repeated their mantra until they reached the temple where a reception was arranged. After the reception, there were *satsang* and *bhajan* which lasted until 10:00 p.m. Then the Mother began to give *darshan* to the thousands of people who had gathered in the temple in order to receive Her blessings. The Mother sat until 2:00 a.m. giving *darshan* until the very last person was individually received.

Chapter 14

Remembering God while eating food

23 June 1984

During lunch two brahmacharis were serving the food while another one led the chanting of the fifteenth chapter of the *Srimad Bhagavad Gita.*[18] Only a few were responding as others kept quiet. Quite unexpectedly the Holy Mother stepped into the dining hall. She was a bit angry at seeing the lack of *sraddha* of the brahmacharis.

"Why is nobody chanting the *Gita?*" asked the Mother. Then came more words of practical wisdom: "One can learn patience if he remembers God even while sitting in front of food. Food is always a weakness for human beings. Nothing enters the mind when we are hungry. We forget what is around us and start eating without caring about others. Once hunger overpowers us, we loose all patience.

"Hunger deprives one of all patience. Even if God suddenly appears in front of a hungry person, he wouldn't care. If one observes a family in the home, one can see the father, son or daughter getting angry if the mother is a little late in serving food when they come home hungry from work or from school. This lack of patience due to hunger is a weakness. At times like this one may lose all discrimination and pick a fight with another person, no matter who it might be. A spiritual seeker should not fall prey to this weakness. He should be able to remember God

---

[18] In India it is a customary ashram practice to chant from Chapter 15 of *Bhagavad Gita* before partaking of food. This chapter embodies the quintessence of *Vedanta*, and it also discusses the digestive processes and the vital energies involved.

and to maintain his mental balance and calmness in front of food, even if he is extremely hungry.

"The human mind is very attached to food. Food nourishes the body, and since we are attached to the body, we are attached to food. The craving for taste is tremendous. Altogether, food is a weak point as far as human beings are concerned. So to maintain patience and remember God while seated in front of your favorite dish is nothing short of working on your attachment to the body.

"In addition, children, remembering God before you take food is a very good reminder to make us aware that we eat to know God, that this food with which the body is nourished is an instrument to serve Him, to pray to Him and to bow down in front of Him. Once again, our remembrance of the Supreme Principle will be refreshed. We always forget God; therefore, we should try our best to refresh this memory at all times. We should try to remember God from moment to moment until it becomes effortless. Consider the time you sit in front of food as a very good opportunity for that.

"Children, always remember and be aware that you are here for God-Realization and not for 'Ashram realization.' The purpose of chanting the Gita before our meals is for each person to remember God, not because it is simply a custom at the Ashram.

"The mind, body and intellect will be purified if you eat food, after having offered it to Brahman, the Absolute Principle. The negative vibrations in the food, if there are any, will also be removed if you chant the *Bhagavad Gita* and the purification mantras with one-pointedness. By doing so, atmospheric impurities will also subside."

The Mother is beyond everything, yet at this moment She was putting on a mask of anger in order to teach the residents. For a teacher such masks are needed. One brahmachari laughed while listening to the Mother, thinking that behind this mask is the 'real person' who is not at all identified with this mask of anger. (In reality, there is no 'person.') "For Mother this is also a play," he was thinking.

The Mother turned and admonished him, "Don't laugh. What makes you laugh? Do you think Mother is joking? What good will it do you if you think that this is only another mask of Mother's and that She is not identified with it? It does not help you to simply 'write this off' as just another one of Mother's *leelas*. By thinking this is just another mask, you are taking things too lightly. This is not a silly matter. You should consider this seriously."

The brahmachari was stunned to see the Mother reading his mind clearly. Before he could express his astonishment, the Mother continued, "Children, do you know the value of food? Do you know how many thousands there are in this world who crave for just one grain of rice to appease their hunger while you laugh and enjoy yourselves sitting in front of this food? Even today before taking food Mother sheds tears, thinking of those who are thrown in the midst of poverty and starvation without having even watered-down rice gruel to appease their hunger. And here you sit and laugh. How can you do that? This is equivalent to laughing at those who are starving. Children, think of them. Let your minds be filled with compassion and love for them. Then you won't laugh. You must learn to shed tears for them. You need to have real concern for them and to be able to share their sorrow. When will you attain that renunciation? Childen, food is God. Have due respect for it."

The Mother paused for a while. After a few moments, She turned around and spoke to the devotees who were standing near Her, "These children have never experienced the hardships of life. They have not experienced what real life is. They were well taken care of at home. They were masters in their homes; they only commanded and never learned to obey anyone. Now they should get good training to become ideal servants of the world. To make them understand the seriousness of life, Mother puts on a display of anger."

Mother got up and went into the kitchen. She returned with a few pieces of cooked tapioca root in Her hands. Mother fed each person with a small piece. Now Her mood was different. Again another mask, the beautiful mask of an all-caring, all-loving Mother.

The Mother's statement that She sheds tears thinking of those who are stricken with poverty and starvation recalls an incident which happened in the beginning in 1980. One day Mother was not eating. All the pleading to make Her eat failed. There was no apparent reason for Her fast, and no one knew know why She was not eating. Mother did not even drink a glass of water. Although everybody tried to find out why, Mother remained quiet. She seemed deeply absorbed in thought, sometimes crying, as She sat alone on the banks of the backwaters. Finally at ten o'clock that night Mother took a little food.

Disclosing the reason for Her fast, Mother said that a few neighboring families were starving. There was nothing to eat, and they could not catch any fish that day. Learning of their distress, Mother did not feel like eating. She wanted very badly to send some food to them, but these families had no empathy towards the Ashram. They were, in fact, dead-set against the Ashram. Years earlier, in the days when the few residents of the Ashram themselves hardly had anything to eat, Mother had sent vegetables and rice to these families, but they refused the food. Therefore, this time Mother said, "Regardless of their attitude towards the Ashram, Mother would have sent them some food. However, Mother knows that they would not accept it, and by rejecting the food offered, they would be incurring bad karma. Mother does not want that to happen. Whatever attitude they may have about the Ashram, they are also Mother's children, aren't they? Mother must have the patience to bear with them. Who else will have the patience if Mother doesn't? Let us not harbor any bit of hatred or anger towards them. Let us pray to God that they will grow spiritually. Anyhow, now they have gotten something to eat. That is why Mother also ate a little food, to participate in their happiness."

At three o'clock in the afternoon Mother was getting ready to go to Quilon to visit a devotee's home. Some devotees were going with Her, and this time Mother did not ask Gayatri go with Her, even though Gayatri always traveled with Mother wherever She went. No one knew why Mother did not ask her to go, and Mother offered no explanation. Gayatri felt deeply hurt. Heartbroken, she stood at the edge of the water as the boat carried Mother and the devotees across the backwaters. Reaching the other side, the Mother was about to step into the car when She suddenly told one of the devotees, "Go and fetch Gayatri. She is very dejected. What a pity! This cruel Mother has not called her. How can a loving Mother forget a crying child. Her sorrow is Mother's sorrow as well. We are not going without her." Thus Mother's heart poured out love and compassion for Her daughter. In a few minutes Gayatri came. She was very happy. She still shed tears, not out of sorrow but out of joy, thinking how quickly Mother had responded to the prayer in her aching heart.

Mother reached Quilon by four o'clock. The family members were exceedingly joyful to have the Mother in their home. Immersed in their love towards Her and forgetting what was the proper way of welcoming a *Mahatma*,[19] they simply stood gazing at Her. The children embraced the Mother, and She caressed

---

[19] When a Great Being comes to the threshold, it is the custom in India to show due respect to this person by washing the feet, placing a garland on him, and waving a camphor flame before him.

them and affectionately asked them about their studies and other things. The Mother went to each member of the family and to all the neighbors and friends present. Lovingly patting a person's back, rubbing another's chest or sympathetically talking to still another, the Mother made every single person very happy.

At the *bhajan* in the evening, the family members, friends, neighbors and others who had come from the nearby area all participated. As requested by one of the women devotees, the Mother sang

Amme Bhagavati Nitya Kanye Devi

O Mother Divine, the Eternal Virgin,
I bow to Thee for Thy gracious glance.
O Goddess of the world
It is just Thy play to create the world
And save it by undoing it.

O Thou Whose nature is as the shadow of the Real,
The Cause of Life, O Thou Who art full of Maya,
I bow to Thee.

While the Mother sang with rapture, the young lady who had requested the song, burst into tears as she could not contain her tremendous love.

After supper at around 10:30 p.m., the family members wanted the Mother to watch a video movie which depicted the stories and experiences of great devotees of the Divine Mother. To fulfill their wish the Mother agreed to watch this film with them, and as She watched it, She became uncontrollably intoxicated with Divine Love. One of the stories was about a fisherman who had an innocent, pure love for the Divine Mother. He was illiterate, but he had an intense longing to see Devi in flesh and blood. The Mother's mood completely changed as She watched this story.

She jumped up from the seat and started dancing and singing. The sounds which She made while in that rapturous mood were varied, but they cannot be transcribed into words. In ecstatic laughter, the Mother embraced and kissed some of the girls and the elderly lady next to Her as She sat down again.

After watching the video for a little while longer, the Mother got up and went to Her room. She was still in an exalted mood as She left. It seemed that the Mother wanted to avoid seeing the movie anymore, for it might carry Her away into a totally uncontrollable state.

Chapter 15

A miracle in court evidence

27 June 1984

The hour was almost noon as a middle-aged gentleman approached the temple. Brahmachari Balu greeted him and the man, Mr. V., revealed, "I have been here twice before. After the first two visits, there was a long gap. But still, my devotion to Amma has remained strong. In fact, without Her grace and help, I would have been behind bars by now." He paused. Brahmachari Balu asked him whether he could bring him something to drink. "Just plain water," he answered. When Balu brought the glass of water, he found him sitting on the south verandah of the temple. After drinking the water, Mr. V. continued, "I was in great trouble when I came to have Amma's *darshan* that first time. Actually, I came to visit Her to pray for Her guidance and blessings in order to get out of the serious trouble in which I was entrapped."

The man told his story. Apparently a case of fraud had been falsely lodged against him by one of his relatives. Since this relative's family were very influential people, they were able to fabricate the necessary evidence to expose him for fraud. Mr. V. knew that if he were found guilty, his life would be ruined. He had a wife and three daughters and their lives too would be in disgrace. With his family's reputation ruined, he felt that no men in this world would have the open-heartedness to marry any of his daughters. For himself, it was a matter of life and death because he felt that if he lost the case he would have no recourse but to commit suicide, and if he did, his wife and children would follow suit, feeling that their future was doomed. Mr.V. did not disclose any details about the case, but Balu could tell from his manner of expression that it was something that would have been a total disaster for him and his family.

Mr. V. said that the public knew he was innocent and knew that his opponents, selfishly motivated by vested interests, were deliberately trying to destroy him and his family. Yet such strong and convincing evidence had been fabricated against him that he had no way to refute it or defend himself. There was no legal action he could take to expose their fabrications. He expressed to Balu, "So I had no recourse in which to save myself and my family from the impending catastrophe, but my faith in God, in Mother Kali, was strong."

"One day," he continued, "one of my friends told me about Amma. He even related to me some of his personal experiences with Her, and this instilled faith and confidence in my heart, torn and pain-ridden though it was." My conviction and faith that Amma was the Divine Mother Kali Herself gave me strength and courage. That was what brought me here to meet Amma for the first time. She really conquered my heart and assured me that I would win the case. I am convinced that Amma is Kali, and subsequently She has clearly verified that to me through experiences I have had since meeting Her." The man paused.

Balu asked, "Did you get your problems straightened out?

Mr. V. proceeded to disclose how he prayed to Amma and continued to pray, even though, with each court hearing, it was more and more difficult for his lawyer to refute the points of accusation lodged against him. Everyone thought he would lose, and soon his own confidence and courage became weaker and weaker. He began to wonder, "Are Amma's words not going to come true? Has She abandoned me?" Yet his faith in Amma remained unperturbed. He continued to pray and supplicate Her every day, undergoing trials of burning in the furnace, never certain about what his opponents would do to him. Finally, when the verdict was reached, he won the case.

"I knew I was going to win because who can refute Amma's point, that key sentence, that key which locked the doors from the impending doom," he said. Words choked in his throat as Mr. V. wept. With great difficulty he controlled his tears and wiped his face. Balu sat and waited, wondering about the last part of his statement about the key sentence.

Upon regaining his composure, Mr. V. cleared his throat and said, "I know you are wondering how it happened. Amma made it happen." He proceeded to relate what had taken place late one night in his living room when he and his family were at the point of despair.

"Sitting in the armchair, I fell asleep. After awhile I was awakened by a strong light and a divine fragrance which pervaded the entire room. My children and my wife were sleeping on the bare cement floor. They did not seem to be aware of what I was experiencing. I wanted to awaken them but could neither speak nor move. As I was gazing awe-stricken in wonder, the light solidified into the form of Amma in flesh and blood! She came up to me and affectionately caressed me, smiled at me and in a gentle voice said two sentences. The first sentence was a hidden and unrevealed point concerning the case which I call the 'key sentence.' Secondly, Amma told me, 'Go and tell this to your lawyer right now, immediately after I leave.' Then She gave me some sacred ash as prasad and disappeared without another word."

As he returned to regular consciousness, he saw that he was still sitting in the armchair and that his family was still sleeping on the floor. After a few moments of re-adjusting his awareness, he saw that he was holding the sacred ash in his hands. Here was proof of his vision. He called his wife and children, and told about the vision and showed them the ash. The divine fragrance, which was similar to that of jasmine, still lingered in the room, and they could smell it. He glanced at his watch and noticed that the time was 2:30 a.m.

"Taking my motorbike," Mr. V. recalled to Balu, "I rode to my lawyer's house five kilometers away. When I told him about the hidden, unrevealed point which Amma had told me in the vision, his face brightened. I told him the whole story about Amma's appearance. He believed it totally because he, too, was a believer in God. The following day in court, my lawyer argued the case on the basis of this new point which finally saved me."

Since it was almost one o'clock, Balu requested that Mr. V. come to the dining hall to have lunch. Gently refusing, he said, "No, not now. How can I eat before having Amma's *darshan*?" He went to the *darshan* hut to sit and wait.

The Mother came to the *darshan* hut around two-thirty. Mr. V. was the first to have Her *darshan*. She received him, exclaiming, "Ah, son, Mother knew that you would come today. You won the case, didn't you? Mother is happy." Mr. V. fell at the Mother's feet and cried aloud. He embraced and kissed Her feet and then put them on his head. He literally washed the Mother's feet with his tears. Like a child wailing for his mother, Mr. V. continuously called out, "Amma... Amma... my darling Amma! O Amma! You have saved this poor destitute from hell."

Such a touching scene deeply affected all those who were present, and they found it difficult to hold back their tears, even though they were not aware of what this man had gone through in the last few years. Bending down, the Mother gently lifted him from his prostrate position and made him put his head on Her lap. She held him there for a long time. Mr. V. slowly regained control of himself, and the Mother had him sit by Her side where he remained in a meditative mood for the rest of the *darshan*.

As the Mother received Her children for *darshan*, the brahmacharis sang

Samsara Dukha Samanam

O Mother of the World,
Dispeller of the sorrows of transmigration,
The shelter of Thy blessed Hand
Is the only refuge for us.

Thou art the refuge of the blind, lost souls,
Remembrance of Thy Lotus Feet
Protects all from danger.

For those deluded ones
Who wallow in the dense darkness,
Meditation on Thy Name and Form
Is the only solution for their wretched state.

Cast a glance
With Thy beautiful glowing eyes on my mind,
O Mother, Thy Grace is the only means
For reaching Thy Lotus Feet.

Then the Holy Mother Herself led a song

Govardhanana Giri Kutayakki

O Cowherd Boy
You have turned Govardhana Hill into an umbrella
You have made Radha Your dear friend.
O Krishna, You have transformed my heart
Into Gokulam (Krishna's sporting place).

O Enchanting Player of the flute,
Your divine music turns shadows

Into silver-blue moonlight,
Your endearing Name, O Giridhara,
Fills the mind with auspiciousness.

O Madhava, Your different moods transform
The sorrows of the heart into nectar,
Your beautiful and pleasing Form
Fills one's life with love overflowing.

Half way through the song, the Mother slipped into a rapturous mood. Her eyes were fully closed and Her head was tilted a little to the right. The Mother remained still. Lying on Her lap was a woman devotee, who lifted her head up to look at the Mother's face. Seeing the exalted spiritual mood of the Mother, the devotee gently moved back and sat in a reverential mood with palms joined.

Although the brahmacharis and devotees have seen the Mother ascend to ecstatic planes while singing *bhajans*, giving *darshan*, or chanting the Divine Name, each time it is a new experience. They sit in meditation or look at Her as their *Ishta Devata* or wait in anticipation.

Some time passed as the Mother remained in that divine mood, and when She came back to normal consciousness, the Mother resumed giving *darshan* to the rest of the devotees.

A question about tantra

While the *darshan* continued, one of the householder devotees put forth a question, "Amma, people who follow *tantric sadhana* think that it can bring quick results. They also think that since everything is divine, there is nothing to renounce. They do not condemn the body as the *vedantins* do.[20] For them, the body is

---

[20] Tantric sadhana is the path to attain the state of union of Shiva and Shakti through the acceptance of everything as divine. The vedantins or followers of

dwelling place of *Tripura Sundari*;[21] therefore, they consider it pure. Amma, please say something about this.

The Mother said, "Any spiritual path, whichever it may be, involves renunciation. Without practicing renunciation the desired benefit will not be obtained. Mother does not believe that a Perfect Master guiding *tantric sadhaks* allows them to do with their bodies whatever they like. Even if they consider the body pure, that is no excuse to indulge without discrimination and self-control.

"All paths can bring quick results if they are practiced properly and sincerely with *lakshya bodha*, not only the path of *tantra*. Quick results do not come as a matter of mastering complicated techniques. The path of devotion is the least complicated method. However, all paths lead to the same goal, and all paths incorporate devotion or love as essential to the practice. Even in the *tantric* path love plays a major role. How can one progress without love?

"Now about condemning the body. No path condemns the body or the world. They do not condemn the body in *vedantic sadhana*. After all, how can one perform spiritual practices without a body? It is ridiculous to think that the body is unimportant. Not torturing but training and taming the body is what is needed. A beginner cannot simply declare, 'Everything is divine, including the body, and therefore, I am going to enjoy and indulge.' He is not going to reach the goal that way. A certain amount of self-control is absolutely necessary. Otherwise, what is the difference between a *sadhak* and a person who keeps on indulging in sensual pleasures? Realization will not come just like that.

"Realization will come if one can concentrate totally on one's own Self, forgetting everything else and not letting in a single

---

the path of Non-Dual philosophy, the philosophy of Oneness or Vedanta, are characterized by their stress on renunciation as a means of negating duality.
[21] An aspect of the Divine Mother.

thought. Even to build up a very muscular body one needs years of constant practice. How much effort is involved to become a good karate master or a wrestling master? How much effort is involved before one becomes a good musician? Nobody has ever attained anything in this world without making some sacrifices through renunciation and constant effort. Everything we do involves some rules and regulations. So why do people claim that renunciation is not needed in the case of the highest attainment of Self-Realization? Mother cannot agree with them on that point. They may say that they are the Self and that God is within them. They may say, 'You are That. You are the Divine,' and things like this. But they can keep saying things like that for aeons and aeons, and nothing will happen.

"You can get as many people as you want to support you and hail you, telling you that you are Brahman, but that will not bring about Self-Realization. You will still be the same old person. Consider those who have attained Self-Realization, and think about the lives of the great saints and sages. They were the exponents of renunciation, and they did *tapas* and strived hard to reach that state of Self-Realization. Those who have attained it will not speak. They do not go around saying, 'I have attained it. I am Brahman.' Neither will they say, 'No renunciation is needed. You are That already. It is within you.' People who say such things are shallow. Shallow people like to talk. Shallow people do not speak from experience. They have not experienced the depth, because where there is depth, there is no speech. There is only silence. If those who are Self-Realized speak at all, their speech touches the heart. It purifies and transforms the listener. Their words go directly to the listener's heart. However, when those who say that God is within them speak, their words remain on the surface, in the intellect for some time, and disappear until they hear it again the next time.

"Mother would say that *tantric sadhana* is one of the most misunderstood and misinterpreted paths. In the name of *tantric sadhana* people start drinking, engaging in sex and other licentious and irresponsible behavior. They say that they are offering it to the Divine Mother, but ultimately such people get totally carried away by such indulgence. Their ignorance about real *sadhana* becomes denser and denser, and so they argue that whatever they do is correct.

"What is involved in *tantric* worship is an offering. The fact is, the principle behind the worship is what is to be offered. This offering is not external; it is internal. You offer your individuality, or your ego, to the Divine. Furthermore, the references to sexual union in the worship are not to be taken as something to be done by a male person and a female person. It is the final union, the union of the *jivatman* (individual self) and the *Para-matman* (the Supreme Self). It is symbolic. It symbolizes the union or the integration of the feminine and masculine qualities – the union of *Purusha* and *Prakriti*, the merging of the mind into the Supreme Reality. It is the attainment of a perfect balance between the inner and outer natures of the *sadhak*. It is the experiencing of and becoming established in All-Pervasiveness, which ensues from the union of Shiva and Shakti.

"In that state the *sadhak* transcends everything and merges with the Supreme Principle. That Supreme Oneness is the meaning of sexual union in *tantric puja*. This union of the masculine and the feminine happens within you. It is not external. This union of Shiva (Supreme Consciousness) and Shakti (Primordial Energy) happens when the *sadhak's* purified semen, which has transformed into *ojas* (pure vital energy) reaches the top of the head where the thousand petalled lotus is located. The use of sexual imagery as symbolic imagery in *tantric sadhana* is an external, figurative depiction of this inner transformation. Sexual union is the closest symbol that can give the idea about this eternal union of Shiva and Shakti. Both aspects, Supreme Consciousness and Primordial Energy are within us.

"All human beings are sexual, and therefore, all are familiar with the experience of sexual desire, the longing for union with the opposite sex. Thus by employing something that everybody can understand, that is, the terms and symbols of sexual union, to express the essential quality and process of eternal union, the sages have tried to give us an idea of the process of inner union. But human minds are so crude and lowly that they misinterpret the whole thing and bring it all down to a vulgar level, misusing it or using it as an excuse for licentious behavior and illicit actions that can cause harm to others as well as themselves. *Tantric sadhana* must not be practiced without the guidance of a Perfect Master."

At about 4:30 p.m. the Mother went up to Her room and then came down again an hour later to go to the seashore for meditation. Meditation on the seashore in the divine presence of the Holy Mother was always a joyful experience. All the residents and visiting devotees traced Her footsteps to the sea, following Her in a long procession. The Mother sat still, facing the ocean as everybody gathered around and sat, preparing for meditation. The sun, after having traversed the great span of the sky, was now about to take its daily dip into the ocean. The waves gently flowed onto the shore and leisurely ebbed back to the sea, humming a continuous lullaby. Whether Mother was concentrating on the ocean, the waves, the setting sun, the horizon or infinitude, or whether She was diving deep into Her own Real Self, it was difficult to say. From the calm, serene look on Her face, one could assume that She was traveling in Her own world of solitude, a world about which others knew nothing.

Everybody sat in deep meditation. The Mother never shut Her eyes; they remained wide open without even a single blink.

She sat perfectly still, never moving, with Her hands resting on Her thighs. Her face was radiant with a blissful smile.

As usual the local children of the fisherfolk gathered around the Holy Mother, standing and watching from a respectful distance. They waited and continued to look at the Mother and Her children in absolute silence. Strangely enough, these usually noisy, active children, who liked to run and shout as they played with the sand and waves on the seashore, always kept quiet whenever the Mother came out to meditate. Of course, the Mother never forgot to give them some sweets before She left the seashore. On this occasion as well, She made the children happy by distributing toffees to them. One by one, the children went up to the Mother to receive a piece of candy. Sometimes a child might be a little shy or reluctant to approach the Mother, and She would beam a bright welcoming smile and urge him or her to come. Invariably the child would overcome the shyness and happily accept the candy.

Since it was almost time for the evening *bhajan* at 6:30 p.m., the Mother and the group started to return to the Ashram. On the way back the Mother stopped at the spot where She first used to receive devotees in Krishna Bhava. The spot is marked by a little shrine made of thatched coconut leaves, and even today the villagers light an oil lamp at this shrine. A small banyan tree grows by the side of this small temple. On one of its thin branches the Mother used to assume the *Anantasayana* (the famous reclining posture of Lord Vishnu on the serpent Ananta) during Krishna Bhava. Inside the tiny shrine pictures of both Kali and Krishna have been installed. The Mother bent down and looked inside the shrine as She gave an explanantion about it to the devotees.

As She continued to proceed towards the Ashram, the Mother met a fisherwoman who was coming from the market across the river. A little chat ensued as the Mother conversed with her like one ordinary village girl talking to another. It was very interesting to watch, for the Mother used the same terms and gestured in the same manner as the village woman.

Then, perhaps to clear the minds of a few devotees who might have been puzzled or might have had some doubts about this manner which the Mother had temporarily adopted, She explained, "The villagers will not feel comfortable if we speak to them from our level. They simply do not understand the attitude of a *sadhak*. If Mother walks away without paying any attention to her, the village woman might feel that Mother is haughty or too proud to speak to her. Mother doesn't care if she thinks that, but they feel happy and satisfied when Mother talks with them. So it should be done in their language; otherwise, there is no use in talking. We should be able to go down to their level to make them happy. They are ignorant. If we philosophize, trying to force our spiritual ideas on to them, presenting the subject in very polished language and talking in an erudite way, it will not impress them at all. Speak in their language; act in the manner they do, and they will appreciate it."

Soon after the Mother had completed Her statement about the villagers, and hardly had She and the group moved a few yards, when we heard the village lady's remark about the Mother in a loud voice. She was telling another lady whom She met on the path, " She is still very loving. That nature has not gone from Her." Upon hearing this, everyone in the group smiled, glancing at each other. It seemed that the Mother was demonstrating Her words in action.

The evening *bhajan* began with the Mother singing

Sri Lalitambike Sarvashakte

O Omniscient Mother Lalita,
This humble child bows down

At Thy All-Auspicious Sacred Feet
Victory to the Mother
Who is the embodiment of Beauty,
And Who is an inseparable part of Lord Shiva.

Victory, victory to the Mother.
Verily, the Absolute Brahman personified,
Victory, victory to Her
Who is very dear to Lord Vishnu.

O Mother I salute Thee, Mother of All Creation.
O Mother, this child of Yours
Is not familiar with any methods of meditation;
Don't You see me roaming in darkness?

O Mother Ambike, come and constantly dwell
In the lotus of my heart. Leave me not,
Not even for a twinkling of an eye.

This human birth has been bestowed upon me
After having passed through
Hundreds and thousands
Of other births. O Mother, let me offer
This rarely bestowed gift of human form
At the altar of Thy Lotus Feet.

O Mother, I might have committed numerous errors,
And maybe I am the most condemned
Among Your children.
Even then, O Mother, being the very embodiment
Of compassion and love, kindly forgive me
For all my faults and flaws,
Remove all my mental weaknesses.

Meditation with the Mother on the seashore followed by devotional singing, carried everyone to sing and dance on the wings of pure love. The Holy Mother says, "To remember God one should forget the world. Remembrance is nothing but forgetting." This is what happens to the devotees and disciples when the Mother sings. Forgetting all their worries and problems, they drink in the ambrosial bliss of the Divine Name.

Mind and no-mind

After the *bhajan* and *arati,* the Mother was sitting at the front of the temple surrounded by residents and a few visiting devotees. She had on Her lap a little boy, the son of one of the devotees. The boy sat quietly on the Holy Mother's lap as his mother simultaneously cried and laughed with joy, exclaiming, "How fortunate is my child to sit on Amma's lap and to be touched and caressed by the Divine." The Holy Mother was trying to feed the child a piece of banana. He ate the whole piece and then continued licking and biting the Mother's finger. The devotee mother then commented, "The child wants to eat you up, Amma."

"Mother wants to eat him up," came the Holy Mother's counter-point.

She continued to talk about children and their innocence, "Children are untouched by *maya.* Their innocence conquers everyone's heart and soul. Who can refrain from loving a child? Even the most hard-hearted person will love a child. This feeling of love is due to the child's innocence." The Mother handed the child back to his mother.

"Look into the eyes of a child. You can see God there. You can see your Krishna or Jesus or Buddha in the eyes of a child. But once the dormant *vasanas* start manifesting, the innocence will disappear. *Vasanas* are not completely absent in a child. They are there, but in the unmanifested state. If it is unmanifested, it must manifest one day or another. This is the difference between a child and a yogi. Even though there is innocence in a child, the child still has *vasanas* in the unmanifested state, waiting to manifest when the right time comes. A yogi, through spiritual practice, eradicates the *vasanas* completely. He becomes totally innocent, such that there aren't even any unmanifested *vasanas* lying dormant. The yogi has no *vasanas* to manifest because he kills the very source of them. He cuts out the *vasanas* by their roots, so they stop sprouting. He is clean and pure. He flows like a river, unhindered and unperturbed, into everything and without any difference.

"The mind should disappear. You should become 'no-mind.' A person who is in the state of 'no-mind' might dwell in the world of diversity, but in reality, he is in God. You might see him act or speak, but he does neither. He is actionless and has no speech; he is still and silent in all circumstances. But your mind will impose a mind onto him. Your mind will impose a body, speech and action onto him. You yourself are divided; therefore, you will try to make him divided also. Yet, try your whole lifetime, put forth all your effort and call the whole world to help you, and still you cannot divide him. You will become exhausted and collapse, trying to do the impossible.

"Undivided people are always strangers to this world. Ordinary people will not let them live freely to speak the truth. They will try to bind them or put chains on them. But you cannot bind them nor can you chain them down. The world cannot understand Great Masters. Whatever is not understood, whatever is beyond the ordinary intellect, people want to destroy. They consider it as strange, unreasonable and illogical. Their egos cannot bear it. Not having an ego is unknown to them; therefore, they want to get rid of such egoless phenomena. They are afraid. They fear that such people will destroy their ego and make others egoless as well. If the whole world becomes egoless, then the big, inflated egos will have no existence. They want the ego and the world to exist forever, for without the ego and the world, they cannot possess, acquire, enjoy and indulge. For them life is for that, not for becoming egoless. Know that the *Mahatmas* are not here to destroy but to create – to create a positive, healthy and intelligent attitude about life. They let you live and enjoy, but they teach you how to live life and enjoy it.

"Ordinary people crave name and fame; therefore, they want to fight against the egoless, pure and innocent saints. For this reason, some who are established in that state of Self-Realization and who choose to remain in the body will create an ego with which to 'fight back.' But this kind of ego is a shadow ego or the mirage of an ego. It looks like an ego, but in reality no ego exists. If you observe closely, you can see that there is no ego in them. You might detect that it is non-existent, but they keep the appearance of an ego to frighten and threaten the big, inflated egos.

"Krishna did that more than anyone else. He kept the apparent ego until the end. He wanted it so that He could live in the midst of vagabonds and wicked people. Whenever it was needed, He used it as a weapon to strike back. Otherwise, how could He fulfill the great cause of restoring the declining righteousness? Even His endeavors at peace-making failed due to the unshakable egos of the blind king and his sons. Eventually they even tried to put Krishna in chains, and this forced Him to strike back with His universal ego, the Cosmic Mind. He then revealed His universal form to make them understand, "Do not play games with Me. I am everything. I am fire; I am the entire universe. Be careful. I will not spare you if you continue your game." This manifestation needed an ego, the biggest of all egos, the very substratum of all minds, that is, "I am everything. I am the Universal Mind." In order to warn them, to threaten them and to disarm them, He had to show it; otherwise, they would not have let Him work to continue His life's mission of establishing *dharma*. The very purpose of His assuming human form would have been defeated.

"Therefore, to teach the world, to discipline people and to put things on the right track, the Great Masters have to create an apparent ego. But they are far beyond. Deep down they are untouched, pure, innocent and silent."

The Mother stopped for a while. Everyone was drinking in the wisdom which flowed from the Mother. The little boy that the Mother had cuddled was lying fast asleep on his mother's lap. The Holy Mother looked at the child affectionately for a few moments with a beautiful smile on Her face. She reached out and lovingly caressed the boy's face. Just as the Mother did that, the little boy innocently smiled in his sleep. Seeing the child smiling, the Holy Mother said, "He's smiling. Maybe he is having a beautiful dream." The child's mother remarked, "That beautiful dream must be you, Amma."

Glossary

Certain words are the same or similar in Malayalam and Sanskrit. Thus *Abhyasa* and *Brahmachari* are Sanskrit whereas *Abhyasam* and *Brahmacharin* are Malayalam

Acchan: Father

Agamas: Scriptures

Amma bhrant: Madness for Mother

Ammachi: The Mother. *Chi* is a word indicating respect.

Anantasayana: The image of Lord Vishnu laying on the serpent Ananta which represents infinite Time.

Anoraniyan Mahatomahiyan: Sanskrit for "Subtler than the subtlest, bigger than the biggest," a description of Brahman, the Supreme Reality.

Aparigrahyam:"Incomprehensible, "an epithet for Brahman.

Arati: Waving the burning camphor, which leaves no residue, with ringing of bells at the end of *puja* (worship) indicating total annihilation of ego.

Archana: A mode of worship by repetition of one hundred, three hundred or a thousand names of the deity.

Arjuna: The third among the Pandavas and a great archer.

Ashramam: Hermitage or residence of a sage.

Ashwamedha Yagña: An elaborate Vedic sacrifice using a horse as the offering.

Atma(n): The Self

Avadhut(a): A Realized Soul who has transcended all social conventions.

Avatar: Incarnation. Great Souls who are fully aware of the purpose of their birth and their identity with God.

Balavat: Having the nature of a child, alluding to the nature of a Realized Soul.

Bhadrakali: See Kali

Bhagavad Gita: The teachings of Lord Krishna to Arjuna at the beginning of the Mahabharata War. It is a practical guide for common man for every day life and is the essence of Vedic wisdom. *Bhagavad* means 'that of the Lord' and *Gita* means 'Song', particularly, an advice.

Bhagavata(m): The book about the Incarnations of Lord Vishnu, especially Krishna and His childhood antics. It upholds the supremacy of devotion.

Bhagavati: The Goddess of six virtues, viz, prosperity, valor, auspiciousness, knowledge and dispassion and lordship.

Bhajan: Devotional singing

Bhakti: Devotion.

Bhava: Mood.

Bhava Darshan: The occasion when Amma receives devotees in the exalted state of the Universal Mother.

Bhava Roga: The disease of birth and death.

Bhrantavat: Having the nature of a madman, alluding to the nature or appearance of some Realized Souls.

Biksha: Alms.

Brahman(m): The Absolute, Whole.

Brahmachari(n): A celibate student under training of a Guru.

Brahmacharya: Celibacy

Brahmatvam: The state of being Brahman, the Absolute.

Chara: Spy.

Darshan: Audience of a Holy Person or deity.

Deva(ta): Demi-god, celestial being

Devi: The Goddess.

Devi Mahatmyam: A sacred hymn in praise of the Goddess.

Dharma: Righteousness.

Dhyana(m): Meditation.

Gita: See *Bhagavad Gita*

Gopas: Cowherd boys, companions of Sri Krishna.

Gopis: Cowherd girls, known for their supreme devotion to Sri Krishna.

Grihasta: Householder

Grihastashrami: Householder who leads a righteous life.

Gunas: Good qualities. Also, the three qualities of Nature: Sattva (Clarity), Rajas (Activity) and Tamas (Dullness).

Guru: Spiritual Master / Guide.

Gurukula(m): Residential school of a Guru

Hanuman: A great servant devotee of Lord Rama who crossed the sea by jumping over it with the power of constant remembrance of the name of Rama.

Hari Bol: "Praise the Lord."

Hatha Yoga: Gaining mastery over the body as a means of Self-Realization.

Ishta Devata: Chosen or Beloved Deity.

Japa: Repetition of a mystical formula (*mantra*)

Jivanmukta: A Liberated Soul

Jivanmukti: Liberation.

Jiva(n): Life force

Jivatma(n): Individual Soul

Jñana: Spiritual or divine wisdom

Kalari: Temple. Also, a training ground for the martial arts.

Kali: The Divine Mother. She is depicted in many forms. Her auspicious form is called *Bhadra Kali*.

Kali Yuga: Present dark age of materialism.

Kalli: Thief (feminine).

Kama: Desire or lust.

Kanji: Rice porridge.

Kanyakumari: The southern point of the Indian subcontinent where there is a temple of the Divine Mother as a virgin.

Karma: Action.

Karma Phala(m): Results of action.

Karma Yoga: The spiritual path of detached action, of dedicating all the fruits of one's actions to God.

Katala: Chick peas.

Kauravas: The hundred children of Dhritarashtra, enemies of the Pandavas, who fought in the Mahabharata War.

Kenopanishad: One of the main Upanishads or texts on the philosophy of Non-dualism, part of the Vedas.

Kirtan(am): Hymns

Krishna: Principle Incarnation of Lord Vishnu

Kundalini: Spiritual energy depicted as the serpent power coiled at the root of the spine which rises to the head by spiritual practices, leading one to Liberation.

Lakh: One hundred thousand.

Lakshmana: Brother of Lord Rama.

Lakshmi: Consort of Lord Vishnu and Goddess of wealth.

Lakshya Bodha: Constant awareness of and intent on the goal.

Lalita Sahasranama: Thousand names of the Universal Mother in the form of *Lalitambika*

Leela: Divine play.

Loka(m): World

Mahabharata(m): Great epic written by Vyasa.

Maha Kali: A form of the Universal Mother

Mahatma: Great Soul

Manaso Manah: Sanskrit for "Mind of the mind," referring to the Witness Consciousness or Brahman.

Mantra: Sacred formula, the repetition of which can awaken one's spiritual energies and bring the desired results.

Marga: The path.

Mauna(m): Vow of silence.

Maya: Illusion.

Maya Rupam: Illusory form.

Mol(e): Daughter. *Mole* is the vocative form.

Mon(e): Son. *Mone* is the vocative form
Mudra: A sign by hand indicating mystic spiritual truths.
Mukta: The Liberated One
Namah Shivaya: The Panchakshara Mantra meaning "Salutations to the Auspicious One (Shiva)."
Namavalis: Songs consisting of the Names of God.
Narayana: Lord Vishnu
Narayaneeyam: A devotional hymn about Lord Vishnu's Incarnations, a poetical condensation of the *Srimad Bhagavata*.
Nishkama Karma: Action without expectation of results
Ojas: Sexual energy transmuted into spiritual energy through spiritual practice.
Pada Puja: Worshipping the feet of the Guru. As the feet support the body, it is the Supreme Truth that supports the principle of Guru. Thus His feet are the symbolic representation of that Truth.
Palum Vellam: Milk diluted with water.
Pandavas: The five children of King Pandu and heros of the epic *Mahabharata*
Parabrahman(m): The Supreme Absolute.
Paramatma(n): Supreme Self.
Prakriti: Mother Nature or Primodial Nature.
Pranayama: The practice of controlling the mind through breath regulation.
Prarabdha: Responsibilities or burdens. Also, the fruits of past actions manifesting as the present life.
Prasad(am): Consecrated offerings distributed after *puja*.
Pravrittika: One who acts.
Prema: Deep Love.
Puja: Worship.
Pundit: Scholar. *Pundit-mon* is the Mother's affectionate way of addressing a scholarly devotee, literally "Scholar son."

Purana: Epic.

Purusha: The Supreme Self. Also means "male."

Puttu: Ground rice and coconut steamed in a cylindrical vessel.

Raja Yoga: The Royal Path of Union with the Supreme.

Rama: Hero of the epic *Ramayana*. An incarnation of Vishnu and the ideal of Righteousness.

Ramayana(m): The epic about Lord *Rama* composed by the sage *Valmiki*

Ravana: The villain of the *Ramayana*

Rishi: A great sage or seer.

Sada: Always.

Sadachara Pravrittikayai Namah: A name of the Divine Mother meaning "One who enforces good conduct.."

Sadhak(an): One dedicated to attaining the spiritual goal, one who practices *sadhana* (spiritual discipline).

Sadhana: Spiritual practices.

Sadhu: Mendicant.

Sahasranama: Hymns consisting of the Thousand Names of God.

Samadhi: State of absorption in the Self.

Samsara: The world of plurality, the cycle of birth and death.

Samskaras: Mental tendencies accumulated from past actions.

Sankalpa: Creative, integral resolve manifesting as thought, feeling and action. The sankalpa of an ordinary person does not always bear corresponding fruit. The sankalpa of a sage, however, always bears the intended result.

Sannyasi(n): Ascetic who has renounced all worldly bondages.

Saptaswaras: The seven notes of the Indian music scale.

Saranagati: Surrender to God.

Sari: A long piece of cloth worn by Indian ladies.

Satguru: Realized Spiritual Master.

Satchidananda: Existence, Consciousness, Bliss – the attributes of Brahman, the Absolute.

Satsang: Company of the wise and virtuous. Also, a spiritual discourse by a sage or scholar.

Sattvic: Of pure quality, goodness.

Shakti: The dynamic aspect of *Brahman* as the Universal Mother.

Shiva: The static aspect of *Brahman* as the male principle.

Sita: Wife of Rama.

Sloka: Sanskrit verse.

Soundarya Lahari: Devotional hymn by Sri Sankaracharya addressed to the Divine Mother.

Sraddha: Faith. Amma uses it with a special emphasis on alertness coupled with loving care of the work in hand.

Sri Guru Paduka Panchaka: Hymn of Five Verses to the Guru's Sandals.

Sri Rama: See *Rama. Sree, or Sri,* is a mark of respect

Srimad Bhagavatam: See *Bhagavatam. Srimad* means 'auspicious'

Tantra: A system of Indian philosophy that teaches one to look upon all Creation as a manifestation of the Divine.

Tantra Sadhana: The practice of Tantric disciplines.

Tantric Puja: Worship conducted according to Tantric principles.

Tapas: Literally "heat." The practice of spiritual austerities.

Tapasvi: One engaged in penance or spiritual austerities.

Tapovan(am): Hermitage, a place conducive to meditation and tapas.

Tattva: Principle.

Tattvartha Svarupini: A name of the Goddess meaning "The Embodiment of all spiritual principles and their meaning."

Tattvattile Bhakti: Devotion rooted in discriminative knowledge between the eternal and the ephemeral.

Trimurti: The Divine Trinity of Brahma the Creator, Vishnu the Preserver and Shiva the Destroyer.

Tripura Sundari: A name of the Goddess meaning "the Beautiful One of the Three Cities (the three qualities of Nature)."

Tyagi: Renunciate.

Upanishads: The concluding portion of the Vedas dealing with the philosophy of Non-dualism.

Upasana Murti: The form of God which one is meditating on or worshipping.

Vairagya(m): Dispassion, detachment.

Vanaprasta: The third phase of life devoted to austerities and a secluded life.

Vasana: Latent tendency.

Veda: Lit. 'Knowledge', the authoritative Scriptures of the Hindus.

Veda Vyasa: See *Vyasa*. As he divided the one *Veda* into four, he is also known by the name of *Veda Vyasa*

Vedanta(m): The philosophy of the Upanishads which declare the Ultimate Truth as 'One without a Second.'

Vedantin: A follower of the Vedanta philosophy.

Vedic Dharma: Injunctions on the righteous way of living as pre-scribed by the Vedas.

Vishnu: All-pervading. The Lord of sustenance.

Vyasa: A sage who divided the one *Veda* into four and composed 18 *puranas* and also the *Mahabharata* and *Bhagavatam*.

Yagña: Sacrificial rites and rituals.

Yoga: Union with the Supreme Being. Popularly used in the sense of a set of exercises to make the body and mind fit for spiritual practices.